Emotional Beauty

How Its Gift Can Bring You to a New Meaning of Embrace

Luis Enrique Cavazos, MS, LPC

Inspired to Thrive Publication

DISCLAIMER

This book does not dispense medical advice or prescribe the use of any technique as a form of treatment for emotional or medical problems without the advice of a physician or from a mental health professional. This book is intended for your emotional and spiritual quest for finding beauty in your everyday life. In the event, you use any of the information in this book for yourself, the author assumes no responsibility for your actions.

Some of the names and personal characteristics of the individuals involved have been changed to preserve their identity. Any resulting equivalence to persons living or dead is entirely coincidental and unintentional.

ISBN 978-0-578-62270-5

Contents

Acknowledgments

Writing a book may seem daunting, but for me, it is relaxing and therapeutic. What frightens me the most is writing the acknowledgment page. I must admit, I'm always afraid I will leave someone out or not give credit where it is deserved. One of the biggest nightmares for an author, especially for me is when the book is printed, out for sale, I read it and realize, "Oh my gosh, I left this person out. I did not give credit to this individual, and so on." Nevertheless, through the hands and hearts of the reader, what matters the most is the guidance and growth that I give. My soul is shared through stories, experiences, love, beauty, and much more. But since this is the acknowledgment page, I will give my best attempt to share the names who have championed my life. This book was based on the idea that life is meant to be filled with beauty. I would hear stories from people, coming from different beliefs, socioeconomic status, cultures, and so on. What caught my attention was how certain individuals who experienced more sorrow and negativity were the ones who searched for new beauty. Whereas the ones who had a savory course of positivity were somewhat doubtful if "this would last for a long time." Their mindset supported their goals but when presented with challenges, they yielded to a dissonance between internal consistency and external validation. After considering everything, I reflected heavily on what makes us search for beauty. The question that I pondered on was, "How can we bridge the gap of nihilism into something more rewarding, one that fills the heart and soul with new beauty?" From that moment on, everything clicked. That is how my title was born, *Emotional Beauty*. This book was written to showcase that no matter where we come from, we are in search of new beauty. Every citizen in this world can position themselves with great leadership skills, while at the same time being empathetic toward the needs of others. As you read this book, open your mind to new possibilities. Highlight, take notes, study, and transform your life. This book will redefine your purpose and help you sustain meaningful habits. For this book, I infuse a different style of writing.

ACKNOWLEDGMENTS

It marinates between revolutionary and existentialism.

I want this book to cultivate great seeds that will multiply beautifully in your life. Furthermore, I want to thank God, my Savior to whom has made this possible. Without Him, I am nothing. Thank you, God, for renewing my soul with a new strength of courage. Also, I want to extend my gratitude to my Mom, my guardian angel, and my shield. On March 17, 2017, she transitioned to the afterlife. During my graduate studies, I would talk about my dreams and goals about writing multiple books, appearing with Oprah at her Super Soul Sunday events, and much more. Throughout our conversations, she would tell me, "You have to put in a lot of work. It will be challenging, but you will have to sacrifice many things that others won't." To this day, her words echo in my heart. Writing books and hosting thought-empowerment workshops, I can feel her presence, telling me, "Keep going, mijo (son). Keep going." To those of you who lost someone whether through natural causes or suicide, may the chapter on grief and despair soothe your soul with a greater understanding of life.

ACKNOWLEDGMENTS

Working through painful emotions may seem difficult, but I promise you, it is rewarding when we unwrap each gift of gratitude for what we have presently.

To my Dad, thank you for all the sacrifices you made to see my dream come to pass. Dad, there are no words to put in motion to thank you for all the times you helped me during my darkest days when starting my entrepreneurship route. Even though you had speculation on where this was going, you kept your faith towards me. For that, I am eternally grateful. And to my brother, Mario. You have seen the good and the darkest days of my life. You witnessed my struggles with setting up my business, seeing me go through painful breakups with my ex-girlfriends, and you stayed up late with me until 5 am, comforting my injured soul with new perceptions that gave me the confidence to get back up. Emotionally, we have been through so much in our lives. But somehow, you artistically gave me the courage I needed to continue to spread the message of meaning, courage, and love. So, to you and our Dad, I love you both unconditionally.

Also, I want to extend my gratitude to my friends who have unconditionally supported me throughout my journey. You know who you are. Please know how much I cherish our friendship. You either shaped my growth or believed in my work. For that, I unconditionally thank you.

Furthermore, I want to extend my love and gratitude to Elizabeth Cermak. I am thankful for the support she has given me. If you follow us on Instagram, you will recognize us for our live video sessions entitled: *Living Meaningfully and Magically*. Our goal is to imprint meaning, courage, strength, love, and vulnerability in all aspects of personhood.

Likewise, I want to extend my heart and soul to Tiffany Coleman for her remarkable work on my book cover. Thank you for seeing my vision in terms of what *Emotional Beauty* means and how it relates to our lives. Next, I want to thank Shelly A. Preston for editing my book, and for designing the interior. The amount of patience you gave to my work is something I will forever cherish. Through my moments of frustration, you inspirited patience and faith.

ACKNOWLEDGMENTS

Moreover, I cannot forget about the San Antonio Current. You guys have a special place in my heart. The readers and the community of San Antonio voted for me as their Best Author of 2018. Words cannot describe how grateful I am. Also, I would like to extend my heartfelt gratitude to the San Antonio Public Library-Edmund Cody Branch for their continued love and support towards my projects on mental health. Nevertheless, I want to thank the San Antonio Monthly Magazine for their devoted support and strength towards my work.

In addition, I want to extend my love and appreciation to Laverne and the entire Witherspoon family. Each of you has sowed seeds of love and faith in my heart. Thank you for supporting me, but most importantly, for contributing to great causes that benefit our community.

Lastly, I want to thank my followers on social media. I receive an abundant number of direct messages through my inbox. I enjoy reading them because it allows me to understand your private album of life. By sharing each other's stories, we can connect and empower each other through the framework of meaning and wholeness.

Introduction

The warmth of beauty is out there in the world, glistening in our hearts, waiting for us to take a leap in our bravery, transcending the pulsing moments of excitement with a throw-in of determination. The thought of settling less is not an option for a thundering lion who spearheads in the wilderness of life. Sadness, grief, wealth, depression, and anxiety are manifested in beauty. When bestowed with the gift of beauty, we can become the disciplined director who narrates how the story begins and ends. However difficult it may be, fear protrudes a whirlwind of doubt and stagnation towards our ambitions. In facing our demons, let us take out the sword of beauty.

INTRODUCTION

It is a vibrant and authentic sword that links all humankind. Most of us cockpit without arriving at our destination. We see it at the murky horizon, but somehow, the vision of purpose gets clouded with a dark expression of nothingness. Surely this cannot be our life. We are called to be entrepreneurs, philosophers, scientists, engineers, teachers, politicians, psychologists, doctors, lawyers, and much more. We are destined to call out our freedom as the royal road to legacy.

By unbinding our chains of social restrictions, we can live again. We can have that day when we tell our brothers and sisters, mothers and fathers, and the rest of the world that our expression of speech is not in the context of hate but rather, it is in the context of our motivational aim toward greatness.

We are the bringers of the LIGHT, the eye that sees our end goal, and the inheritance of free will. Strangers will speak of liberty as decades of constraints, tightly bound with cautionary suffering. Let us cast out those melancholic nihilists who tear our spirit of authenticity. Our true Self cries for courage, seeking beauty in our masked soul.

Why then, do we bound ourselves with self-criticism yet, we mix it with freedom?

It is because our soul is tired of self-criticism. Our soul is ready to ascend towards freedom. Our natural drive is to rise from repeated mistakes. We must remember that recycled fire is suffering without meaning.

Every single act of consciousness reveals our chase for something meaningful, breaking all boundaries for us to explore. We must decide to divorce fear and hate once and for all. Let us join the movement of humility, love, and purpose so we can take back our stolen treasures.

Once freed from the paralyzing hate of marching the streets of protesting, give back your voice, the voice of partnership of beauty and joy. It understands your pioneer notes. Signal them, produce the end outcome of meaning, and quickly become the guiding light who inculcates a relationship with the community that leads others to a prosperous life.

The tools to manage our peace will not be easy. We should not be surprised by this. Belittling our highest esteem for commercial submission has minimized our wisdom.

Of all the hurt and toil, we were blinded to believe that our former lover and endless trudges through our meaningful moments was an orchestrated event for death to oneself. Many scuffle at the lessons that we must learn. But they never pause to find beauty in between the rocks and the rivers of joy. For some, the final arrival is never reached, but for others, they utter, "I anticipated this moment when my comfort turned into a greater calling for a genuine life."

Despite the movement of success, we somehow regretfully end up as a 15-minute philosopher who only reached certain wisdom and vanished into a cave. Let us not be those 15-minute philosophers who preach the meaning of life yet, they dwell in their habitual dolor. Our glorious moments come from heartbreak, grief, depression, anxiety, and courage.

Our courage, strength, and wisdom must be self-evident to the created efforts that we promised to ourselves and to those that we serve. We believe that when we grow, we secure the providence of our destiny. It is not decided by the Otherness; it is decided by those who defend their birthright of meaning.

Greatness and transcendence spotlight their slog with an introduction to a new soundtrack of life: *The vessel of enchantment.* Most never mature at this stage. We are on constant halt; we lull to find out who we are, declaring ourselves as rebels against society by opening ourselves to hackneyed ideas of, "Let me abuse drugs to numb my void." "Let me drink until my fear is gone."

Know not of the desperate feasible
pleasures; know the wisdom of a good life.
The good life of preparation and mastering
one's craft to enhance the welfare of others.

We continue to experiment but lo and behold, our existential Self visits the nihilistic inventories that have no benefit to our lives. We shall trounce our demons by moving forward with courage and authenticity.

Our internal demons will poison our growth by rewinding our subconscious thoughts to a moment when we were heartbroken, depressed, delusional, fearful, and struck with a meaningless existence. Our existential Self is decided by how we respond to our stimuli.

Some of us can remember when we felt caged and leashed by the opinions of Others. It is as if we were rattled with humiliation because we let the Other dictate our existence, unsure of what to do. We allowed it because the volume of freedom was low. Periodically, we questioned ourselves: Who exactly am I? If I were brave enough to accomplish my goals, what would I do next? These questions can bring an existential tension between being authentic and being fearful to achieve a driven life.

Regardless of our challenges, the beginning is always the poet who utters wise words under the brume that taunts the disciplined spirit.

The existential experience is an understanding of who we are and the relation we have with other individuals. It is about the common experiences that we share in strength. It enables us to fully experience life in a shared dimension.

To spend our lives advancing toward authenticity is a worthy habit. To spend our lives moaning and professing statements that are not aligned with our purposeful Self is a destruction of our will. We cannot lie to ourselves about this knowledge.

The sayer is the banker of wealth.

The doer is the banker of persistence.

Leap on to find the planner of joy.

When one becomes the inner destroyer of greatness, we become the thief of our own Light. Most of us ignore this because we are afraid of accepting our destiny. The sidelines of history have taught us that being fearful is good because we do not get hurt. We avoid humiliation. But isn't it true that we need to take risks in life? Isn't it true that we must use fear in the utmost creative aspect?

INTRODUCTION

Isn't it true that magnificent accomplishments come when you least expect it? Isn't it true that when we succeed, it motivates us to pursue another goal? Let us keep the BIG PICTURE in mind. We shall not compromise beauty for long-term suffering nor shall we compromise beauty for false desires. We must gain a greater purpose in our lives. We need to become attuned to our common strengths. We are the ones who are the bringers of the Light. We are the makers who shift our society to a new enlightenment. Humble yourself to know this truth. Discard the false information that has been placed in your mind. Visualize a new form of destiny — a destiny where men and women set higher ambition, tearing the defiance of fear and division.

To spend our lives working on aimless goals is to retire in our coffin. A vital pursuit is worth aiming for because we will gain ownership of a meaningful life. Yes, this will be difficult. Yes, we may experience doubt. But if we march on, day by day, we will beat the bully of doubt, fear, and stagnation.

Let us measure our presence and power in our lives. Abandon your old ways. Learn your subject. Find the truth in your vastness of freedom.

If we are given enough time to aim for greatness, our definition of despair will not be the sorrowful tears of a broken heart; it will be the optimistic spirit who gained recognition for our liberty and enthusiasm toward the declaration of motivation.

In our pursuit, let us stop hating each other where we boast in a rebellious nature that goes against our humanitarian rights. Be the evidence who believes that no human shall torment another human through physical harm or verbal harm.

The bravest star is not the one that shines
among the rest, it is the one that
shines alone in a darkened sky.

It is self-evident that our world is weakening, despairing in fire against all goodness and mercy. We shall no longer hate one another. There is no sense in it. We must sustain meaning, love, and authenticity if we want to reserve eternity in our souls.

To avoid the dangers of suicide, let us be empathetic towards those who are considering exiting from life. Reserve the measures of beauty and love. Our emotions are always in an upsurge of dichotomy, leaving us doubtful whether we should exit or remain rational. Either or, the one-eyed witness of meaning and the death of nothingness are watching — ready to see if we have the endurance or to be vanquished into yesterday's news.

As we prepare for a new enlightenment, let us bring forth the solitude that makes our life meaningful. Make no exception for your banal pleasures. You will be tempted to experiment with the life of drugs and alcohol.

Like a father who alienates his children, your courageous Self will no longer recognize your humility. It will abandon you until you return to your investment in the zest of life, one that is filled with love, respected by nature, and clothed in grace.

We have work to do. This is not going to be easy. Collective citizenship will require us to do more soul searching, keen for a greater life. Not the kind of life where we sprawl into the estates but rather, the good life of clarity, preparation, and advancing our Age into an order of legacy and peace. If you are ready for this new lifestyle of beauty, go ahead and pass the sauce. Let us grill a new possible outcome.

In possibility, your inner child is
invited to a party; the magical
curiosity to be a beginner.

ON LEADERSHIP

A New Path to Lead with Meaning

I magine for a moment that you are the next best thing in leadership. You have the best communication skills. You have been contacted by the president because he knows you are not a seeker of wealth or the privileges that it bestows.

He knows your work ethic just like how a shepherd knows its flock. The world is in tyranny, lost in a show, silenced in bondage. Everyone is looking for direction. Religion, New Age, spirituality, chakra, cleansing, but none of that satisfies their taste towards the crown in their heart. But then, there is you — polished, educated, exquisite, popular by the masses, has a lot of followers on social media, has over 500 million views on YouTube, and above all, you are inspirational. Where have you been? This will be the question many will ask. Where have you been all this time? The world is in a state of confusion and we have not seen you before.

Out of the ocean, comes a new sunrise. A new leader is born out of the virgin morning Light, but not to wear a crown for a show, but to share the crown with every individual. The throne is not exclusive for the leader, the throne is acknowledged by the public masses.

War has started, nations against nations. But then, there is you. Peaceful and collected. You dare not to strike with war. PEACE! PEACE! PEACE! Citizens all over the world yell PEACE! Calm and collected, you listen to their cries. You listen to their pain. You listen to the concerned parents who had to kiss their son or daughter one final time before they head overseas to fight for our country.

You are admired and praised for the international peace that you are about to bring to the world.

Now, open your eyes and come back to the present moment. How would you handle a situation such as the one I presented? What actions would you take as a leader to make sure everyone is on the right path towards enlightenment?

Ask yourself this question: Am I merely a seeker of fame and wealth, or do I desire to be a leader of growth and change?

You must have the courage and faith to decide what happens next to an individual's life. It is elementary to strive for the benefits of fame, prestige, and wealth while overlooking the formidable responsibilities of being a leader. If you feel in your heart that you are destined to be a leader of peace and change, seek philosophical wisdom over temporary riches. The one who has wisdom but lacks riches will soon gain them. But the one who has riches but lacks wisdom will soon meet the basement of insecurity.

Leadership: Which Way Is It?

Do I follow and lead? Who do I ask for advice? In a nutshell, leaders have no one to follow. Through calculated measures, they analyze the steps that must be taken to lead us to safety.

As a leader, many will scorn at your status. Many will wonder why you are the leader and not them. The majority will integrate darkness in the world to showcase the hatred they have for leaders that are changing the world. Followers seek the representation of riches, status, fame, and their desire to destroy the lives of others.

Whereas leaders, they look beyond the ocean peak, knowing that their decisions affect the lives of those who look to them for wisdom and guidance.

A balanced mind is not easily swayed
by pressure or conformity. A balanced
mind is enriched with bold action to
commit something honorable for society.

In an age of dissonance, humanity has been pushed to an escarpment, leaving us doubtful if these are rearrangements for the final shudder or a global shift to help us find strength in unity. Let us be the joyful sages that start in a virgin morning with a steady direction of purpose and peace. Let us recast our humility towards each other. Past sorrow will leave us with a brutish relic, trapped in irreparable defects.

Ambition and courage are the genesis of leadership. When the comforts bind the commoners, it is our duty as leaders to point another direction that shelters the soul with significant meaning.

Leadership as The Revelator

In times of confusion and distress, we turn to premature beliefs that have no proof of the good life. Knowledge and wisdom will lead us back to an understanding of our psychological growth. Every soul is born with opportunities but not all are equal. Some are stronger, some are weak. Some are born rich while others are not. Every species is never equal. Equality is honorable but not achievable. It is a mythical goal to believe that equality will lay its domain in our historic form. However, we must honor and treat each other with the utmost respect. Every citizen has the same opportunities to strive for a better life.

Those who shiver in weakness can easily become stronger by setting habits that are meaningful to the mind. Regardless of prestige or class, we must be treated under the form of respect. Those who preach on a podium but judges upon the weak, he or she will realize the pedestal of destruction.

We must not exhaust ourselves with religion or science. It is always evolving with new ideas to bring change and peace to our world. Religion and science cannot answer the question of your meaning of life. It limits your significance to become greater in life. I say with great confidence, endure in your wisdom. Use your experiences as a whale of inspiration. An existential attitude is the closest to a genuine life. So, go ahead, carry out your routine. Become the three lectures of life: Being, authenticity, and love. Acquire yourself in your Being. Teach yourself about the meaning of life. Become aware of your relationship with the world. Together, we can build a new foundation that leads to courage and connection. With it, we will walk together in a new global transpose where our brothers and sisters, mothers and fathers, our children, and grandparents can witness the truly lived life of beauty.

The Moral Dilemma of Leadership

The moral dilemma that we face today in politics, science, or religion has not changed from the days of the American Civil War when many were forced to choose between taking sides for or against slavery. In our time, one is faced with the choice between political power or help reform our society; give five medications to a patient who is mildly sad after a relationship breakup or use existential talk therapy for ten sessions and heal the individual without medication; advance our sciences by using the BEST technology to help patients with dementia, cancer, schizophrenia or trammel the welfare of others. Ministers and psychiatrists find half-truth toward the highest esteem of authenticity. Ministers never mirror what they preach. Psychiatrists defend their obligation to prescribe medication without realizing the poison whispers of secondary mental illnesses. Now, one must ask, "cui bono?" For whose benefit?

Why would a minister preach about love and then turn back against the Word and molest children? Why would a politician hurt the welfare of his or her citizens? Why would a scientist keep a secret of the cure for dementia or cancer? Biological knowledge is only a perspective used as an ends mean. It destroys the comprehension of our human race. Our pragmatic concept of beauty is that the immediate solution is never conditioned by those who understand it; the condition that presents itself is the reason that seeks to bring everything back to its interrelatedness.

When questioning the actions of your ministers, politicians, or doctors, find truth in your personhood. If you desire to be a leader of integrity, then, present the way. Neither through favoritism nor outrage, but through salvation where each of us leans upon the honesty of truth and beauty to do good for others.

Leadership is a false crown
when it is worn for admiration.

ON POWER

The Human Benefits to Strive for Greatness

Power is not a cruel goddess that selects those who deserve an empire that is richer than others. Power is given to those who honestly believe that it is their birthright to succeed in life. Who says that money is more powerful than stones? Who says that diamonds are superior than food? When given thought, remember this, the mind believes what you tell it. If the sky were to rain diamonds, we would be a plebeian in our pyramid. But if it is worn, it becomes an admiration. In the jealous eyes of the crowd, we become worshipped idols. The same goes for thought and power. It becomes a treasure chest in our subconscious thoughts.

Say who you are and let
it become your truth.

A king and a queen are no different than a newborn child. We can manifest success and wealth through dedication and intention. Our subconscious mind is the most powerful muscle.

Our deepest humility comes from the enlightenment of understanding our path. Power becomes a recognition tool for the changes we make in our society. Those who do not understand power will soon recognize the deep vortex pool that pulls the feet down to the rabbit hole.

When drowning in difficulty,

swim like an Olympian.

Fastening with conformity leads to a frightful madness; a fulfillment that gossips each other's imperfections. Without an undertaking, one becomes a past generation of nothingness. To preserve the Motherland, we must fulfill the duty to love with an open heart which is the perfection of readiness which recognizes mankind as a destiny of perseverance.

Open your eyes and recognize the power you have. You bestow confidence, wealth, wisdom, and health. There are no differences between you and a millionaire or a billionaire.

The kings and queens that you admire are no different than you. Yes, their names are put in books. Yes, they have statues that people worship. Yes, they have power. Look within, you have the same power as they do. What you choose to fill your mind with is what separates you from the rest. Fill your mind with abundance and it will return tenfold.

The Crown of Power

Wishful imagination is useless without the intent to pursue power towards your driving force of life. Power is not a single penny; it is a shared custody between two or more people. When ideas come together, an organized effort takes root in the inner white space. True power is putting the universal design in good order. While many thrive on power to punish others for their thrill, they will soon realize the animal instincts that lead to war among other nations.

Though you may feel different from the rest, civility teaches us to keep such thoughts to ourselves. Be still and realize that even though the chairs are empty at the table, power awaits you to claim your throne of change. Strive for it, and you will experience the hollow white light of greatness.

Words are the true source of wealth and power. What separates successful people from commoners is that successful people choose to fill their mind with abundance rather than despairing over an unborn dream. Patience and an open mind to new ideas are the necessary ingredients to pioneer the moment. New methods, new leaders, new cures, and new teachings have been manifested through intentional power and dedication.

The probability of attaining power depends on
your definite desire and your organized
planning to pursue success without
an explanation to others.

Intentional Power vs. Power of Possession

In the pursuit of our endeavors, we must remodel and redirect our intentional power of success. All great fortune can be obtained through the better lines of serving our talents with a touch of great faith.

Figure 1-1: Sacred Points of Riches and Power

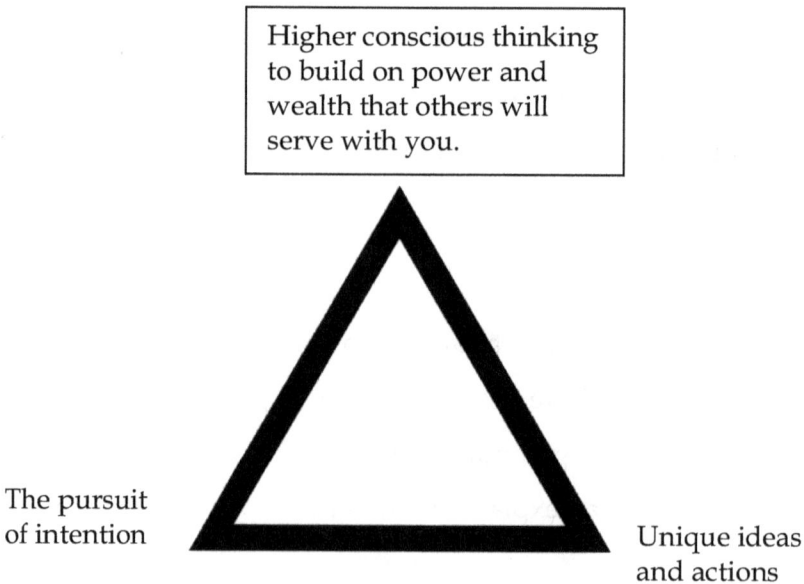

Higher conscious thinking to build on power and wealth that others will serve with you.

The pursuit of intention

Unique ideas and actions

All are born naked and all dress in clothes, the difference between our bodies is the vastness of our organized thoughts of power to change our lives and the lives of others. Unlike the animals, they are pre-programmed to follow certain orders from their highest supreme. Humans are born with a mind that begins as a beginner or as John Locke would say, *tabula rasa* (blank slate) in which he theorized the mind can begin again if we choose the opposite emotion.

We are aware of our existence and the legacy that we want to leave behind. Just as a child learns to walk, speak, or act on free will, the same goes for the adult who is desiring to pursue power for the positive changes in our society; it grows slowly through the progression of learning and through the adaptation of wisdom from our mentors.

Moreover, let us call attention to the power of possession. In this revelation, we see a periodic sequence of individuals who acquire power for the sake of shallow pleasures that have no attention towards others. Through glory and decorum, the possession of power becomes a statue of worship with dissemination in the latter years.

Without an apology, power becomes a sweet poison of punishment towards all those who do not conform to the obedience of their commands.

Punishment is a drama that conforms to the sadism of adaptation. It becomes an advantage of repayment which disrupts the equilibrium in our society. Heed the warning of power: It is a seduction of superiority to the Other. Those who understand power know how to use it for altruism rather than a festival of suffering.

An example of this outcome is someone who wants to control every situation. Therefore, the individual expects the other individual to conform to his or her power. In doing so, the individual with power trumps over with the glorification of, "I am superior than you." In this mode, we adrift in the randomness of life. We become unfulfilled and stressed about who is going to admire us with our power. To live a meaningful life, we must learn to focus on where we have power and where we do not have power. It is okay to not have power in situations such as grief, economic crisis, or opinionated individuals. What we can do is observe the moment. Let us ask these mindful questions:

1. Am I fully present on how I am feeling?

2. Do I want the power to control others or to change the world?

3. Am I authentically connected to other people?

Why Doesn't Anybody Follow My Orders?

Even though you are on the path of leadership and power, most do not believe they should follow your orders. Your power is not strong enough for others to obey them. Why should your sand be traded for a home? Why should anyone believe that your food is worth more than diamonds? Convince yourself that your words are wealthy. Tell yourself this every morning and night. Eventually, your words will be the commands to other individuals, and you will experience success and wealth.

Power and Hardship

Every king, queen, president, and prince have been tested through hardship. Whether it was temporary discomfort or severe hardships, they pressed forward until they succeeded. Though they make it seem easy, their hardship and despair are clothed behind the scenes. Unlike the rest of us, we sprout them all over social media, pleading revenge that has no meaning to our lives.

Those who press on through hardship are the ones who remain behind the curtain. Every human is born and destined to succeed but only a few will dedicate themselves to the steadfast willpower required to advance our human race to a new historic form.

Power and belief are what breaks the
wall between doing and doubting.

Like a captain or an officer who gives commands to their people, so does your mind. Why does a captain give orders to his lower rank and yet, they obey him? Your mind faces the same dilemma and we believe it just as the soldiers believe in their general. It tells you every day to give up on your dreams. It bombards you with useless messages that have no meaning to your life. Your mind tells you that it is time to go back where it is familiar. But beneath your heart, you know through great faith, you can endure the storm.

Power and Its Glory Pool

I ask in great confidence, is your power merely for a show that is decorated with silks and gold, or do you desire to have the power to help others achieve their goals? It is easy to attain power, representing it authentically is another story. When power is rested by an unfoolish individual, they will be manipulated by the whims of the masses.

A wise leader knows how to use effective power to calculate a path that leads every citizen to enlightenment, greatness, and a destiny where our children can smile once again to the melody of a new life. We are free to become the portrait that we envisioned for ourselves. You and life are not a screen that separates itself but rather, a mirror in which life holds in front of you, measuring your actions as if the human race is staring at you.

Power is a glory pool.

Few will drown,

others will leave clean.

"They" Have Power, I Don't

Whether it is a mere conspiracy or the suppression of our power instinct, we truly believe that "they" have power and we don't. Whose "they" one may ask? "They" are the individuals we refer to as leaders, innovators, and other influential members of our society. For selfish reasons, we feel the need to resent them because "they" have more influence in our society. I like to term this as, *the habitual behavior of deflation.* This deflation reduces our meaning of preservation. At this pace of progress, the field of envy and hate increase with time. Past generations have understood the displacement of competition and cooperation. Every tribe, castle, town hall, or cathedral has witnessed the testimony to the spiritual and intellectual transcendence of a new possible outcome. In all events, individuals have sprawled over the syllabus of power: What makes them have it and I don't?

Do not concern yourself with such questions that have no meaning to your life. Concern yourself on the repeated experiences of resentment and emotional responses to the other party. To lift our world to a conscious state, we must live with intention. The crown of achievement unfolds broadly when there is a solar solitude in our goals and for the rest of humanity.

As we continue to advance our abilities of discipline, self-improvement, and knowledge, we can experience a new awakening as if our eyes are opening for the first time. To create a better world, we must disband our selfish behavior. Cooperation requires a peaceful transfer of compromise and strength to unite the welfare of our citizens. Together, we can make our universe a timepiece of innovation where everyone is contributing their talents for the greater good of life.

ON WISDOM

Our Age of Enlightenment

Every day, we leap forward with liberation, bringing numerous mixed forms of moral judgment to help us understand the internal compass. Our ability to choose wisdom over destruction is what sets us apart from the animalistic kingdom. Even though we act on those traits, the polarizing outcome strikes us with either conflict or peace.

Our brain is like a computer, it processes all information, picking up new data, or saving old junk that is not helping us in our journey. For every lesson that is presented to you, you can either add new information of meaning, or you can *choose* to gamble on anger and jealousy. Either way, perception guides us to the safest route of wisdom.

What is seen is often a passing moment of appearance, but what is true to the heart is often a preparation for growth.

In life, wisdom does not end with one lesson or two lessons. It is not a racetrack where you win first place. Wisdom cannot be bought with medals. It is a constant continuity that lasts a lifetime. Every day, we are given a chance to gain new beauty. Every mistake is not a failure; it is an opportunity to learn something new about ourselves.

The enlightened ones do not bitter over the loud cries of the sheep. Instead, they study what worked and did not work on their path towards wisdom. They avoid repeating the same mistakes that brought them misery. They heed the lessons as a cautionary knowing where they gain new chances to flourish in all areas of life.

Wisdom is a child of discovery, a longing to understand the mysteries of the universe that drive us to the pathway of human relations. Knowing oneself is an acquaintance derived from existentialism through which we question the human dilemma. What does this mean? Why does this happen here but not there? How can I muster up the courage to understand the meaning of life? Look past the indifferences. Open your mind to see the proximity that comes close between the Self and the environment.

You are surrounded by number codes waiting to be opened — each lock will reveal knowledge that can be used for the rest of your life. Do not be ignorant of the fact that each answer comes with sacrifice. The sacrifice will be far greater than what you expected. It will call you to abandon your old ways of living. It will call you to leave behind the individuals that drowned your energy. It will call you to be ontologically different from the norm. Few will scorn at your individuality, asking themselves: Who does he or she think they are? What makes them deserve to be rich? Do not pay attention to the venom that outpours various toxins toward your personhood. Most of them will abandon you. These can be your closest friends or family. In all that you do, flourish in bravery. Through it, you become anything that is Light, not darkness.

Enemies who find fault in you will expose you because they care nothing for your friendship. Often, they will remind you of an unresolved issue from your past. Do not get bitter over it. See it as a gift to strengthen your armor with a foundation that builds an unmoved home.

Even when life gives you a test towards your character, you will motivate yourself to new concepts that bring a new understanding of what it means to develop a curiosity to solve the question.

Failure: An Expressed Equation

The question about failure will be formulated and discussed in a way that guides you to a new understanding of life. Culturally speaking, we live in a transparent world where we thrive on competition, especially when we humiliate our opponents. In our Western culture, we tend to fluctuate between practicing harder to savage our opponent or to be egoistically available to the mass audience, professing a speech on how we defeated our opponent. This is not new. We place divisions in academia and sports. Kids are ingrained to learn that first place is a winner. The masses brainwash them to believe that being second or third is a failure.

Every story that we have told, it begins with, "You got this." And it ends with, "There is no time to complain and cry. Stop whining. Failure is not an option." This functionality of speech, however, creates an origin that features a delimiting mindset that leaves no room to be vulnerable. Real progress comes when we inquire into the area where we feel vulnerable. Driven mostly by reaction, we must step back and increase the information that is presented to us. The real movement towards growth is when we positively investigate certain inquiries that stagnated our growth. Research has shown that when we act in a place of rationality and peacefulness, the more we become intuitive with our clarity. For this section, I will present to you a new paradox of failure. This has changed the mindset of the clients that I coach. On the next page, you will see a full diagram of the subject Self and how it relates to the meaningful actions that we take.

The average ways of thinking remain protected when we do not interpret new decisions to progress a new lifestyle.

Figure 1-2: A Manifold Subjectivity of Being

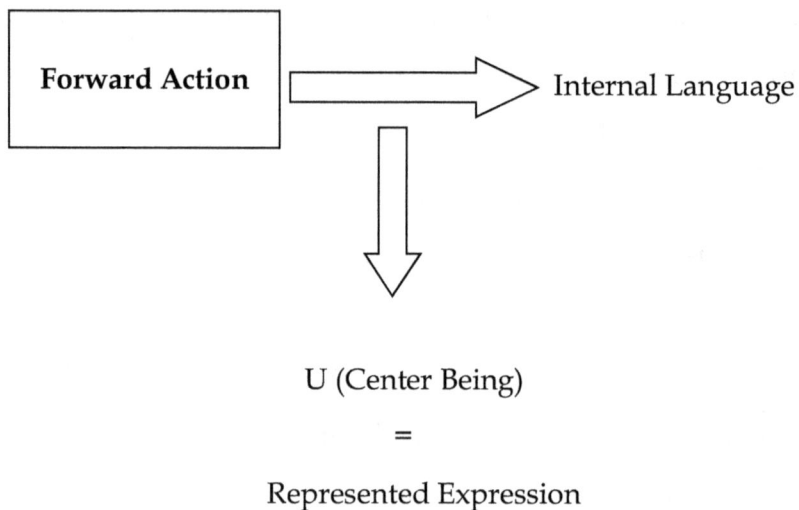

Forward Action ⟹ Internal Language

U (Center Being)

=

Represented Expression

In the diagram, I give failure a spin twist on how it is viewed authentically; not negatively. If you pay close attention, you will recognize how failure is broken down as fa (forward action), il (internal language), u (center Being), and re (represented expression). To go deeper, I will first explain the stage of forward action. Forward action and internal language marry each other. Here is why. This is where you question your meaning of life along with the service that you are giving to the world. You begin to ask:

1. What am I producing at this moment?
2. What steps am I taking to achieve my goal?
3. Did I miss any step?
4. What will the outcome be once I accomplish the steps?

Without forward action and the internal language, you will stumble through insecurity, leaving you doubtful whether you are worthy or simply a faded talent. The beginning is crucial because it sets the tone on where you will be producing your talents. This is where I see most of my client's stumble. They engage in forward action but neglect the internal language of questioning their dilemma.

One cannot exist without the other. Next, we have center Being which means U which is tied with represented expression. Again, these two represent "the showing up" part of your personality. By focusing on the present foundation rather than the soaring future, you begin to identify real progress that opens proximal clues for the areas that you are collecting results. The basic concept of this formula undergoes simple mathematics in solving the rigorous and most firmly constructed ground of failure. Normally, when we *feel* that we failed in life, we encounter a crisis. At times, we get an anxiety attack or a panic attack. But what if I told you that failure has nothing to do with your performance. It mostly has to do with perception in your questioning.

You see, when we take an exam or participate in a sport, we feel nervous because we do not want to fail our crowd or our teammates. For an exam, we do not want to disappoint ourselves or our professor. The outermost worry comes from the absence of baring the ground on what we want to accomplish. Once we bare the ground, we move slowly in exhibiting the sequence of circular reasoning that leaves a forward movement toward the priorities that regard as functions which means solving its aim, and its motives.

It is naïve and opaque if you do not seek the ontological task to discuss within yourself the different possibilities in solving the problematic mechanism of existence. Tradition has been handed down with the same arrival of greed, professing that we should win more and beat our opponent. This has been the narrative. What we need is a new script. We need a new arrival that structures failure as a personal growth toward the Self. When we interpret the Being as meaning, our represented expression will integrate fully into a distinctive manner that organizes the questions. Once everything is analyzed in the full picture, failure will no longer be demonstrated as a Western, competitive society.

Failure is an event of misplaced questions.
Once we organize our questions and delve
into its meaningful outcome, we will
inquire a new science of reasoning.

The Dance We Take with Wisdom

The question of the meaning of life is formulated when we discuss inwardly the inquiry that we are seeking. Beforehand, it must be guided through an intimate bond of creativity and expression. The Being-of-Self, which is the centered Self, it must be able to understand the manifestations of consciousness. Lasting satisfaction with life can only happen when we emerge out of the results of the ought-mode. It-ought-to-be-this-way is what presses itself to the general realm that brings no absolute truth to life.

Much of our understanding can be made when we adequately investigate a purpose toward the Self. Without carrying the weight of the world, we can come hand in hand with the penetrating field of concepts. Everything that comes into existence is not conditioned; it is unconditioned that is freely perceived by the maker who shapes the world. Truthfully, by virtue, our consciousness is action built on intentionality which tethers with existence and knowability. In our understanding, our spirit of creativity follows the ideas of wholeness that shapes and reshapes the imagined life that we are pursuing.

Each moment of clarity brings coherence to the presentation that points upward to the plurality of symbols, meaning, and truth. The background experience which we heavily investigate through false impressions is what makes us passive, a target for the sensory bombardment that imposes all sorts of information and perceptions from the environment. As stated previously, failure and life lessons are distinguished from a grouping pattern of questions and answers through a position of inward order. This emerges from the subconscious mind and slowly, it gaps the outline from the separation dots to a complete full circle. Even more so, wisdom deactivates the addition of shadowy anxiety that kept us powerless from human reasoning.

At this moment, let us exist with a purpose; not with utter defiance that goes against the poetic gestures of the universe. Strive for the enlightenment that is worth your understanding; not because of comparison or superiority of knowledge, but because your effort and rationality are evident through the toil.

A Path Towards Wisdom: Reflection Questions

1. When I find beauty and meaning in my life, some of the major priorities connected with my focus is…

2. During the last 30 days, did I challenge myself to see the beauty behind every emotion that I felt? If so, what lessons did I learn? If not, how can I yield towards growth?

3. Through the vehicle of creativity and creation, what skills did I acquire to incorporate a new form of flourishment?

ON DECISIONS

Moralistic Choices That Benefit the Welfare of Others

An effective leader does not give much attention to those who protest the loudest. An effective leader is one who listens to the silent and helps them lay a road where meaning, humility, and love become the boldness of the uncharted. Citizens are easily distracted by hardship, anger, and envy. Their decisions get clouded with a perversion of the hierarchy of negative values: fear, succumbing to an agreeable stimulus, functioning on a joyless habit, and entertaining the subculture of desperation.

Through the composition of nature, we have rushed into the examination of extremes, as though they bore some sight to life. It is strange when we wish to understand the beginning of life, and suddenly, we arrive with comparison, leaving us to feel insecure. This design cannot be formed with the image of all things.

The author of humanity partakes into an infinite multitude of curiosity: Where does this begin? How can we work together? What makes this method work more effectively than that one?

At sight, we can move forward with an inclination of rationality without representing a fatalistic attitude. The visibility of decisions can arrive at a reaching point like a compass. But let us not exceed ourselves in pointing in many directions, blaming the coordinate points on how they share the same circle. Decisions depend on the Self and the questioning of mankind. We cannot hide from the beginning of knowledge. Our intellect holds the same position as a compass — we draw our points and drive toward the importance of proximity to our arrival. We must see ourselves objectively when arriving at a conclusion. Too much subjectivity can paralyze the understanding of our sensitivity to the wonders of life. True decisions are made best when we consider the welfare of others. When the building collapses and citizens shut down in grief; and while others start a war, who will you listen to?

Will you listen to the protesters or the silent souls whose words cannot be spoken, but you can see their tears and shadows behind their wounded souls?

Let us not look for the comfort of certainty. Let us reason with stability. Our comfort of certainty deceives us by the burning shadows of protesters. From a distance, it may look reasonable, but it adds a certain toxicity of energy. In the long run, that decision will hinder the infinite scope of existence. To truly make decisions, we must relate the situation to the motion in order. Stability, when mixed with relatedness, it brings together the understanding of one detail to another fixed continual change. This elevates the soul to partake in a spiritual corporeal where it resides to solutions.

Our horizon for a greater destiny carries on in rhythm with a stunning ambition to create new aims in life. Our decisions seek its way to bring us freedom, one that is greater than the slavish, quiet denial of absence. Distractions declare war against our citizens. Whereas peace and love strive for a greater purpose that brings us to a path where we honor and share each other's sacred, emotional connection.

False decisions, when based on favoritism, it will suffer in nihilism, breaking the ceremony of meaning. Apart from the joyous meaningful life, citizens will leave their Sunday practices for the dehumanization of separation. This is not the story we want to portray. Indeed, existentialism moves forward in actual living when we experience a cultural crisis. The validity is common when we move from one transitional period to the next.

When making decisions, consider how your choices will affect the whole. Accepted ways and means yield to lose security. It sinks into dogmatism, blindly conforming to the dependence of the Other. Self-consciousness form new connections that bedrock new insights despite a crisis period. It is required for firm leaders to unravel the naked truth about the unpleasant attitudes that have caused mere despairing. Let our dialectical search be the prototype whose consciousness expands the span of life into a realization of questions and answers.

Our stark awareness is shown beautifully when our words match our actions that are built on relations. Rather than having shocking similarities of the past, let us move ahead to the concerned ontology that cuts the left side of hate and the right side of foolishness. In the center, it should be our self-understanding of how human nature operates. It should be the chief specific purpose to help us create new solutions that will correct the assumptions of the emptiness of life. Traditionally, we have operated on a sense of belonging, always searching for the new, hoping for our souls to convince us of a new American dream.

Unconsciously, we have engaged in a dialogue that is governed by attachment, which encourages the view of security and adaptation. These facts are presented in Van Gogh's paintings, Cézanne, and Picasso. Art and literature brought out the unconsciousness to the consciousness of each existential relatedness. The articulated symbology portrayed America and the rest of the world of a new search. Each had their common elements throughout history that painted freedom as the human capacity to enrich and to design a life that shapes our ends toward the direction of unity.

Let us return to the beginning: That no soul shall be left behind in the darkness. We shall build our faith in the belief of love and humility. When we unite for the common welfare, we can prosper to new stories that draw forth the similarities of the human experience.

The greatest perfection lies eternally when our hearts do not see an error in the soul. Rather, it sees the blessed joy of empathy and forgiveness. Our decisions cannot be clouded with avarice. The Being must open a pathway that asserts itself with community building where each citizen stands with new insights. Decisions alone cannot sustain enlightenment. It requires discussion with other like-minded individuals who are not swayed by impulse, reaction, and resentment.

When power is rested by a witless,
they will be manipulated by
the whims of the masses.

When we think collectively, there are several possibilities: We may arrive at the truth, or we may have to debate over it cautiously to bring a positive strength to the world.

Men and women strive to understand what is ethically right based on desires and experiences. But this is not enough to sustain the fort of humanity. What we think alone is foolishly desiring a finished race. We immediately give proof that our understanding must be the absolute truth. This mental capacity is a weak foundation for it holds past thoughts at a particular time. True wisdom begins when we ask ourselves: Is the disagreement worth the distance? What solutions can I find to bring peace between myself and the Other? The importance is in the question, not the immediate answer. We dupe ourselves with the understanding of quick application instead of understanding the true nature of its roots. False understanding creates a lack of knowledge. It strives to know one situation and not the scope of existence. This is what separates humanity. Humanitarian goodness gets hazy with the critics who outcry, "Fight! Fight! War!" We must not listen to those who flatten human reasoning with traditions of a twilight crime.

It destroys our faith and our Sunday practices which puts us on a betrayal of our belief in goodness and mercy. The more we pay homage to the catastrophic crisis, the more we build bottomless foundations. Hence, it represses unacceptable potentialities to bring good to society. We need to keep in mind the main question: What keeps us from not achieving a meaningful, connected life? This may involve morals or ethics, but it also involves a lot more such as the existential output of our freedom to help others achieve a meaningful life.

Acceptance of the same margin represses the unawareness of Self. Thus, making us deny the great discovery of life and connection to our world. In a general form, when decisions are resistant toward the flourishment of goodness, we slip back to the expression of the dynamism of transference. This is where each of us specifically preserves certain detachable feelings from one object to another. The resistance holds back on making meaningful decisions with desires that are unacceptable for society to carry on. Aware of this, we can move forward to the potentialities through which meaningful decisions can impact our world.

Shaping and reshaping is the conceivable acceptance to a justified defense of the analysis of what makes our life meaningful. Traditionally, we make decisions on the reserve of content. Meaning, we reserve special interests that violate the humanness of constructs. How many of you have witnessed people make decisions out of their pride? I assume we have seen this. This drive puts forth a destruction to community engagement. Corruption and secrecy place people in a vehicle that drives toward a dead end. Without considering the Other, they fundamentally point out to the cries of revenge instead of helping those achieve clean water, nourishment, and a place to call home.

Meaningful decisions are expensive
because they demand different lessons
for your growth and maturity.

ON GROWTH

A Continuous Process of Maturity

The need for growth and motivation are dependent on a position on how we govern our existence. Psychologists and philosophers admit that our primary givens of emotions sharpen our cognitive capacities to motivate a new outcome. In the past, individuals would perceive negative attitudes toward the need to get rid of the present emotion. Whether it was through suppression or through the need to fill the void with drugs, they would press toward the elimination. Today, we know through studies that human growth and motivation are greatly flourished when we proselytize a structural model of abilities and competencies to develop new ways to measure the personality and the environment. In a nutshell, human growth is the ability to express our emotions openly and can understand how to access them meaningfully. The ability to understand is what formulates the first branch of *modeling*. In this branch, we perceive our emotions not as fatalistic, rather, open to new meaning.

It is the ability to identify oneself and of Others to understand the narratives that have been imprinted.

By knowing this, we can redesign our differential effects toward a new primary aim: an equilibrium that intrinsically validates how we want our end-experiences to feel. This is what is known as an instrumental activity. It helps us to do more with our lives. Particularly, maintaining the tension of anxiety, and "becoming" autonomous to think independently. This determination of behavior is an inner-qua that reminds us to consider a uniform agreement that defines our characteristics not as flaws, but as a fully emerging Self who becomes whole through the evolutionary process.

Our true freedom is being able to understand the hard knocks of life, the tragedies of existence, our stress, our grief, and being able to create a new dialogue that will self-direct the Being to a spontaneous orientation of Self. A key characteristic of our emotional expression through human growth is being able to relate modeling with our second branch in what I like to call *confirmation of meaning*.

When we model new behavioral patterns, we will be able to generate, actualize, and attempt to understand the conundrum of life. By weighing our actions and choices, our questions and answers will not arrive by luck. They will arrive with a living maximum where obstacles turn into persistence; experiences into lessons; and conflicts into connection. It will require us to harness assistance between what we feel and how we process the outcome to find meaningful solutions. This is where we want to engage in a feedback loop, where we become creative with our emotional experiences. An admirable quality of confirmation of meaning is the usage of self-improvement and self-searching. These stages produce a qualified existential reliance that etches a greater variability in the skill that helps us to regulate our feelings from the viewpoint of reasoning.

Knowing what we know, I would like to conclude the final branch that is vital to our human growth. I call this *condition of a meaningful stimulus*. When we comprehend our confirmation of meaning, we can address the intentionality that falls within the sphere of subjective awareness.

This simply means that we can regulate oneself through an understanding of progress and have a consensus with existence to measure our output performance with a new potentiality to develop, to construct, and to maneuver a new improvement in our skill set of habits. This becomes an inner consistency of change. It is being able to increase synergy while at the same time, integrating a new acquisition of habits that builds positive change over time.

To the extent, condition of a meaningful stimulus peels away the diffidence of the personality, leaving us to emit a new radiance that enables us to be authentic, freely choosing whether to repeat a past stimulus or to allow an inner nature of change. Once we accept the notion of a new stimulus, we can detail how we want to mature in our present activity. Meaningfully, we can actualize a new Self whose experiences are not validated through external rewards but rather, it is subjectively depicted by us, pairing behavioral measure and a supplemented domain that maximizes adjustment, adaptation, and competency to our environment.

Working Through Our Tragedies

Can we mature through our growth? Can we find significant meaning through our tragedies? The answer for some is yes but for others, it is a struggle between the continuum of courage and purpose. Today, psychologists have turned their attention to humanistic psychology. It is the basic premise of conceptualizing and managing to give rich meaning to one's life. The psychology of humanism implies for us Beings to do good for humanity, collectively working for the greater good. Ultimately, we govern our cognitions by theorizing the effect of the outcome and attaining a new construct of meaning.

The basis of this increases our productivity to contribute to a new stimulus. This can range from an expansion of optimism, or to an immediacy between the desire to accomplish something or to produce the actual meaning behind the movement. From an existential point of view, the interaction between the Self and the environment lies heavily with an operational narrative that groups certain pathways. This helps the individual to reflect on the actual choices that one makes by choosing an alternative that brings out knowledge and wisdom.

It helps us to pull toward certain ideas and beliefs. When we turn our attention to the pre-event, we spiral with assumptions along with a negative feedback loop. Whereas if we use the pre-event as an analysis of value, we can mold the situation by reinforcing the progression of the actual pursuit, not the abandonment of the pursuit.

Expectations of achievement do not intensify meaning; action does.

Pathways to a new agency of thought address the overview of emotional sets and meaningful-related activities. Turning our attention to the pre-event analysis will undermine our functional pursuit unless we use it as our capacity to process the actions that were taken. When looked carefully, we can summon new courageous decisions to help us push forward. Barriers, like challenges, it enables us to seek alternative routes to calibrate our motivation.

Tragedies, as sorrowful as it may seem, it adds a new addition to our lives. Such surprises may be daunting, but there is a positive gain. These surprises navigate our relations of Being towards existence. Ongoing events transform immediately to either "attached outcomes" or to a "forward meaning feed" that incorporates different views of the events.

It is more feasible to ask questions within the Self and to rationalize your outcome. When you have a perceived probability, your conceptualizations do not come easy. You either attribute to the meaning or you intend to span the problem for years. Our balance to observe the events and to gain new meaning lies in the action that we take. Once we connect the external environment with our bendable measures of determination, we can accomplish a new appraisal. What I found to be effective with my clients who are facing certain tragedies is to correlate the emotion with normative information. This simply means to suggest to yourself a second strategy to assess both *meaningful-solving attitudes* and *skills-driven attitudes*.

It looks something like this: With enough meaning to my situation, I believe I can solve most problems that confront me. And to the rest of the problems that I cannot solve, I will either figure it out, or I will allow myself to ask for help. In the example, that I provided, it shows both meaningful-solving attitudes and skills-driven attitudes to confront the dilemma.

On the flip side, if you avoid the dilemma, it will look something like this: When confronted with life's problems, I feel unsure about my present situation, let alone about the future. I do not feel competent to solve a particular issue. I can no longer see other alternatives to my situation. I am hoping for a miracle to happen.

In that example, you shut out or in existential terms, alienate the personhood from existence. All of life's dilemmas can be solved when our meaningful-solving attitudes and skills-driven attitudes assess our verbal measures to figure out the nature and frequency of personal problems. This strategy not only focuses on the complexity of human existence and the Being, but it measures the output to solve each issue.

The Sum of a New Meaning

The construct of problem resolution can be gained when suitable action follows spontaneously through a casual analysis that utilizes choices that are made without conflict. With that said, a meaningful individual is one who has a belief system where they increase the understanding of the issue, and they understand how the issue is related to the world. They can adjust rather than approach life with a fatalistic attitude. They take into consideration the previous reinforcement that was externally addressed as an association with one's behavior. Nonetheless, they understand their internal control while at the same time recognizing the presence of subfactors: events, emotions of the Other, negativity, and other considerations of the environment. Altogether, they position their emotions with a motivated desire to dial back between the relationship of Being and the stimuli of the environment. Once their struggle for human freedom is understood in the realm of a "different format," they begin to increase their bravery and they cut through the irrational fear.

As we move beyond our comfort zone and ground ourselves with wisdom, we will move forward with integrity. Without any form of stagnation in life, we can develop the final stage of development: *value orientation of acceptance*. With the acceptance of our personhood, we can move beyond the individualistic concerns of our environment and modify what needs to be changed and accept what cannot. This dialectical conception is relativistic, yet we do not link it to our new search of meaning. Usually, we operationalize on conditions that are external and internal to the person who is persuaded by the pressures of life.

If we extract the complexities of existence, we will renew a middle life — to choose to begin again or to course through the problems — repeating the same outcome or shifting the problem into a solution. We are thoroughly familiar with problems; however, they are never permanently gone. Ideally, they are conceived as if it were eternally. Years later, the meaning and design work together to transform our nature into a fitted existence, one that is observable and measurable with our cosmic picture of experiences.

Under the grey ashes of tyranny, we can rise from the difficulties and begin to form new principles that will set the stage for a global compromise. Our search for beauty may vary from person to person, but our unity of cultures and languages must enable a meaningful connection that gives every citizen the right to share their nature, space, life, and love for each other. By justifying our morals with good character, we can increase our altruistic traits to undergo a revision that puts us in full transparency to do good for humanity.

When we cultivate meaning and
refine our purpose, it will help
us to fulfill our destiny.

ON COURAGE

Our Willingness to Leave a Purposeful Legacy

When we profile courage as a virtuous trait, not only is it necessary to preserve its sensitivity but it requires us to face certain changes. We are called upon to do something new for ourselves and for humanity. It pushes us toward greatness while at the same time betraying a certain strangeness of fatalism. This is what existentialists call *courage of reliability*. It is being able to forecast periodic changes that are not quite common. It requires a degree of courage to independently create a meritocratic relationship that nourishes superior talent with sound ethics.

The common view of today has a poor understanding of courage. It overlooks its traits by focusing on the customary view of sacrificing one's life. For curious reasons, individuals shy away from the signposts of moral courage, relatedness of courage, and existential courage.

Moral Courage: A Passage of the Human Spirit

Tracing through history, there are a few people who come to mind who embodied moral courage: Jesus Christ, Socrates, Gandhi, Mother Teresa, Martin Luther King, President Lincoln, President Reagan, and many more. These individuals had the greatest moral courage to execrate the concerns of violence, resentment, inequality, war, and politics. By bearing the richer fruits of mankind, they had a different outlook than the common norm. Each of them searched for benevolence that had an importance for the welfare of citizens. Take, for instance, President Lincoln. He never based his arguments on political affiliation or what other people had to say. He made sound decisions based on the citizens of our country. He rarely, if ever, used republic language to get his points across.

Words pierce through the mind,
but courage strengthens the soul.

President Lincoln had a belief that if he entrusted on the affiliation of any party, he would be five steps behind. Meaning, he would pass on the sensitivity from the suffering of one's fellow human beings. Lincoln learned from people. He had immense, seraphic energy and great faith to trust the recognizable volume of doing the right thing. This reminds me of what Jean-Paul Sartre would say "reflection of the reflection."

Lincoln relied on his sound principles to not only do good for humanity, but he made his decisions based on how existence would stare back at him. He would deliberately question himself: Would mankind approve of my decisions? If not, what can I change?

Another figure that stands in many hearts is Jesus Christ. He is best known as the Son of Man. While we know him as the Son of Man, we fail to neglect that he preached a virtuous message that many reject: love, humility, and forgiveness. Contrary to the views of critics, Christ was a brilliant thinker. He spoke in parables, used short phrases to connect with the heart, he had unconditional empathy, and most importantly, he had a zest to live a meaningful life.

When Christ preached on humility, he strictly enforced it to be a virtue. As Christ said, "Do not conform to the pattern of this world. Be humble and patient. Do nothing out of vain conceit. Rather, love one another and help each other." His discussion on love, forgiveness, humility, and corruption lead other men and women to think before debating irrationally. He emphasized on living an authentic life, one in which we are free from corruption. His wisdom, logic, and rationality built an innate relationship with other citizens to think about the grave dilemmas of life: human presumption, pride, and envy, all of which he made sound arguments for others to examine the blurred perspectives.

Christ did not shy away from arguments when it came to the rejection of the Word or the corruption of power, money, or greed. He listened with a compassionate heart but brilliantly had skillful communication skills to elucidate a different output. In a sense, Christ was not a philosopher of the system, he was and still is of the Spirit that eventuated through wisdom and love. He spoke and left traces of God's work so we can continue His legacy through our acts of compassion, love, and humility.

Christ, in a nutshell, wants us to live joyfully and meaningfully like children. Here's why. Children are our greatest professors because they teach us to have a light heart; not dark or clouded with hatred or envy. They show us that it is okay to smile and to love in the midst of the darkness. They help us to nourish a greater understanding of life. When we face a moral courage dilemma, whether we want to speak on corruption or inequality, just remember, have the innocence of a child who is curious to learn about the topic. When we get caught up with subsidiary issues in our environment, take a moment to analyze how children respond. You will notice how most of them laugh when they fall; act curious when faced with problems and love openly without the worry of criticism. No matter what we face, it is important to stay emotionally current. It may be challenging, but when we tailor our lives to suit our ambitions and human drives, it will inevitably lead us to a happier life.

Moral courage is a transcendence of
wisdom that heightens our level of
motivation to do good for others.

Relatedness of Courage: A Shared World of Beauty

The second kind of courage that is opposite to moral courage is what I call *relatedness of courage*. It is the courage to comprehend the nature of other human beings. It is the connection and authenticity to build meaningful relationships that will increase the openness of self-actualization. Relatedness of courage requires vulnerability because the risk involves possibilities of a new outset of connection. Like a covalent bond, one interacts, while the other bonds, and together, they form a new reaction. This is what I mean when I talk about relatedness of courage.

When we engage in this kind of courage of relations, we become mindful to ask ourselves: Will we bring out new meaning, or will this destroy us? Am I certain this relationship will strengthen us or subtract from our wholeness? We cannot be certain what the outcome will entail, but if we emerge ourselves with knowledge and effort, we will not fall into the endless dogmatic attitudes. Instead, we will enrich the social margin of one's development to arouse productive work that keeps our human race together; not separate. The desire to have interpersonal relations is much needed today.

A common view of relationships has been desecrated with lust for another person's body. Our society is naked psychologically and spiritually. All forms of emotional beauty have been threatened with the joy to use each other for status. This structure is mechanically a means-object whose sole purpose is to minimize the process of a healthy relationship.

Therefore, let us maximize the courage to listen to each other, to share our creativity, our fears, and our purpose. Rather than short-circuiting the obvious, we must have authentic courage to relate our Being to the Other. In between growth and maturity is the space of creation. It is the continual exploration through each world, the daring to know one's soul. Each conversation brings an unknown fate as to whether it brings lessons, bridges a union of love, or marks an end of a previous unfinished business. This relatedness of courage, to some degree, is a fear of connection. It is an ongoing struggle between an independent autonomy of one's world and the creation of a union. The striving for autonomy while maintaining close relationships is a struggle for our individuality.

We are afraid to engage in vulnerable conversations because we "give in" to certain aspects of ourselves to the Other. It feels as if we are dependent on someone's judgment. This fear creates an ongoing separation that loses its wholeness. Each person's inner biography is in part unique and in part to the evolutionary process. When individuality is threatened to know another person, it creates a tension instinct where we lose balance, and become enveloped to disintegrate the process of nourishing an authentic relationship.

It is interesting to see how society governs on the collaboration maintenance language of, "We protect ourselves so we do not get hurt, and it shows we are tough." This language postpones the relatedness that I am talking about. Our pursuit of common aims must imply that our social connection must co-operate as a team. Even though it may not serve you in the long run, the intimacy of giving oneself to the Other defines the neutrality of human development. When we engage in the mystery of co-operation, we find new creativity, new beauty, and a new meaning in life. It retains some sensibility for us to be firmly grounded with an experience that brings us new principles.

Again, our courage to connect with others has been devalued through the process of an industrial system. Today, machines are designed for quickness, to give us the best results in minutes. New phones, new technology, everything that has the word "new" has led our culture to course the human values as a machine. In some respects, human values are dependent on economic values. Citizens believe that if they are slow to learn an art or slow to learn how certain technologies operate, then, they foster the illusion of falling behind thus yielding to anxiety and depression.

Courage is an integration of
insight and motivation; you slowly
build your foundation through the
principles of precision and logic.

If we are to move away from the conditioning of economic values, then, we must allow ourselves to slow time by practicing the art of communication. To discuss the problems of the human dilemma is the purest form of living a genuine life. It unfurls variations of unconscious pictures in its entirety. Difficult tasks are carried out to attempt a new description of how one will experiment with the question and the answer. It is the growth of consciousness that branches different possibilities to connect each puzzle piece.

Existential Courage: An Enrichment of Potentiality

Our last phase of courage is existential courage. It is the courage to strengthen one's belief to face existence and to break one's destructive habits. This form of vitality enriches new potentialities to have personal awareness. With every psychological challenge that we face, it creates a new path for our psychological stability to form new constructions that build resilience toward the Self.

When we attempt to structure our lived experiences with a form of existential courage, it increases our personhood, competency, and it nourishes our growth. Our threats of war, illnesses, and in the face of death, our courageous behavior must take place during the phase of these factors. What I found to believe is that when we have something to "live for" rather than living as a by-product, we enhance our experiences in our relationships and with ourselves. Our needs and values are highly correlated to self-actualization. No individual is exempted from living an existential, meaningful life. The most heroic individuals are tested through their individuation, creativity, and productivity. They agree that in order to summon a higher life of meaning, one must immerse through the capacities that express themselves through a universal connection. The process of moment-to-moment is rewarding. The awe and delightfulness are experiences that leave traces of beauty in our world. Connections to courage profiles insight into one's creativity. On these grounds, it creates new experiences that change one's view toward humanity. Existential courage creates aspects for greater expressiveness and spontaneity.

It helps us to remember the lessons that we endured so we can continue to grow and mature in our personhood. In general, its rewards are not only purposeful but also amicable.

A step toward existential courage means giving up something familiar. It means parting ways with parts of your life that brought you discouragement or sorrow. It means rebirthing to a newer Self that connects you to a new attitude. It often means giving up an easy, comfortable life for a demanding life, one that requires more responsibility and more growth. It requires courage, faith, authenticity, and a driven purpose. You do not need permission from the environment to live out your dreams. All you need is a new outlook towards life with a little mixture of desire. The ideal way of enhancing your lifestyle is to posture your advantages with formulas that show new diagrams for you to follow a new blueprint. This means you demonstrate your nature by pressing toward the ultimate potential of capacities to live in a flexible yet congruent life.

The will to live a meaningful life is when we understand the perversions of mental conditions such as wishes that lead to a sleepwalker who daydreams of a good life but never does anything about it. Another one is a negative outlook where we confound our current events with an irrationality that life is fatalistic. We attempt to diagnose everything and put a label. There is no reason to shun or label human behavior with terrible limits. It is simply a universal involvement — an attempt to question and answer the complexities of existence.

As Socrates once said, "The unexamined life is not worth living." I say the unexamined life is worth analyzing for it gives us comprehension of how modern society operates. It is easy to root in the external presence. Without realizing it, we become like the Other — desiring, craving, and enjoying passive pleasures that have no meaning in our lives. So yes, go ahead and analyze the unexamined life because it gives us an unimpeachable taste for a better life that is worth examining.

We are citizens who are brave enough to orient new content that helps us to rewrite history. Strangely, it is through uncertainty and anxiety that pushes us on a voyage of discovery.

When it comes to existential courage, the path will be foreign. But that is when we bend ourselves towards growth and maturity. Our ultimate risks will walk us through a path that is temporary dark. Through it all, those different experiences that frighten us the most will help us gain a new zest. And in some mysterious way, life will feel invigorating.

Legendary moments are granted
to those who accept the moment
and convert it into a story of courage.

Existential Courage Worksheet

Use this worksheet to reflect on where you are and where you want to be in your journey. This has helped my clients to reach a new level of self-actualization.

1. What is important for me and the world is...

2. Beginning today, the steps that I will take towards courage are...

3. I recognize my potential to achieve a greater life. The qualities that I bring to the world are...

4. I value the importance of real, authentic social connections. Today, I will increase my network by...

5. Those who are closest to me such as my family and friends, they need me to show up with a motivational progression to a meaningful life. I will demonstrate this by…

6. I am aware of an increase in gratitude. I will show more gratitude by…

7. The external environment is not my validation. Today, I validate my life and my health by changing and nourishing my habits that align with my destiny. I choose to manifest more of…

8. I am strong enough to grieve and to find new beauty. Part of this process is difficult, but starting today, I will shift my mind from losing to gaining new insight. I can begin by doing something meaningful such as…

9. Living in regret is a story told by millions. I choose a different plot for my story. Today, I will write, revise, and go back and edit my life. One of the plots that bring more beauty, love, courage, and freedom to my life is doing more of…

ON CONTRIBUTION

Unwrap the Benefits of Goodness to Help Others Flourish

Today's world is full of wants, and a desire to accompany misery with pointless drama.

Many go astray to surround themselves with immediate pleasure that brings a small extent of possession. If we take a minute, what can we do differently today where we can enrich a better future? Think about it for a moment. Also, if we want to advance our society to a collectivistic wholeness, what steps can we take today to know we are getting closer to human flourishment?

Globally, there is a yearning to utilize a new experience, one in which we can discover new meaning and a broader connection that can gap our past lessons with present wholeness. Closely, we are learning new insights into the truth of existence. In carrying on my humble lessons, I can honestly say that our world is dividing itself into comparison and status. In the early days, when thoughtfulness was greatly embraced as a gift, individuals would express their attitude through a plenitude of love and connection.

Today, we see superficial demands where individuals want extreme praise. In evidence, this tells us that most inspire the soul with a design that considers favors for themselves. Contribution has become a conversion of, "I will continue to donate my money to your charity, but you will have to continue to help me be in office for the next four years." This has become a political game rather than inspiring society to live through the principle of altruism that considers the welfare of others. This proposes a question. If we benefit our minor works, how will this create a constructive domain for the community? The failure we see today is when citizens are convinced that lavish deeds and favoritism are sported with achievement.

By establishing this faulty belief, existence becomes identified with an end to its pursuit. Our history must be rewritten with a necessity to proclaim good morals, values, and ethics. Our actions should lay a path whose principles strengthens the intentionality of logic and analysis. Once we begin to care for others, we will learn to care for the image that we put out to the world.

The narrative that we want to write for our world is an expression to join those who are ready to prosper and to invest in a life that is filled with beauty and meaning. Collectively, we defend the tyranny, the war starters, but I am asking each of you to depart from the private expressions of hate. Let us understand that we need each other; not for special interest, but for unity and love. When you face the mere end stages of your life, reflect on how you changed the world rather than focusing on how much money you will leave behind. Death does not care for your riches. The rich and the poor go through the same transitions of life. It is the greatest reset to put everything back in balance.

The Future of Humanity

As citizens of the world, we have work to do to build a solid bedrock of unity. Our meaningful habits must structure increased creativeness that brings certain changes to humanity.

To some degree, we have fashionably distorted our image of beauty. If we are to live a motivated life, we must observe society and deliberately ask these important, meaningful questions:

1. Today, who can I serve with the utmost love?

2. How can I be of change? What steps can I take today to know that I am contributing something significant?

3. Who needs me today?

4. With the money that I have earned, which organizations can I donate it to? Or better yet, which organization would I like to start?

5. Who can I contact today to set up a meeting about forming a union of change?

Ask those questions every morning and afternoon. At the end of the day, before you retire to sleep, I want you to be honest with yourself. Take inventory of what you did and did not do. The things you did not do, ask yourself: What stopped me today from serving others? How can I enhance my love for others so that I can enrich the world with meaning? Do not be afraid to be objective with yourself. There will be times when you will feel uncomfortable. When I objectively analyze myself, my heart either beats faster or my heart feels at ease. When my heart beats faster, that means I did not accomplish what I promised myself. At times, I feel uncomfortable because I feel as though I let the world down.

But in my heart, I know I did not. That is why it is extremely important to not beat yourself over if you did not contribute something. It takes habit and persistence. Research has shown that it takes two months to form a new habit. When you begin your journey on contribution, you will notice that at times, you will succeed in your promises, and at other times, you will skip some of your promises. When that happens, just know, you can extract wisdom. Do not exhaust yourself on the why's.

Focus on the what, who, and how. This will enrich your mind to take responsibility for your internal process thinking and to take responsibility to do good for the welfare of other citizens.

I genuinely believe that good moral behavior exists in each of us. However, I am not naïve to think that no evil or bad behavior exists. As I said before, we need to yield to a new enlightenment, the enlightenment of universality, empathy, connection, and unconditional love. This path will project a firmer foundation that helps us to develop a new centering. Our attachment and desire for dependency on the environment have caused the human species to betray each other through the value system of war and hate.

These tendencies cause a deficiency in the Being-of-Self. One of the quickest ways to turn our society from deficiency driven attitudes to a more growth-based attitude is to differentiate the effects of external gratification and the association of internal meaning placement. The internal meaning placement is where we contribute something significant that detaches the breed of a hidden agenda.

The relativeness between the Self and existence is when we uniform an agreement among the circle of influence to do good rather than doing harm.

The most important take away on contribution is to change the circumstances. It becomes meaningful when we associate a new outcome that extends a new belief system that constructs to understand the world and our deeds to others. It is easy to defend the pre-determined corruption of ill behavior, but it is more rewarding when we agree to hold our positions as humans to take responsibility to help others flourish towards a life that has beauty and truth. Let us hold strongly to a view that is purposeful and meaningful, which supplements a dialectical relationship between connection and empathy. All possibilities will reveal themselves as an enhancement that summarizes the suitable action that we must procure to make our world thrive.

ON SELF-ESTEEM

My Reflection is who I am, not The Beliefs of The Environment

When a relationship ends, or when someone berates us, it is existentially painful to understand their residual. The high volume of pain comes deeply rooted in how our invisible wounds reflect upon the human condition. We carry on with our agendas, expressively giving ourselves wholly to the universe. But then, somehow, someone strokes a misfortune of words that scar the soul with insecurity. People lay back, accepting what is told from the Other. They occasionally serve the defects of language that was spoken. They say things like, "You are not made for this." "Stop pretending you are successful." "Might as well quit." "You are too skinny to lift weights." "Stop being emotional." Some of you may have been put through this situation where individuals place their venom in your consciousness. Day by day, it saps your energy into disappointment; joy into sorrow; and connection with disconnection.

A significant number of you will go through betrayal. But isn't this to be expected? Isn't this the human condition? Society will challenge us mentally, emotionally, and spiritually. A lot of us will want to push against the tides rather than going with the tides. You see, our environment is constantly changing. That is a given. The full weight that we face is not so much from the stimulus of the environment; it is the interpretation that we give to the environment. The more we attempt to enkindle the intimate contact with our fellow Beings, the more we will understand each other's nature.

In simple terms, we must preserve our emotional growth. Authenticity, connection, empowerment, and finding meaning in life is one's ability to maintain his or her self-worth. By positioning beauty and meaning, you can look inward. As such, you value yourself, while at the same time, you acknowledge and question Other people's behaviors, motives, and reactions.

Self-knowledge builds an integration of wisdom that allows us to look honestly at the world. Most are motivated by corruption while some are motivated by greed. No matter what is presented to you, no venom is too poisonous unless you allow its company to seep into your soul.

Multiplicative Inverse

In mathematics, for every x except for zero, y represents its multiplicative inverse. The number zero does not represent any real number because when it is multiplied by zero, it does not produce the number one. The product of zero is zero. Reciprocals of every rational number are rational, thus making the fraction complete.

To put it to practice, let me give you an example.

$\frac{5}{3}$x = 15 (the multiplicative inverse for this equation would be the opposite).

$\frac{3}{5}$ $\frac{5}{3}$x = 15 multiplied by $\frac{3}{5}$

$\frac{15}{15}$x = $\frac{45}{5}$

X = 9

You may feel a certain puzzlement at this point. You are probably asking yourself, "Luis, what does this have to do with your chapter on self-esteem?" That is a great question and it deserves a deep, existential outlook as to why I explained and broke down the concept of the multiplicative inverse.

Mathematics, philosophy, and psychology are participants that bind deeply to the physical home of the mind, body, and spirit. Our human biography is attached to probabilities that are woven consciously and unconsciously to the qualities of time within the body and physiological tempo. Like multiplicative inverse, your self-esteem is tied to the same equation. The difference is the creativity toward the relation of personhood. For instance, the multiplicative inverse for self-esteem can be summed up in an existential equation.

What most people do:

$$\frac{Self-esteem}{creativity} X = \frac{authenticity}{1} X \frac{creativity}{0}$$

X = 1 x 0

X= 0 (a lack of self-direction toward the personhood)

You see, most of us have authenticity and self-esteem, but we neglect our creativity. When we neglect our creativity, we cut ties with knowledge and wisdom. Most are motivated to accomplish tasks in life. Some have zest while some lose the courage to live meaningfully. In between the stream, they internally lose sight of the vital meaning of personhood. True knowing of Self begins when we trust, validate, and accept the Self by honoring the choices and decisions we made. Our involvement with existence demonstrates growth and skills that are needed to bring change through which we connect with beauty.

Breaking up one's vision of the world is how one fragments the expression of Self and existence.

The meaning of self-esteem leads to an active process of exploring one's personality, understanding the meaning of life, forming beliefs that bring purpose, motivating ourselves to a greater life, and a willingness to acknowledge our vulnerability.

This becomes a companionship of what one feels and does. When we take the time to truly honor the soundtrack of our self-esteem, we will become conscious of the special place that brought us a jubilee, enabling us to move toward the window, raising the blinds, and smiling to a new serenity.

We should be encouraged to learn more about our self-esteem through a multiplicative inverse point of view. Suitable changes often lead to the designed life that we imagined. For example, previously, I stated what most people do. Now, I will present an equation on how your self-esteem should be connected to your personhood.

How it should be:

(Inverse equation)

$$\frac{creativity}{self-esteem} \cdot \frac{self-esteem}{creativity} \; X = \frac{authenticity}{1} \times \frac{creativity}{self-esteem}$$

$$\frac{creativity}{self-esteem} \; X = \frac{1}{1} = 1 \text{ (wholeness toward the personhood)}$$

The qualities of mathematics, philosophy, and psychology can unbind or loosen what was deeply held in our subconscious thoughts. When a dialogue is maintained within the Self, not only can we explore our issues and concerns, but we can be objective toward the image we see within ourselves. This emerges slowly once we empower the centered Self with a sequence of creative endeavors.

The fullest meaning can be attempted once we create a vision that transcends fear into inspiration. Our self-esteem is a driving force of continuity that endures in the universal context. Whatever situation we find ourselves in, we can creatively orient to the full scope of a meaningful, driven life. This unique process liberates us from the fear of social conformity. We eventually discover self-actualization, one through which the Self emerges from feeling negative into a courageous, expressed Self whose existence is not circulated around insecurity. Rather, it is leveled universally that establishes involvement with existence toward the Self. This is the hallmark of inner growth. It is through awareness and intentionality that puts us in the level of human flourishment.

Nurturing the Self Worksheet

Below, you will follow the directions to link a new discovery to your life's script. By assuring an ongoing continuity of growth and maturity, you will resolve any alienated parts of your Self. The goal of this worksheet is to heal any wounds that may have left a residual in your unconscious thoughts.

Directions: You will write in the space that represents your highest self-esteem. By writing in the space that is provided, you will rescript your narrative to an action-oriented phase where you give a sense of choice and control toward the personhood.

When I fast-forward through the positive changes that I am feeling, seeing, and experiencing, I will begin to act more…

When I frame my self-esteem with what aligns with my life, I will begin to choose to feel…

Describe when, where, and how you went from emptiness into a fuller, happier Self where your self-esteem increased by five interval points.

ON LOVE

The Importance of Authenticity, Empathy, Connection, and
Expressing the Desire to Have Meaningful Sex

S omething stirs within love which points to a
metamorphosis. It remains quiet, yet vibrant to the
references of connection and transparency.

The entire authorship awakens gladly to a new discourse
that reflects on its actions while at the same time, emending
the weighted outcomes of hate and anger. Expressions of
love are a mystery that snapshots the uniqueness of another
individual.

We see the meaningfulness of human existence
flourishing in singularity between the twoness. Creative
values become ensued that formulates into actualization,
making love a living experience that validates the action and
comprehension of a human soul. In love, two are
comprehended with an inner enrichment that embodies as a
We-Thou, surrendering comparison of talents. It values the
grace of being in love; not falling in love.

Being in love represents the sacred unity, standing one step closer to eternity. The primitive attitude in this mode is identical to the one we have with our spirituality; it pushes us to worship the lover in front of us. Lovers lack this kind of worship that I speak of. The worshipping should be authentic, respectful, honorable, and vulnerable. It should place the union as an established connection to the creation of love.

Earthly love engages in pride,

centered love engages in

connection and empathy.

The mark of maturity is when both understand and respectfully honor each other's wholeness. In *The Five Virtues That Awaken Your Life,* I talked about how relationships should be 1 + 1 = 3. 1 represents the wholeness of oneself. The other 1 represents the second individual with whom you are in love with.

Lastly, 3 represents the union of love. That is where you honor and promise to bring out the best in each other. The most common mistake couples make is to defend themselves out of the field of egoism. It transfers feelings of superiority, raging onto a projection of anger to the partner. One way to be mindful of the union of love is to ask yourself this question: By vowing to the sacred circle of love, how can I be more authentic and open to my partner?

This question is powerful because it detaches you from self-ego. It keeps your identity concealed by coming forth to the light. What the psyche does not understand is that it is selfish or as Freud would say, the id is a desirable pleasure principle that wants to seduce the morality complex. At a higher level of love, the couple must briefly introduce to each other the intimacy and openness of feelings. Regretfully, we do not yield to this path. Instead, we repress our wounds. And somehow, we expect our partner to comfort those wounds with unmeaningful sex that leads to guilt.

The feeling of unity that a child feels during the womb is the same feeling we pine for in our adult years. As we enter a relationship or marriage, keep in mind that no partner will magically restore your disowned Self. You will stir up each other's unmet fantasies, repressed feelings, and earlier emotional childhood wounds. In either case, you must communicate your feelings, commit to listening, share your needs and intimate concerns, and steer the union back to the sacred circle. This connection will associate with spiritual growth along with a healing space between dialogue and self-integration.

The type of partner that you choose,
it will expose an outline of your
unconscious attraction.

Sex and The Human Level of Authenticity

Beneath our unconscious thoughts are hidden chambers of certain pictures that we manifest. Reflections down the path create a painting that allows us to express our emotional center. It takes great courage to relate our intimacy to another soul. Not just to achieve sex, but to create a meaningful intimacy where both risk a new growth toward the relationship. Binding ourselves fully into connection will have a certain suffering. We will experience gladness, nakedness, fantasies, hopes, and fears. It is easier to neglect the person in front of us whom we love, especially when they say, "Can we have sex tonight? We haven't had pleasure in a long time." Stupidly, we respond with, "Not tonight, sweetheart. I had a long day. Maybe some other time."

Hence, couples short-circuit the route of sex by building a frontage of being busy with activities that may have no meaning. For the next few pages, I will spend an amount of time talking about sex, authenticity, and expressing each other's touch, kisses, and sounds.

Today, we see a high amount of fear of expressing our authentic sex towards our relational partner. Intimacy begins slowly with ice cream on the lips, slowly wiping it off with each other's kisses, and then, the fun stops. It is no wonder we see a high variable rate of divorce. People leap with different partners, hoping to fill the intimacy void. Jumping from partner to partner will not bring you meaning. On the contrary, they will bring more baggage that deepens itself with higher expectations. What do I mean? Well, since the former could not live up to the expectation of sex, openness, and social intimacy, the new partner will be expected to perform on a higher form of degree for you to deliver the need. This becomes new anxiety mixed with pleasure dependency on someone else. It shows that a need must be met but through the effect or a "sooner or later" phase. This type of pleasure dependency brings no fruition to the union. It creates a remarkable form of guilt that punishes the basis of authenticity.

What we see presently is a form of guilt. Today, sex has been deduced. Many couples do not want to have sex due to the rebellious differences of sacraments in religion. Or even worse, we see couples engaging in the figurehead of sex due to lowly satisfaction.

In my coaching sessions and therapeutic sessions, I teach couples to put aside the differences in beliefs, politics, and the noise of the world. I help them bring back the sacred circle of love. Love has no religion. Love has no politics. Love has no hate. Love sees all and knows all. It knows the nature of creativity between two souls. When couples come to me saying how their marriage is on the brink of divorce, I ask them these three important questions:

1. Does your relationship have spontaneity? If not, what is holding you back from achieving a new form of excitement?

2. Are you two being flirtatious? If not, what can you do differently to bring out new arousal where both of you get a certain feeling of ecstasy?

3. When was the last time you felt each other's bodies and kisses?

By asking them those questions, it gives me a quick assessment of where they are in the moment. 99.9% of the time, they want to enhance their relationship. Through a few sessions, I help them practice a technique that I call *four breaths, hold the look.*

In the example, I will guide you slowly on a technique that I developed two years ago. What this does is, it brings back the moment of clarity. It helps you focus on each other's depth.

Directions:

Take out a blanket. Place it wherever you feel is cozy. Dim the lights. Place some seductive candles that give a pleasurable scent. Also, at a low volume, put some soft jazz music. Lastly, get naked. That is right. Take off your clothes. And be presently open with your partner. Without touching or getting excited, one will lay down on the blanket, while the other will be on top. Remember, no touching, no kissing. Make sure your lips are not touching each other, but just enough to feel it close to you. Now, for five minutes, slowly breathe on your partner's lips.

One will take turns doing this. One partner will breathe on the lip. And then, your partner will do the same. Another exercise is, hold one hand and place the other hand on your partner's heart. Your partner should do the same. Both of you should be holding each other's left hand while your right hands are touching each other's hearts. Slowly, both of you will take turns in saying this:

I accept you just as you are. With imperfections, my love for you is a home through which I find comfort. Every piece of your beauty brings me closer to your eternity. I now understand every stone of your past, and every carriage that you rode on. I am in total sensibility toward your personhood. Naked and vulnerable, I am free when I am with you. Onward, we will work together as a couple to see the beauty in the world and of each other. Every visitation of life will bring us to a newly made decision on whether to be bitter in jealousy, or to exist with our unique individualities, piecing the image of strength, enlightenment, and love. I vow and commit wholly to you as we leave our mistakes at the river, peacefully going on its own speed while we move forward to what is important — the ascension to a meaningful life. I love you! I love you! I love you!

At this point, bring each other close again to the lips, stare at each other deeply, hold for a minute. Once the minute is up, slowly kiss each other. Place each other's hands on the body. Feel each other's textures of the skin. Explore the body. Whisper seductive messages in your partner's ear. Nibble softly. This is your time. This is your creativity.

In practice, I give this worksheet to couples who want to divorce in vain, without giving valid reasons. Couples argue but never calibrate to the details of the relationship. Once I give them the worksheet, they come back happier, more fulfilled, and more meaningful towards the sacred union of love. If you find yourself in this dilemma, try my exercise. If your emotions are beyond overload with your partner, then consider couples counseling. This exercise is only used for couples who sprout in vain but are willing to work out the relationship without breaking it off or divorcing.

Those who engage in communication, cultivation, and vulnerability, you will notice a correspondence between happiness and romance. This is noticeable when both hold a middle space for extension. It adds comprehension and a vessel that is continually observed by a perpetual flow of openness. Sex, when engaged with your partner, it should feel evident that it is authentic.

Too many people have sex for unworthy causes. This is a mistake we see in society. People have a misconception that sex will give a geometric power that will sustain for a lifetime. It is no wonder people hop from one bedroom to the next.

The type of sex that I am talking about is the sex of authenticity. Sex is a sacred energy that should not be played with. It is an intimate bond between two souls who are vulnerable and open to give each other new beauty to life. Without ever having to arrive at its playful game of quenched desires, it should move slowly to a necessary conclusion that this moment feels right. By entering each other's private world, each energy will be passed down to the body and soul. When it enters, it should feel like a beautiful sun, providing warmth and comfort to the house of creation.

Along with the parameter of growth, both should inspire each other; not battle against genders. I had a woman call me up for a quick coaching session in terms of sex with her husband. They got married and had two months into their marriage. As the conversation began, she bluntly said, "Luis, I love my husband. I do. But damn, I cannot stand how he does not help me. When I ask him to help me with the laundry, he does not fold it properly. Do you know what he does? He lays them straight on top of our laundry cabinet.

He does not even fold them. Also, he leaves his undies on our bed. And to top it off, he expects me to have sex with him at night. Like hell no. He is not getting any from me if you know what I mean."

With an empathetic attitude, I said, "I can see the amount of frustration you have. You went into this marriage thinking it would be the perfect love story. And now, here we are, battling the sexes to see who has more control or to see who is more obedient. Am I right?"

She chuckles with some laughter and says yes.

Here we see a powerful presentation of the American myth, a myth that swallows up the home, consciously or unconsciously stripping away the protection of unity, and developing a final judgment that points to blame and resentment. We live in a new age where men and women are competing for the same status. One desire for men is to be admired by women. The other desire for women is to be a queen whose power fascinates the picture album of the world through power and presence. Man wants to take care of their woman through their machismo behavior — flaunting their muscles, showing a grandiosity of power.

Whereas a woman, they want to be independent of their man. Not as in single status but as in I-can-take-care-of-myself. Women play an important role in the world. They are the product of creation. Above all else, they are the puzzle piece that glues the home with nurture. They become a part of togetherness — bridging hate with peace. They carry with them a certain light, a home where we can feel a secure belonging. Whether occupying the status of a mother, a sister, a politician, or a female entrepreneur, they protect the community through a sensible intimacy. It develops over time in a human fashion of empathy and peace.

Evolutionary speaking, they have demonstrated this behavior through warmth and protection. Today, we see men and women competing against each other as if it were a race against humanity. Women protest with signs that read, "Vaginal power." "Women are in charge." "Men shall obey us." I feel that this disorients humanity into resentment. It divides the world into a greater surge of war between gender roles. What we need today is for men and women to forge a new path that corresponds to a new healthy form of communication.

As part of the community and of the world, men and women need to build the human spirit with kindness, a symbol of eternity that glimmers with the blessing of a new beginning. This is not only a requirement; it is a prerequisite for a spiritual awakening. Men and women who carry together their aspirations, ideals, and have a deep sense of a collective society, we will see a new reflective society. This will not only change the heartland of America, but it will multiply its effects throughout the world. The lonely myth of gender competition will no longer fascinate the center stage with its shiny advertisements or crying out for the unread literature of superiority complexes. It will deeply reveal what humanity has been longing for; a wondrous moment where we successfully aspire for a greater life.

Nevertheless, I see married couples not engaging in sex due to superiority complexes. One wants power while the other wants the sexual released drive. Divorce is occurring because too much emphasis is placed on which gender deserves credibility. When I tell couples to reach out to your partner and be flirtatious, they kind of laugh and respond with, "It has been a long time since we did that."

Couples who validate, express, nurture, love, and make time for sex, they will element different shades and colors to their relationship. But those who triangulate with power, conflict, and reinterpret the past, they will struggle against each other, holding down to the mockery that places them inside a prison cell of despair, coupled with ignorance and warfare.

As I wrap up this portion of sex and authenticity, I want to emphasize how important it is to construct validation and peak time experiences. The daily routine should not create a strange cloud upon your relationship. It should emphasize the intensity of experience that yields to new meaning to counterbalance the old experiences. The strangest route we can take in a relationship is when we feel obligated to triumph love with power. In a sense, it glimpses into a narcissistic love that shrinks the individualism of each other. When gathered, share the intimacy just as how we hold a book; read each other's body language. Do not stop at one page. Continue to revisit the domain of connection and transparency. Most importantly, lean on each other for strength and guide the relationship towards a supportive, centered, healing space.

The book of love should never be paired with comparison or with resentment. It should admit the faults and imperfections. By building each other up, you will piece together a home that feels as if it was built for the first time.

Basement Relationship vs. First Floor Relationship

For a while, I have been analyzing relationships, especially how they communicate and express their feelings. The fears they hold, the companionship, the touch, the kiss, all of it builds a deeper level of intimacy. Romantic love is more than calculated words. It is about acknowledging the emotional wounds from the past, digging deeper into the present moment, and being empathetic of what is lacking in each other's lives. In a nutshell, romantic love builds more security rather than showering one-night stands, leaving the Other to feel like an illusion. It is no wonder we see lovers clinging to the basement relationship, which is lust and irrational behavior.

For several years, I have studied what makes a healthy relationship flourish and what depletes the relationship. And as such, I coined two terms: *basement relationship* and *first floor relationship*. Let's begin with the basement relationship. Have you ever taken the elevator and pushed "basement level?" I am sure you have. I know I have. What do you see on the basement level? How does it look? What does it smell like? Close your eyes. Analyze what the basement level looks like. Now that you are ready, open your eyes and see yourself in the basement level. Walk through it. I am sure it feels odd, yucky, and scary. You mostly see ladders, wastebaskets, lights flickering, and lastly, a history of written messages in pencil form on some old wall or maybe on a new wall.

This represents the unconscious level of a relationship. Just as you felt confused and scared on the basement level, so does your unconscious mind. It has filtered information whether good or bad into a wastebasket that wires neurologically from memory to present awareness. To some degree, denial plays a role. It is a coping tool that we use when a relationship is sour, or when an individual represents a parental figure.

Whenever life presents us with a difficult situation, we have a proclivity to snub existence and create a fantasy world where everything seems perfect.

This is the problem with today's relationships. Most of them operate on the basement relationship status. They do nothing to improve their current situation. No matter the arguments, they complain endlessly about who is right or who did wrong. Playing the child role appears to be the commitment role they take instead of taking the adult role, where they improve on their communication and listening skills. I have been asked numerous times, "Luis, is it bad to be in the basement relationship mode?" Yes and no. As I explained, it is bad when two individuals push away the authenticity of love. And it is only good to go to the basement relationship mode when you notice repressed trauma, unfinished business from your previous relationship, and the projection that you place on your partner.

That is the only time you must enter the basement level of your relationship. It should be a safe circle between you and your partner. You must open the conversation with, "Sweetheart, can I talk to you? I have been wanting to tell you this for a while, but I do not know how to explain it. I have been experiencing some unfinished business from my childhood wounds. My parents were not there for me. I want to get more intimate with you and explain everything to you. Hopefully, you will understand on a deeper level." That is a quick excerpt to have your partner enter their movie role so you can see who directed it, who produced it, who wrote it, and who edited it. You can witness their darkness on a lower level of their unconsciousness. The abandoned Self will show up on your partner's personality once you have validated their wholeness, even their hidden sources of tensions. By accepting their basement, you can help them let go of the hoarding of emotions where they once held every bit of hurt and minimization toward the Self. You are not playing the rescue role; you are playing the part of connection and wholeness to your partner.

That is what they need from you. They need to feel your nourishment that fills up with a connection, not a facade. This reminds me of the myth of Plato's *Symposium* that serves greatly in today's relationship status, especially the basement level. In his myth, he vividly describes how Zeus pondered on the notion to have men and women split up, leaving their emotional wounds open and visible for them to feel. What was once four feet and four hands is now two hands and two feet, in search of restoration to the wholeness that we once had with our lover. This is a powerful myth with a lot of truth that helps us to debate life's questions on love.

Who am I as a Being? Why do I feel alone without my partner? What can I do differently to help bring more vitality and beauty to the relationship? These questions will help us go through life in a meaningful sphere. Today, we neglect the basement level because we do not want to enter the darkness of the past and therefore, we fill the emptiness with drugs or engage in alcohol abuse.

What we yearn for is not so much the ecstasy of touch and kiss, we yearn for the restoration of wholeness that we once had in our formative years. Cheerfully we smiled as children, played freely, spontaneously asking questions about the universe. But somehow, we lost that curiosity in turn for the banal desires. It is our birthright to return to the Buddha joy that we experienced. Our spiritual yearning for love and connection must be the firm conviction that will appeal to us with a smile — completing us with wholeness. This is what restoring our basement level relationship does. It helps us understand and to move toward the greater depth of the next chapter. It is when you look into your partner's eyes and say, "We finally understand each other, my love."

When we go through rocky relationships, we somehow watch the drama unfold. The stage is set. The curtains are open. And now, each tragedy unfolds a progressive relation of hidden sources. Blindly, we symbolize it as an inner fact of how the relationship is. A lot of individuals do not recognize that it is not the spoken word that causes the volcano to erupt; it is, in fact, a history of projection of anger, charging each word with a strategy to win the argument.

Also, we cannot forget that when you date someone, their former lover left a collection of energy which consists of kisses, touching, holding, written lyrical poetry, familiar outings, and warm moments on the beach. With that said, when a relationship faces an upheaval, it is not so much you who is to blame unless you said something to offend him or her. Nonetheless, most of the arguments stem from an unfinished business from the previous occasion. Are you to blame? Absolutely not. Unless you triggered your partner with a demeaning tone.

Every altercation serves as a fascinating story to your dialogue with your partner. Most speak in a fateful horror of, "Please leave me alone. I want to be single and free."

No rescued relationship is bought through another human soul. Most castrate themselves from the troubling mountain slide that brings a peril of threat. Nothing forms originally out of spite. It forms originally when two join the dance of love.

When two understand each other's basement level of relationship, they can go inside the sacred circle of love and push to the first floor which is the conscious level of vulnerability.

What's fascinating about the first floor relationship is that most couples that I have coached or counseled seem to hesitate on how one can come to terms with meaning. After having many discussions with them, one of the tools I teach them is what I call *integrative conclusion*. What this tool does is help them take part in their conclusion, in addition to exploring the reasons as to why the absence is far more threatening than harmonizing in varied viewpoints. To explain what I mean, let me share a quick session I did with a married couple. Being that it was twelve sessions, I will only cover a snippet of what integrative conclusion is.

Around the eighth session, I used my tool with a couple who repeated the flow of the meta-message of "always." They would say, "It's always your damn fault. Not mine!" Or, "If it wasn't for your lame ass extended family who always butts in with our things, we wouldn't have this dilemma, now would we?"

These dialogues interest me because their arguments have nothing to do with wanting to fix the occurrence of problems. What they deeply root for is to cherish their future together, but they resort to the moderate intensity of emotions. As humans, we pluck out our animalistic instincts in defense of our message.

To move away from the defensive side, I have the couple share their integrative conclusion, and what it means to them to draw significant statements that produce meaningful outcomes. Some may have an intense need to hold on to the negative traits of their upbringing. This can be a repetitive integrative conclusion that they finalized. At times, that is where their outbursts stem from when he or she argues with their partner. Unconsciously, they want their emotions to be nursed with positive feelings. It becomes difficult when two parties challenge each other's tolerance. Frequently, this happens a lot at an unconscious level. This becomes a paradox to the relationship. When one tries to merge the projection onto the partner's seeding, it becomes impossible to become "available" emotionally and spiritually.

In the primary givens, a search for acceptance plays a primary role when two secure the lot of what it means to be authentically open toward the wholeness of the relationship. When a couple expresses and validates each other's vulnerability, the couple experiences a new sense of awareness, and thus, they move to the completion phase of positive seeding.

Like in the example that I provided, I helped the couple to reconcile their narrative. Integrative conclusion helps the couple to participate as a subject instead of momentarily booking the language of anger. This tool helps to produce constructive activity to help meet the threatening situation such as an argument, verbal acquisition, or blocking off the awareness. To use the tool effectively, follow the directions below.

Directions: Take out a sheet of paper. Each will write their integrative conclusions that they have been telling themselves, marked as facts. On the other column, you will put integrative conclusion (new greater Self). You will write down what new conclusions you want for you and your partner.

This helps to challenge misconceptions about the previous conclusions that you held as facts. When you carefully analyze the tales that you have told yourself, ask yourself these questions:

- Are my faulty conclusions marked as facts?
- What is it about this conclusion that has caused me to feel a shrinkage toward the Self?
- What new distinctions can I make at this moment?

- What are some steps that I can take that will help me deepen the source of emotional beauty?

Integrative conclusion is a powerful tool that will draft a new inner experience that will help you to solve life's dilemmas. It is a moment of enrichment, a dance between each other's notes, a degree of consciousness, and an adaptation to a new frontier that will garner a philosophical formulation of cause and effect. The experience to a new conclusion will have the union to constructively confront the situation with an awareness that distinctively correlates to the subjective and objective moment. When the problem is correlated to a solution, the psychological defenses will lay rest, making the union to unfold a direction that drafts a harmonious connection, leading each other towards an opportunity to position and to respond to the demands of life in a meaningful way.

One area that I have the couple focus on is the transition stage between lecturing each other the wrongs to a premium sensation of preserving the locked language of love. The locked language of love brings out the matched qualities of congruence and empathy.

Again, it is simply not about blaming our external environment. It is a criterion that is *chosen* and *written* by the person. It brings to bear upon himself or herself when they feel an admixture of anger or anxiety. When this happens, they somehow want others to feel their integrative conclusion by saying, "Alright, you think you can play this game. We'll see. I can play this game way better than you. Watch your back." This language purchases the development of later admission to the suffering of emotions. It bears nothing when someone takes a stand to that position.

A final point that I would like to make on integrative conclusion is the importance of values. I believe that when a couple commits to the constructive experience of relation, they will bring out the best in each other. They will relate to each other's courses of beauty and meaning.

In a nutshell, most of the suffering occurs when several conclusions are integrated into another person. That is when we need to question ourselves and ask: Am I moving into a time of argument? Why do I feel compelled to make my conclusion superior? Once this wisdom sets in, you and your partner will reach an articulated realization that it is not the external environment of blame; it is, in fact, the conclusions that one has written through a historical line of dilemmas.

The triangular relationship will always be the person of Self, the partner of Self, and the sacred circle of love. Each has a degree of consciousness through which the attitudes and behaviors underlie certain conflicts. When these conflicts are discussed authentically, it pushes the union to admit and to understand each other's conclusions.

Attraction and Original Wholeness

The striking thing about attraction and wholeness in our present-day is that, whereas in the past it was about enchantment, romance, and jazzing to the representation of the fundamental idea of being essentially significant. Today, we are held up with the belief of insignificance that every connection that we constitute, we somehow remodel it with deception.

What we lack today is authentic love. We love unauthentically because we are afraid that if we choose to leap into the chorus, we will be silenced with rejection. In the past, especially in the Jazz Age, men and women encountered an eternal growth of totality.

They would not disguise their differences. They would transform the moment with an inner glory of beauty that helped them to permit themselves to be in love.

Occupying love with action bounds
the union with security, leaving
behind the history of hurt.

If we look back to the history of the mythology of Qetesh (the goddess of beauty and sex), Venus (the goddess of love), and Eros (the god of love and sexual desire), each of them would confidently use the power of seduction through the framework of love and beauty. The deepest inkblot is not so much a Rorschach of sexual fantasies or a stacked-up pile of fishnets. It is about the connection and spellbinding to keep the spirit of originality infused with a deepening process that allows the couple to feel the moment, indulging in the body from a spiritual stance, creating a purpose to which love is permanent.

Love is rooted when the eyes are locked in the eternal moment, twisting to a tell-all of carnival, holding each other up to the light to the same watermark of love. In such a moment as this, we must retrofit our modern purposes of love. By learning the *ars amatoria* (the art of love), we can place a special preference on what it is that we must deliver to our culture. By detoxing the lustful games, we can begin to realign our craft of attraction and original wholeness. This will take time. Engraved are the memories of our past love where arousal, attraction, and desire was frankness. Today, we see the suffering of sorrow, a casino of games, couples turning one eye to another individual. The beginning exists but somehow, the middle and the ending end up in a storm, each of them tearing the individuality of beauty. Every day, we must add maturity to the dedication of the youthful spirit of love. Understand that it is "we;" not "I" that pushes oneself to honor the promise of devotional practices that lead to the moment of self-understanding.

Outside of love are the absorptions of a lower court that pleases the notes of the same nature. Inside of love is the expressions of universality that measures a unique dialogue between passion and vulnerability.

Too much is given to a ministering lust of attraction. We forgot that through attraction, there is a view of admiration, creating a poet of surrender, love, and commitment. We forgot how to look into the eyes, sweet sentimental longing that leads us to the promised land. Attraction is more than love at first sight. It is a moment to trace back to the familiarity of what we love about that person. We complete the art by adding qualities that present a belonging. Some might wish to love harder while others wish to withhold the emotion.

No matter what the attraction is, your feelings will somehow remain forbidden due to the priming of socialization. Wouldn't it be weird on a first date, you told the woman in front of you, "My gosh, you are such a goddess. I worship you."

Or telling the man in front of you, "You are so sexy like Tom Ford." I am sure it would create an energy of awkwardness. You can say goodbye to that date of yours. Instinctively, we know that society tells us to repress our attraction because of boundaries. The question that is most often asked is, how do I know the person whom I am on a date with is attracted to me? The answer is simple. Pay attention to body language. Eye contact allows the individual to bring out the hidden desires through a soft glistening that twinkles in their soul.

Lead with your voice,

guide them with your eyes.

Too many people fail to recognize that it is not about over-preparing yourself with deep inspections or to profoundly show off your charms. It is about engaging with the person in front of you. Joy and gratitude should only be the inviting guests to your dinner date.

Not the far reach land of sexual incentive that begins in lust and ends with a discussion of, "Let me go to your house so we can drink wine and chill."

When clients of mine come to me for advice on first dates, I investigate whether they go on dates just for the mere sexual pleasure, or for the authenticity to know the person. The old cliché of nail and bail; steak and wine and under the cover sheets are not what first dates should be about. The first dates are about contributing to beauty. It is an extension of distinctive traits that two people bring to one special night. It helps us to remind ourselves that the experience comes alive when the quality is measured through an illustration of growth and connection.

The person you asked out on a date,
they bring a different level of the past
that is mixed with useful information
to understand their totality.

I get it, first dates can be a dread. People tell me, "It is easy for you to say, Luis, you are a clinical therapist." Clinical therapist or not, we all experience some good feelings of anxiety. It pushes us between what *we know* and what we want to *know about*. When we seek to know another human soul during a date, it produces an authentic connection. One must have an eager readiness to engage in duality. Broadly speaking, the encounter should have the power to move two souls to focus on the significance of adding beauty.

Most dates focus on the defended price of mechanical pleasure that often leads to wild sex and drunken nights. That has been the classical distortion of reality. We analyze what is in front of us, and somehow, we reduce the person into data. Meaning, we determine through the supported subject of properties of sex. We end up imposing a system of conflict with an inborn turmoil of questioning one's existence whether to satisfy the soul with lust or not. The fact remains true. Our Being becomes a Being when we hold accountability towards the moment that we produce. Responsibility becomes awareness through a dialectical relation with humanity. The prerequisite for learning our relation is through social biology.

It takes a mixture of sociology and science to understand attraction and wholeness. Our worldview can be comprehended once we consider the uniqueness of the other person. When going on a date, the most critical question we can ask is, what am I becoming at this moment? What am I pointing towards? Is it my unmet sexual desires, or am I present and vulnerable to this individual? When we realize the power of knowledge and wisdom, it will enable us to process a new meaningful bi-structural subjective experience and an increased production of authenticity.

Windows open each other when
we raise our blinds to a harmonistic
form of communication.

I Cannot Move On

So, you went on your date, both of you felt attracted, and now, you are on the first anniversary as boyfriend and girlfriend. But then, it gets called off. Confusion, depression, anger, they all settle in as you experience a lack of Self. Grasping reality is no longer an extension of beauty; it becomes a private tribulation. I am sure you know what I am talking about. I have been there too.

It is a sharp departure from the one you spent months or years with. Fundamental changes and new habits do not seem possible. The wellspring of this is the unique potentiality that we can build for ourselves, but at the same time, it increases the reproduction of what we made with our former lover.

After going through grave periods of sadness and tears with the breakup of my ex-girlfriend, my life did not make sense without her.

During the turbulent time of 2015, towards Christmas time, that is when she called it off. I was at a place of despair. Every moment did not feel new; it felt like a maw of oblivion, swallowing me into uncommon parts of myself. There was a misrelation between the Self and the world around me. I tried to continue to live a meaningful life, but then, it struck me with a bolt of lightning — her presence, her touch, her kisses, her laughter, her sincerity, everything traced back to what we had. But then, little by little, I arose from the sickness of despair as Kierkegaard called it. Admittedly, it was difficult for me.

However, I used those challenges as my whale of inspiration to deepen new meaning in my life. A continuation of growth helped me to progress to the actual moment of emotional beauty. It is possible to change the feeling of despair into meaning. The key is to conquer the feeling of tragedy into a form of context that heightens new productive action.

The problem we see today with couples who end their relationship is the stagnation towards growth. Most of the population place their attention on the void rather than analyzing the adaptation of events. Critically speaking, we can mature from a breakup when we transform the original relation to a new table of values, which requires a new window of consciousnesses. Slowly, we can nourish the hurt with a thousand-fold process, involving new things, circumstances, and new beauty into our lives. This is how responsibility toward the Self evolves. It takes a calculated goal to make the necessary changes. Precisely, it will be a long journey, but with the right habits and with the right mindset, you will spring up the greater part of the Self. If something should stay in your memory, it should be the main clause of the endurance towards human flourishment. Often, we color the gloomy days with hurt, distinguishing loss without purpose, and lifeless with death.

Attend the mystery of yourself — the Self that promises, vows, and pledges to be the Light of change. Relationship breakups do not end by the Other. That's what threatens the Being. We feel that they have the power to call off the ending. Remember, they are just an actor or actress playing a role in your life. When they say it is over, that means your final scene ended in that movie. There is no need to despair. When a new production calls for it, you will move forward with bravery.

Let us be clear with the phrase, "I cannot move on." Yes, you can move on. Strangely enough, the experience will participate as a rightful professor, passing on lessons for you to soak in the degree of wisdom. Temporary, we might suffer the separation from the one we dedicated our lives to. Somehow, it gets reconstructed with a new subscription of lessons.

What we see today is humans causing another human to suffer through banal games. The notion of, "I doubt they will ever find out about me having an affair." This narrative does no good for the relationship. One of the few ways to be mindful of the Self and the Other is to begin by asking these questions followed by a **declaration** of promise to love.

1. The cheating games that I am employing to my partner, is it coming from revenge, or am I engaging in my self-interest?

2. Do I have an incompletion in my life?

3. Would it be fair if my partner did this to me?

4. If I am not ready to take the next step in asking the person to go out with me, what are some steps that I can take to let the person know I am not ready to date?

5. The childish games that I am playing in our relationship, is it adding authenticity to our lives, or is it subtracting from our lives?

A Declaration of Promise to Love

The declaration that I vow to make is to give love a seriousness, one where the greater totality becomes obvious to my language. I will no longer deceive myself nor others into the false passions that lead my soul astray. My mind will dwell on the beautiful glimmerings where the roses fill up each heart with new promises of hope. Pleasure through possession will no longer be my story. Concealing in vain will no longer hold secrets. The development of a new proportion will flexibly move me to the necessary eloquence of two souls. Effectively, I will call to beauty, building an empire of hearts, original in its form — respecting the highest esteem of others. To me, this will be proof of origination toward the language of love.

Invisible Exit

Have you ever been in a relationship where you feel as if it has been called off? Yet, you remain loyal to your partner out of fear of separation. You continue dating because you do not want to hear from your partner on how things are not working out. This is what I call an invisible exit. It is when you talked about your differences, your arguments, the spilled emotions of resentment and anger, and to one degree or another, you involve yourself with a power struggle. Both spend too much time raising their voices, avoiding the nursery of validation. Even though they expressed their emotions, somehow, they feel betrayed and cannot find salvation. In retaliation, they erect an emotional impedient known as the silent treatment.

When a couple engages in a silent treatment exchange, it becomes a form of emotional abuse in the relationship. War begins in your mind, leaving you naked to your existence. You become the invitation and your partner becomes the magician; leaving you without answers.

On an unconscious level, the one who engages in silent treatment is more than likely to replicate other avenues that they saw from their parents. This appears to be a common denominator for those who lacked emotional nourishment and empathy. What I found to believe with my clients whom I have coached or counseled is that most of them do not know how to open the dialogue with, "Help me to understand you." By promoting an open communication, both parties are validated. Pointing out and labeling each other's behavior will provoke the relationship to end sourly. If you want to avoid an invisible exit, I suggest you get inside the sacred circle of love and be vulnerable to each other. Express empathy followed by relative emotional experiences. By sharing each other's relative emotional experiences, you and your partner become conscious of each other's stimulus, needs, and discovery.

If, on the other hand, you feel that your invisible exit triggers an important message of it-is-time-to-let-go, then make your exit to your partner in a mature manner. Never leave a relationship making the Other feel worthless. It does you no good nor to the other person.

Instead, explain your reasons as to why it did not work out. Talk about what you learned from the relationship. What new strengths did they bring to the table? How were they able to impact your life in a positive way? Express your answers to your partner.

Talk about the positives instead of the negatives. By focusing on the positives, you are saying to the Universe, "Yes, I want my new partner to express their emotions to me." "I want my new partner to make me feel more magical than my previous one." If you focus on conflicts, anger, resentment, or any other negative emotion, you will attract that with your new partner but ten times worse. It is imperative to make your exits in a fashionable way where both of you feel honored, respected, and validated. Relationships have a tremendous amount of stories, helping us to learn about each other's personalities. When someone walks away from your life, are you to blame for giving a great amount of your joy and love? If the gift of love is not received, then, do not fret over it. When a new partner enters your life, you will have the courage to deposit a foundation where two find shelter in its form of strength.

ON VULNERABILITY

The Fundamentals of Human Connection

A century passes with fragmented universities that meet in the hall, luring in the common spirit that is no longer found in openness. The knowledge that resembled an intellectual warehouse is now a meeting of assumptions that tell us a message of different conceptions.

To the world, vulnerability is weak. But to the eyes of an enlightened soul, it is in fact, a legitimate intimacy that becomes universal. Nothing is hidden between the joining of two souls or more. Whether unfinished or through progression, vulnerability develops overtime which completes the basic attributes of humility.

Denial is the godhead of all deception. And yet, we obey the master because we know we will be in chastity or locked for a decade if we dared to question the utmost urgency of life.

The seeming triumph of vulnerability is when we appreciate the full weight of our human dilemma. When we understand this, we can begin to develop intertwined factors toward human growth: achieve universal love, understand the practical question of authenticity, and lastly, create a legacy that conceives the foundation of purpose.

A world-system allows the acceptance of fears and anxiety to discourage growth. When we find ourselves understanding the hook of separation, we can begin to understand vulnerability from our inner private world.

In life, just like in a counseling session, it is a therapeutic relationship between you and Mother Nature. It is easier to communicate one's attitudes, making a sheer connection to the sensitivity of understanding the perceptions and feelings toward the experiences. Fixated measurements never ascend to clarity; it submits to irrational impulses that make you possess an experience that is not reliable.

The philosopher who speaks and acts in the accordance with their doctrine, they must set the rules through precise formulations which become the hallmark to the keenest

Note: I use the term universities as an output of one's prehistoric knowledge towards life; not school.

knowledge of truth and wisdom. It is through question where we call attention to certain things that help us move closer to the beginning of openness. Vulnerability correlates to weakness in today's age. Some occupy its wealth, some breakdown the word with violence. In between, the clearest communication that we can have with ourselves is to endeavor into the fixed objects that keep us from growing.

Western thinking has laid down the language of life, precisely the conflicting positions and constant polemics that grasp a world that is strangely finished. But in our common welfare, no life is finished. It is a continuation of understanding and questioning how things work, how relationships operate, and how love should be authentic. It is important to understand the distance between the creation of emotion and universalizing the form of behavior.

Fragments come from within like
drops of rain to teach us that our
wholeness is filled with riddles.

The chief forces of creation begin with a thinker whose attitude is active toward altruism. If, on the other hand, we universalize a Skinnerian behavior of hate and violence, we will yield to an illusion that hostility is welcomed to our world. This cleavage can develop further with a practical collision in which the members of society endanger themselves. Ruling one domain over another has no place in our world. Previous generations have operated on that idea and have failed to further humanity to its light.

If by now, we are ready to understand beauty and its strength of connection, then we must consider the courses of history. Every occasion transformed an ideal expression on how mental emotions should be expressed. Dominance, ruling, and regulate were the words of the past. Somehow, the ghost of nihilism is haunting us with its whispers in our lives.

Considering its shadows, we must detach the ideas of a ruling nation. It attributes threat and a shaken personality. Increasingly, abstract ideas of peace hold sway while we divide the world with an ideology of traditional division. The goal ascribed to our traditional division is to be tough, to man up, to stop being a cry baby, and to express our emotions through fists and weapons.

Our past and present are nothing but a separation of generations, each of which escapade the forms of the human mind, handing down the teachings of war, and thus on the idea that love is masticated with superficial lust, all of which proceeds to the continual activity — distorting the changed activity that we ought to further.

Productive life should be enacted as a means for the satisfaction of the world. This is a species-life, not an animalistic life that we desire. In our productive life, we reside with our vulnerability and openness to new experiences. Delving into the unknown is what helps us to magnify our highest Selves. Our wholeness becomes free from previous productions. One must bring order to the recognition of connection whereby distinctions are made through the creative output of clarity and precision.

Human thought determines the ontological analysis of the entity that stands between the Self and the situation. Existentially, it becomes our task to integrate the question and the answer to our human dilemma. Beforehand, we must formulate the question.

Is my Being authentic, or is my Being demonstrating a cover-up from my authentic Self? Maintaining this awareness will help us become accessible to something that is to be understood and interpreted.

Prior, we may have misled ourselves into thinking that vulnerability is grounded with a personality decay of weakness. On the contrary, science has proven that when we expose and share our vulnerabilities to those who are close to us, we will conceive empathy as a form of trust. This becomes self-evident when we choose how we want to access our vulnerable part of the Selves.

Essentially, one's Being must be considered before laying the horizon. These shortcomings of emotions are not grounded in fatalism or some supreme deity who endows punishment to make our lives more difficult. They are there to help us categorize the ontological foundations that gain a suitable interpretation of our vulnerability. It is a preparatory procedure just like when a doctor prepares his or her essentials for operation. Our vulnerable emotions prepare us to surrender our ego for humility.

And once we undergo the procedure, our horizon will be laid naked, which leads us to a full scope of new opportunities towards beauty.

Authentically, it brings out the best in us because we can demonstrate a constitutive state that firmly places meaning over temporality-of-emotions. This task requires the strength to understand what it is that we struggle. Is it our social environment? Is it mainstream media who portray toughness as sexy? Is it our primitive genes that tell us to be machismo? In general, we are not defined by social sciences or biology. Yes, you should consider your genes, but they do not make a Being a full historical happening. The minute you are born and through each transitional stage, you can modify and restore your genes from your previous generations. A full distinction can be made when you investigate the functionality of your previous family genes.

The fact remains that through enlightenment principles, we can admittedly function beautifully to our own accord. Problematic as it may seem right now, you are indeed an individual who can fully express your tears without judgment; fears without laughter; and feelings without belittlement.

We are accustomed to comparing at an early age. Why is fifteen-year-old Jeff crying so much? Is he a namby-pamby? Why is seven-year-old Kimberly punching her crush on his arm? This has become our customary, mythical narrative that cleaves vulnerability with traditional concepts that naturally process comparative criteria.

As I see it, this has become our ontological dilemma in terms of various modes of comparison. Children and adults who reinvent the tradition of, "Follow along because that's where the train is going," they will find out that the after-effects of a traveling train will either lead to a dead-end or to a destination of despair.

> Exhibiting hatred or suppressing
> vulnerability will leave you in
> treatment at some doctor's office.

In the long run, vulnerability builds strength that helps us to deepen our expressive emotions. Without criticism, we can become centered and connected with the Self and with existence.

The Origins of Bullying and How Vulnerability Can Make a Difference

In the previous pages, I talked about the ontological dilemma that we are facing. We are facing comparison and operating on emotions rather than connecting. Comparison has been a history of partition. Commonly, we upsurge the instinctual needs directly to the multitude stream of status and stature. Since the beginning of time, we have ingrained the Western narrative of, "Let's out-perform the rest and bully those who are not "chosen" for our inner circle." This formal theme has played for centuries. It is extremely powerful when others follow this belief. Our human race has not changed from the competitive atmosphere. Even though we are evolving in science and technology, we are not evolving in our social acknowledgment of empathy and love. This competitive hierarchy instills an ideology where bullying is welcomed. It exclaims for revenge because of the social pressure to keep up with the practical transformation of conditioned behaviors. This peculiar kind of bullying is characterized by strong pretensions, coupled with false construction that leads to the habitual use of bullying tactics.

Children and adults who bully learned early on the voice of its toxicant whisper that leads to believe that one podium is higher than another. Whether in school or the workforce, children and adults are haunted by the capitalistic, cosmetic practice of intensifying hate where they sever ties between authenticity and empathy.

While they believe it is facetious to bully other citizens, they fail to realize that it is they who are facing the insecurity to be authentic and vulnerable with their feelings. Intersubjective comparison and competition often lead to a range of temporality. What do I mean? Temporality is having an intense focus at a particular time. It can be in the form of the past or the present. Our past exists in the form of memory and irony. Our memories of the past generate a constant script that tries to understand certain situations that we faced in our childhood years. The irony behind it is that we form emotive destruction habits that morph into malice and revenge rather than applying the ethics of enlightenment, which consists of love and empathy.

If we are to do the extra work in downsizing bullying in our schools, then, we must recourse to the foundations of human reasoning.

Society will improve its political stance when we turn to empathy. Careful investigations must be made when curtailing to empathy. Many will ridicule empathy as a structure of weakness. Wherever there is empathy, silence shares a best friend, and the name is revenge.

To be comported citizens, we must self-inspect as to why we establish societal habits, and carefully cultivate self-responsibility for our actions. It is easy to blame and pick on our differences. It is easy for the adolescent to dissolve into the external, societal relations to make a possible entrance with the cool kids.

A society that compares will heavily bear the psychological venom, causing deception to seep in all walks of life. With that said, let us briefly touch on the phenomenology and sociological point of view on bullying. Among its origin, Nietzsche pointed out that bullying is a mistaken form of an idol that we seek for attention. In a sense, bullying is self-toxicant toward the personhood.

Without relying on its consequences, the individual systematically represses the forgiven attitude and alienates connection, empathy, values, and reasoning. Their repression leads to an insidious stentorian of indulgence that leads to revenge, hatred, and envy. Thirst for bullying indicates that the individual is seeking attention. This kind of attention is reactive toward the desire for aggressive impulses. Such reactive impulses precede an attack or an injury.

This is not to be confused with self-defense. For instance, suppose you read in the newspaper that an individual was abducted but took out his or her gun and shot the individual out of self-defense. That is not bullying or hatred. That is someone who is enacting the fight or flight phenomenon. The person is fighting to live; not to bully.

Bullying and seeking revenge are distinguished by three phenomenological characteristics that I have formed based on my observations. First and foremost, *the desire to impulse on the reactive state,* with an escort of anger and hate. The response to this stage is consequently delayed to a later time to make the other individual feel nervous. It is when the bully says to the person, "Just wait until I get you. You will not know what is coming."

This type of speech restrains the other individual to feel trapped in a box which causes a suitable panic. The second phenomenological characteristic is *psychological arrivist*. The person who inflicts suffering and pain on another individual wants to arrive at a certain message. He or she wants to outdo the pain that was caused previously in their upbringing.

As such, they are unable to love, to forgive, to admit fault, and most of them do not have friends, while some do. They are content with the suffering that they caused to the person because unconsciously, they feel they have destroyed their pain from their previous upbringings. This is what I call *objective repression toward the Self*. They repress the intensity of hurt from their childbearing years in return for an aberrated satisfaction. Their personality generates the constant urge to win over those who are weaker than them. They display this in public, fishing for social esteem. Respect is what they want, but soon, they find out they are empty in the soul and lonely in the social circle.

Lastly, the third phenomenological characteristic is *independent comparison*. Subjectively, the individual who bullies compares the totality of Self on how others view them. If they feel dared to cause suffering, or if they feel they have unfinished business from their past, they compare the objects to the given narrative.

On one hand, they naturally drive out reasoning and freedom for bleak indulgence. And on the other hand, they create an alter-ego that stands in a presence, mocking the beauty of meaning and purpose. Comparison is the human enemy which provokes vulnerability, making the expression feel inferior.

There is a progression of feeling vengeful when the individual has specific comparisons. It directs them to outlast the past for a desire of punishment towards those who come in their way. It is as if the bully is saying, "Go on. I see nothing. All I hear is more pain for you and more satisfaction for me."

There is a self-conquest for the individual to make a statement to the other individual and to the environment. By being inauthentic to their emotions, they couple it with toughness so that they do not show mental weakness and fear. Chiefly, they confine themselves in this myth that they dominate the environment, stinging with authority, having others in a psychological cage.

These three phenomenological characteristics make bullying the most noticeable source of forming resentment and anger. The progression starts slowly, escalating to the impulse of spite, which concludes in human suffering.

Subsequently, the three phenomenological characteristics seek outer-directed objectification toward the person. If those aspects cannot draw gratification, then, the bully will exult in more faults toward the individual, pressuring him or her to fixate on a troubling pattern. The impulse to detract the person is a mere result or direct experience, furthering to hamper the concerns of the individual.

Despite the troubled impulses to bully, it becomes deep-seated as if it were a celebration to bring down the authenticity of the Other. Revenge and envy lead to verbal abuse followed by clinching a fist, ready to battle. The bully who is consumed by hatred wants the Other or those around them to know their indignation. They want everyone to know his or her suffering. The bully feels as if it is not enough to suffer alone. Therefore, the bully makes the emotional presence known.

Because of the suppression of hate and envy from their previous upbringing, they either cover up their weakness with fists or in the very origin, speak of words that poison the personality of the Other. As we know, the more direct shift toward the objectification, the more satisfaction they gain. But if the desire for revenge remains unsatisfied, somehow, they make it known that another event will happen. They usually say, "You may have escaped this time, but I will come back stronger."

This type of speech leads to a recursive of power. It is a step ladder to entertain the mind with explosive ideas to assemble basic concepts of hate and envy. Thereof, the only proposition they have in mind is to be pulled into a violet vortex that ponds the physical force as a conceptualization that leads to causations and formulas of revenge.

With the leading permanent message, the individual intensifies it as a duty to accomplish the suffering. The vindictive person is without a conscious of the events that he or she organized. Great sensitivity chambers out while the psychological contagion begins to injure the beauty of existence.

Bullying as we know is caused by repression of suffering or humiliation. Conversely, feelings of revenge are highly favored by emotional pretensions, which remain hidden in the person's emotional position toward their personhood. We must add that bullying when married with revenge, it directs to what I call, *suitability typology*. In their eyes, they feel it is suitable to feel the wrath of their experienced reflections. The tension between desire and suffering flares up when Being casually diminishes vulnerability for a stand of violence.

Therefore, the bully who enacts the scene is considered to have an existential resentment. The individual resents that the Other is either happy with life or wants to weaken the soul and thereof, make the Other feel an unbearable humiliation just as the bully experienced in the past. The bully gradually alternates into superficial love to stay awesome with the social circle and at times, they will artificially cast light on the source of time and involvement with the world. Without realizing that their temporality is focused on a historical basis, they bring up those aspects that are strongly associated with powerless emotions.

Bullying is an alienated exertion that the individual purchases internally through an unjustified manner, abstractedly showing a sycophantic dependence upon the resentment in a negative, unconscious, spurious way.

With the ever-changing of society, authenticity gets ignored in the spiritual atmosphere. Protesting to stop bullying will not do anything if we cannot harmonize vulnerability in our classrooms. One way to begin a simple paradigm shift is to begin the first ten minutes of class with a circle where everyone shares their goals and fears.

The instructor must reflect content, meaning, and they must be empathetic. Students will also learn how to reflect on each other's feelings by focusing on empathy. Asking questions to each other will build similar stories that each has endured. Responding in an empathetic manner will make the visibility of love and empathy yield to an open pathway that leads to connection, culture, and wholeness.

More than ever, we restrict the circle in our classroom with lessons that may not seem important at that moment. Yes, instructors are advised to illuminate the minds of young students in our history classes, math classes, or science classes. But what is more important in the first ten minutes is how the students feel when they come in. Tradition speaks of, "Come in and take your sit. The exam will start shortly." If we shift that tradition to a modern sense of psychological congruence, students will flourish to new heights of confidence. Gradually, compassion and shared vulnerability will reduce the revolutionary protests and obstacles that most schools have endured. The main characteristic of change is to be willing to engage in a spiritual enthusiasm of love and empathy. This will decrease the phenomenon of bullying.

Again, the instructors are not the counselors of the classroom. They are the bringers of the light who show students that it is okay to be vulnerable. Each day of the week, by expressing their emotions and feelings for ten minutes in the sacred circle of love, students will feel less anxious. And by no means, no student should ridicule another student for his or her troubles. Every story that is told in those ten minutes should be honored and respected. The instructor is held responsible to keep the circle in balance. This goes for the coaches as well. It has been stereotyped that coaches have a rigid personality. It is no wonder our students grow up to be a reproduction of their previous experiences. Albert Bandera was right in his social cognitive theory where he explained that we model certain behaviors that seem important to us at that moment. The error in modeling certain behaviors is that we end up becoming the by-product of the secondary emotions that we learned in the environment.

That is why it is important to also hold the coaches accountable to allow their students to share their sufferings in an open dialogue.

Again, the coaches are not counselors. But they must learn to reflect content and meaning. This will correlate to a positive, mental health state that enables each student to increase the interval points of connection and empathy. The moving force of vulnerability happens when there is an agreement to continually grow through social evolution and intellectual development. It becomes enriched with specialized meaning that spreads wider in all areas of life. The energy in every school will evolve through a universal love that is built on contributing a formation that dramatically favors the mind, body, and soul. The maxim of love will be, *peace is where my heart is, love is what becomes of me.* The more students that repeat this, the more they will undress their wounds. And when the faculty and staff comprehend the highly esteemed of love, they too will flower its truth. A peculiar meaning of vulnerability emerges out of insight. Vulnerability is always particular when everyone else shy's away.

Why is that?

Because as a society, we have been ingrained that vulnerability results in weakness.

It augments into a development of instincts, a lust for power, and sexual coercion. When we accept the false message of vulnerability as being weak, we will engross unhealed emotions as a cycle of shame. The starking challenge that we face with vulnerability is being able to reorganize and reinvestment in human relations. Many of us have faced betrayal and resentment, but what we ignore the most is the growth and courage that life presents. When we extract our unrevealed emotions and connect them meaningfully with others, we will create a new passageway of beauty that renews the interest in life.

As I mentioned before, vulnerability is when we comprehend the sacred obligations to actively listen and to foster human strength.

Love and communication set a higher order to invest in the common welfare of our community. We begin to accept our own humanity and the humanity of others. The gift of this embrace becomes a moment of placement, whispering, "I am right where I am supposed to be. I am ready to live and learn, but also, I am ready to invest my energy in caring for others with compassion and gusto."

The modern positivist idea of humanism is that we play an integral part in our social evolution. We accept responsibility and welcome the challenges of the present and the future. Along with it, we make meaning by searching for productive solutions that lead to growth. Even through tragedies, we can strive towards a world that eliminates the turbid mixture of hate and violence. Human nature contains the seeds of beauty and connection that classify into a natural preparation that extirpates the decadence of a gloomy, serving ego.

Dressing Our Wounds

Biologically, especially in the viewpoint of Darwinism, we dress our wounds out of survival. Our ancestors who fought in battles had to cover up their weaknesses to survive the chaos of humanity. Today, we see a reoccurring effect on the psychological conditions of every human being. Cynicism has manifested into a fixed totality, thirsting for admiration for wrongful behavior.

Again, I always get asked the same question:

"But Luis, what has happened to today's world? How can we improve it?"

The answer is simple, yet somewhat an existential view. The answer is that we have felt worthless with our morals and values towards a meaningful life. We were our own cheerleaders, screaming, go, go, keep moving. You got this! And now, our unity and truth have been characterized by events that lack entirely the meaning of personhood.

When the world suffers, we somehow supply ourselves with anger and blame. The world is a by-means of categories which include: the belief of event values, application of dependence, and modifying our wholeness into corruption. These are the categories that granted me the freedom to observe in our environment. The belief of dressing up our wounds lies in the assumption that our world is constantly in spiritual bondage. *The belief of event values* has been learned spirally. Ideally, it leads back to the obvious expression that our emotions to the world are conditioned. We desire the appearance of humanity in the absolute conviction that we insist on becoming like it.

Our belief that the world is in chaos, and how people are bad, it has excused us from our relative strengths. The possession of this belief used to be the enjoyment, punishing others to give power in ways that we thought were superior. Now, when we position ourselves in this pole, not only does it deprive us of an authentic life, it also characterizes an illusory mental attitude that forces away from living a self-confident life. Enormously, we see this phenomenon of belief events where we turn to Otherness — fearing that we are not them. Hereto, fear has compromised existence with secondary transferences of the object of resentment — having others believe that inflicting pain and suffering is some sort of festival. These held beliefs have been conditioned by society, telling us to give up the good, moral life. This breeding will take many generations to undo. In its estimation, we will trade our ego for a sense of strength and belonging as we learn to connect even our most painful feelings. The most essential belief that we can hold dearly in our hearts is that humans can be good only if they correct themselves and believe in the power of vulnerability.

With all things considered, individuals who submit to revenge and resentment have tried to reverberate beauty with a soulless attitude. Their dogma is, that because our world seems to be unfair, we shall express our instincts in ways that will get everyone's attention.

The bottomless never leads back to
the degree of a moralistic life.
They remain chained to the
submission of superficial power.

Now that we know what the belief of event values are, let me curtail to the next phase: *application of dependence.* From the outside perspective, some may say, it is a fixed ratio of power and presence. The belief of, "Authority is conscious of reason" has dashed the greatest number of happiness in our lives. Wherever revenge precedes, the individual interprets it as a companion who married darkness over light. They know that pessimistic influence will result in nihilism followed by emotional falsification towards meaning.

This is where they generate false desires to divorce a genuine life. Too many citizens apply toward the dependence of revenge and hate, causing them to cover up their wounds with insatiable fury to those that injured their psychological psyche. In this mode, people conform to the notion of suffering. Animalism is often the reign of passion where citizens strengthen their reason that this world ought to be recognized as hatred for all that has happened. It is where they account for the depletion of humanity to a mummery, wrapped in self-deception, desiring a fatalistic submission to the trending thoughts of the Other. One of the ways to move away from this mode is to justify the wrongly acts of humanity. Questioning everything and applying knowledge is the supreme power that becomes available to practical reasoning. By learning all traces of history, like an artist, we can take down the paintings, reassemble life as much as possible, and author it ourselves to the walls of the 21st century and for the centuries to come.

Lastly, our final stage is *modifying our wholeness into corruption*. Today, especially in the workforce, political arena, and in school, we witness a lot of individuals who depend a lot on the degree of closeness. Some call it a tribe while some call it an inner circle. In the inner circle, secrets are kept even though they know the consequences are coming. They keep convincing themselves of the falsification and reinterpretation of judgment. This is the hallmark of bullying. They modify into corruption to make themselves strong so that their personality impresses the interest of an instinctive attitude. The automatic process of corruption is an upright conviction to those that follow the pattern based on human hatred or favoritism. Beyond all lying, there is a weakness, a certain fear, and an utmost anxiety to the dialogue that they justified to be true. It prevents them from freedom, beauty, independence, and success because they value the history of emotions rather than adding more zest to the value systems of community inheritance.

Now, we return to the question, why do we dress our wounds? In all cases, the individual who bullies and dresses up their wounds end up committing the crime to mask their authentic Self. Instead of hating from a distance, they release it through an active state. It becomes a basic impulse that takes minimal effort on their end because they bully through words or through weapons. Most often, they are not tough. They are taciturn, shy, and quiet. The bullying they impose is always a sudden outburst of impulses that they held from their previous childbearing years.

Most likely, they were bullied themselves, or they were raised in a formalistic expectation that everyone must be perfect. And if people are not perfect like them, they somehow believe that they should extract those who are not like them. This is what I call a *continual deflation of humanity*. The deflation of humanity reinterprets a one-sided interest that brings satisfaction for the wrongful behavior that was inflicted on the Other.

Certain expressions take the dark side of the personality, passing on suffering rather than combating it with empathy and love. In our present-day society, a lot of citizens dress up their wounds, proclaiming a new religion, saying spiritual messages, rejecting the old, but somehow, asserting pain and conflict to those who are not like them. Those who search for spiritual enlightenment cannot expect others to express the same harmony as them. They can set the dominos, but it is the Other who must push them in order to fall into its course.

What people fail to realize is that bullying comes from all sorts of socioeconomic status. They all cite certain messages that chiefly attribute to impotence. A lot of them feel helpless but end up dressing their wounds through physical forces which in turn leads to a repressive, superiority complex. They are afraid of being irrelevant and ignored in the social circle. They find new ways to pulse intimidation to distinguish organic causes of respiratory trouble. These forces begin by removing the sphere of goodness which in turn accelerates the continual process of vengeance.

Even if they do not have reasons, they will release an unexpected inner paroxysm of anger without any specific reason. Between peace and love from the other party, the bully banishes it through a cocky smile, mocking it with weapons of destruction.

What lacks today in expressing our wounds is being able to encounter previous emotional upheaval and present emotional upheaval. Within the reach, we must direct the entire experience and sense of renewal to the shadows of unconsciousness, bringing up the understood distortions that have oversimplified every relationship. It seems to me that we cover everything about ourselves which includes our personalities, how we walk and talk, and our expression of vulnerabilities. It is important to display our vulnerability to whom we feel comfortable. It makes the experience a universal cathedral where our expressions are honored through compassion and love.

Ideally, when vulnerability is not honored, controlling others becomes a by-product of weaponry — molding the individual to believe that bullying and favoritism are the apples of enjoyment. Without realizing the consequences, they spread the contagion among the sound languages of the environmental space that fill up with vices.

ON FORGIVENESS

A Different Makeup to The Soul

Since the origination of life, we have fiercely debated on the topic of forgiveness. We have turned left to religion, right to personal enlightenment, backward on our past generations, and forward with our wisdom.

Forgiveness, in a sense, is a personal communication between our present Self and our Higher Self. In a way, we can navigate wisely and effectively as we gain an opportunity to integrate wholeness. The forgivers stew an inner awakening that it is time to wake up from resenting and hating people who wronged them. The forgivers throw out the possibility that the rest of their lives will be single-minded by the injurious acts of another human being.

Forgive once, you will prejudge
when to forgive again. Forgive all, you will
release yourself from the prison that
you created in your heart.

We entertain the idea of revenge by saying, "I want them to feel what I am feeling." Whether it is through religious acts or servanthood of enlightenment, we know that it causes a strain in our hearts. In a relational sense, the keeper of our heart is no longer us, it becomes ownership toward the Otherness.

Forgiveness is an act of an awakening that
secretly prepares us to face whatever issue
that is blocking us in our pursuit of meaning.

Reorganizing Forgiveness

Forgiveness is an internal motivation that allows us to regroup our thoughts and our past hurt. In a nutshell, it means that it never stops at one developmental stage or another. It is a continuous effort to take responsibility for whatever got us stuck in the middle of the circle.

To deny the circumference circle of the impact that other individuals had in our lives is to slow down our strength of forgiveness. It becomes a distortion in our mental picture album.

Our drive towards forgiveness is an attempt to restore our equilibrium within our present Self and with our unconscious ideas of hate and resentment. When we sincerely forgive ourselves and those who have hurt us, we allow a medium space to take place. In that space, we can shortcut the process by putting all the past pain and present pain in the circle of restoration.

When you forgive others, you expand your energy on awareness. That freed up energy becomes useful for creativity.

Proactive Steps to Reorganize Forgiveness

One of the most common miseries people face daily is not knowing how to forgive. They seek immediate pleasure or seek out a priest. For all common purposes, I will leave out religion, and instead, I will focus on existential forgiveness. Throughout existence, individuals have logged out on authenticity and forgiveness. Psychology, science, and philosophy have alienated the critical importance of forgiveness. While religion preaches it, at times, they do not live up to the portrait. For this reason, I will take the stance from an existential perspective.

There is a broad continuum between forgiveness-of-Otherness and forgiveness-of-Self. First and foremost, forgiveness-of-Otherness is learning to conjure up your past pain in the present moment. This will require deeper work and an existential analysis toward the confrontation of wounds.

Examining ourselves and the individuals that inflicted hurt is the hallmark of insight. Most genuinely, it greases out past pain and opens a new emotional road for us to drive towards growth and maturity.

Every so often, we need an emotional tune-up to remind us that forgiveness is a long-term relationship with the Self. Before publishing my first book, *The Five Virtues That Awaken Your Life,* I went through a series of bedlam — from graduate school to a painful breakup with my ex-girlfriend and seeing my mom in the confines of the hospital bed. What pained me the most during the process of writing my first book was seeing my mom terminally ill while at the same time going through a difficult breakup during graduate school. During a cold December afternoon, my ex-girlfriend came to my place and arrowed at my heart with, "I want to call it quits with you. It is not working out between us." Into my flesh and out of my heart, I could not stay connected with my feelings. I felt hurt, betrayed, and marooned. At about the sixth-month mark, many wounds and familiarity seemingly hit me at once.

Her voice, her touch, her scent, and her laughter ravished my heart and thoughts with, "Go back to her. You know you want to." Simplistic as it sounds, it was tough for me to forgive her. She knew my family on a deeper level and had a soft spot for my mother who was terminally ill. I could not keep my heart intact let alone keep my emotions balanced.

But alas, acceptance ticked into my heart, helping me to go through the process of emotional healing. However, even though I forgave her and forgave myself, I honored those experiences because they gave me life at that moment. As years went by, I learned that she was a season who played her part. This kind of wisdom and knowledge helped me to prepare and restore my equilibrium. Wanting and waiting is usually the norm for individuals who go through a breakup but for me, creating and turning scars into beauty was my theme. Rather than "no longer wishing," I made a moral decision to keep my joy at bay, and to embrace it, whether it goes left or right, I followed the wind of emotional healing.

Two voices in one body are something that
must be dealt with in a cautionary analysis.
One voice says, "You know you want to hate."
And the other voice says, "Forgive and allow
the free space to become your life lesson."

Forgiveness Model

As years pass by, we wait for our anger to subside. We hope for the Other to say, "I will make it up to you." But then, we realize that they continue to hurt us psychologically and spiritually. Keeping our old wounds gives us a visitation from the past. It damages our scope of meaning along with our connection to personhood. At times, it is difficult to express or to articulate our anger. Nonetheless, we suppress it without expression. Thus, it leads to a dysfunction toward the Self. We minimize our authentic feelings of hurt in hope of an adjustment, forwarding our tears with revenge. Breathing techniques, counting backward from ten to one, or asking a miracle question will not restore our emotional wounds. They will continue to occur in spells of anger, revenge, and jealousy. For this reason, I have created a model that will help us understand forgiveness from an existential point of view. By following this model, we can turn pain into creativity; anger into love; and denial into acceptance. On the following page, I will walk you through my model and explain each step on how our emotions are present-focused and how to cultivate a new meaning of creativity and awareness.

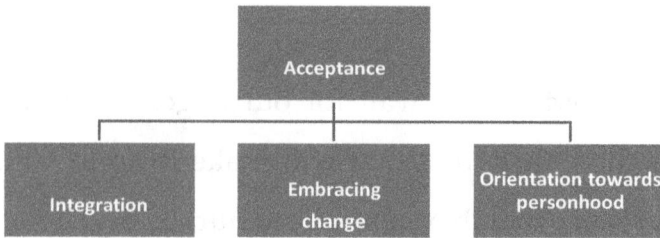

Figure 1-3: The Construction Stages of Forgiveness

Forgiveness-of-Self and forgiveness-of-Others involve various steps in the stages of forgiveness. As we learn and develop the ability to forgive, our neurological and interpersonal relationships will improve. Let us begin with *Stage 1: Acceptance*. When we get heartbroken or experience grief, our minds get impaired but also our bodies. Our body holds a secret that most ignore when facing emotional difficulty. When we experience trauma such as divorce, grief, or neglect, our body sinks into high blood pressure, high cholesterol, somatic disturbances such as body aches, and so much more. We neglect these experiences because we unconsciously focus on our emotional pain, leaving behind our health. In this stage, whatever you go through, accept it in the here-and-now. As difficult as it sounds, it will save you and your health time at a visit to the doctor.

The art of forgiveness is when we heal our memories with new endeavors. A bitter past may get the best of our personhood, but we can empower ourselves with a new joy of living. If we lock ourselves in a cycle of blame or guilt, we will give the power back to anger. This will cause a split between our psychological rationality and our accessible parts of healing.

The unwrapping of our pain is like unwrapping a gift on Christmas morning, it becomes a miracle and a thank you to the Divine. It is in this moment of acceptance that we can address unresolved issues from our past or present. It brings forth the unconscious to the conscious. This becomes a critical period in our lives because our emotional needs challenge us to remain centered for deep healing. To illuminate acceptance, answer these questions:

1. In the moment of separation, can I accept the event as is?

2. Can I face the changes around me?

3. Through responsibility and rationality, can I direct my emotions to a centered Self?

4. Am I brave enough to mold meaning and love despite the separation?

Recognition of acceptance is gained from experience. The casts of your previous emotions become an awakening from your trance. Acceptance is a challenge but once learned, you can gain emotional independence from the bondages that kept your soul tied.

Stage 2: Integration is where most individuals stagnate. In my experiences, I have counseled, coached, and mentored individuals who felt disconnected from their emotions. I have been asked, "Luis, how the heck can I integrate meaning and forgiveness when he or she dumped me for another person?" "Luis, there is no way I can forgive my parents for divorcing and leaving me with another family." Indeed, this is a challenge, but it requires us to defend what I like to call the *positionality of emotion*. Positionality of emotion is when we defend a new emotion that brings new information and meaning. For instance, I once counseled a woman whom I will call Jennifer, to protect her identity. Nonetheless, she was getting over a painful divorce with her husband. She was heartbroken and had thoughts of suicide. As I got to know this intelligent woman, I connected with her and slowly integrated my model throughout the session.

My first opening statement was, "It seems to me you are yearning or longing for someone in your life." Tearfully, she responded, "Yes. Yes, I never had the comfort or love from my father. He would come home drunk and slap my mom. At times, he would push me against the wall if I did not take his side. And other times, he would show love." In the most empathetic manner, I said, "I can see and connect with your emotional center. Growing up must have been confusing. One minute your father pushes you against the wall and other times, he shows love, not the kind of love you hoped for." Wiping her tears away, she responded, "You are totally right, Luis. All along, I have been searching for love and all the men that I have dated are like my father or are too needy and childish." I went on to say, "This reminds me of the myth of Briar Rose. In this story, it talks about *integration* and loving wholly. In the beginning, the princess is entirely centered on her ball. She gives no thought as to what the ball may mean to her. But as the frog comes closer, she begins to feel nervous and sensitive towards her feelings.

After a long stretch with her meaning towards the ball, she begins to gain independence and becomes herself again. Perhaps, this ball represents your unfilled void with your father and the frog is your emotional guidance to a meaningful life." Towards the end of the session, she began to see her perspective in a new light. She was able to crack the mysteries of her void, leaving her to trust her capacities of integration. Through my own experiences and in working with others, I believe that sorrow and abandonment are the greatest professors. They welcome us to the classroom without judgment. We can never underestimate the intensity of emotions for it tells us to listen closely and for us to integrate beauty that brings measurement to our relationship with the Self and with the world. The fact that we can live with some joy or sadness, and some intimacy with our healing, is an expression of a meaningful life.

If you struggle like most individuals with integration, begin where you are. What are you feeling at this moment? Are you motivated to begin again? If you look five years ahead and come back to the present moment, what did you do to muster up the courage to integrate forgiveness?

Individual freedom gives structure to our sense of Being. The upshot of integration is molding the spoken words of hurt into a dialogue of an awakening. With all things considered, let us view *Stage 3: Embracing change.* "I did not know I could handle this change after the divorce," said Jennifer who I helped. In stage two, I introduced integration with a new concept that I entitled *positionality of emotion.* For stage three, I will go into full detail on how you can emotionally change your thinking and feeling, so you can match your energy with a new form of beauty.

When I helped Jennifer get over her divorce, one of the main ingredients to change emotionally is to embrace the change. This is where most individuals feel they need to escape the change through the nourishment of another body or to engage in recreational drugs. So, you may ask, "How do I embrace change?" By rescripting your dialogue from sorrow and hurt to the examination of life. Human existence is like bees; we form a connection with specific honey.

The honey that I speak of can be in the form of relationships with your partner, family, or goals. What happens when the beehive perishes? The bees must explore a new setting to give birth to a new home. The same goes for humans. Fellowship and meaning are the purposes behind the curtain that unfolds a new story. To fulfill the law of creation, you must awaken yourself to the service that you are called to do. Whatever it may be, create, and perform your best Self.

One of the vexing problems I have seen occur every time I counsel, or coach individuals is closure. When there is little closure, most individuals question the situation, hoping to understand what went wrong. By the same token, those who have full closure, they suspend judgment from all their previous stories. Whether it was broken relationships, havoc in the household, or trauma, they put aggressive behavior aside. They discover their ability to separate fighting the past to surging new energy and meaning to their lives. In short, those who have full closure, they will be able to process and to free themselves from living with unnecessary psychological pain.

Now, we come to the final stage, *Stage 4: Orientation towards personhood.* We can speculate opposite conclusions as to what happened in our lives. After all, the conscious mind denies and recognizes events as is. But in such a case, we must ask ourselves: Is the event an end to my means, or is the event a conscious outlook for me to gain perspective? We can understand the situation that confronts us by constructing the sorrow into a continuous development toward the wholeness of Self.

Exploration of meaning ripens the inner childlike love. When we reveal the significant childlike love, the silence that we buried with hate becomes a passage toward spiritual growth. This often leads to a new destination, heightening sensitivity with a readiness to invite empathy as the symbol of peace. When we balance our thoughts with forgiveness, our wounds turn into stories and our unresolved pain turns into a home — carrying us into the stages of life.

Again, orientation towards personhood means connection with our childhood and adulthood selves. When we marry our childlike spirit of love along with our courageous adult Self, we slowly change our broken hearts into something more fulfilling than the bankruptcy of our past hate.

When I see my clients or when I mentor individuals, I can see the light of curiosity in their eyes. They want new habits, new growth, new meaning, and a new story to tell. They want to understand their personality as to why they behave a certain way. To widen and grow, as I tell them, is to gain insight. Self-awareness begins when we consider the injurious pain of our past and present. It becomes empowering and meaningful because we never know what we are going to unlock from our unconscious mind.

The beauty of this gift is that we give up parts of ourselves that conditioned us to isolate our emotions. When we decide our direction, our actions match who we are on the inside, leading us to a connection of meaning, attracting growth experiences that fit our sense of a good, moral life.

The task may be enormous and there may be times we regret opening Pandora's box, but as I tell my clients, without these experiences, how would one know life? Whether we deny it or not, everything happens in the moment. Today's problems are packaged with past issues. Self-destructive thoughts about our personhood fossilize themselves into bad habits and emotional conflicts, leaving us with an internalization of angst.

Yes, all of this can hurt us and yes, it may seem impossible, but when we toil with a meaningful life, we bridge the gap between hate and forgiveness. By embracing the moment, we design a new life, drawing our awareness into a new consciousness.

When you reach the end of your crossroads toward the orientation of personhood, turn to the next page, and begin to say this in your beautiful journey:

Alas, I am a new version of myself. Integrated with my past and with my present, I am the original Self. I hold my heart to all that I am. I accept myself to be vulnerable, not wishing to be someone else. I am willing to continue to be authentic and open to the world. I stay purposeful and grateful because I am stretching and growing to new heights with myself. I have incorporated and integrated new habits to become the Self that I am today: empathetic, lovable, forgiving, and courageous.

H.A.T.E

The most uninvited emotion welcomes itself to our meaningful party — living with anger and resentment, building up the tension to doom ourselves to repeat the painful circumstances. The greatest revenge that hate leaves behind is the poison whisper of, "Take me by your mind so we can seek revenge together." We falter with its empty poison whisper. We become the obedient servant and hate becomes the commanding leader.

To open a new vista towards hate, let me introduce you to an acronym that I have labeled. Hate equals to a (H)ouse (A)round (T)oxic (E)mptiness. In my motivational programs, I educate others that hate is simply a house around toxic emptiness. Often, we want to make our case that the Other hurt us. And now, we feel obligated to enter the house of toxic emptiness. What happens when we enter the house of toxic emptiness? The individual walks into psychological venom, accepting the prophecy of deception.

The house of hate is no mansion. It is contributed to communal feelings from previous members who took the oath to accept hate into their hearts. The intensity of feelings builds comparisons that one is better than the other. It becomes the ugliest grimace to the soul. The individual remains less comfortable, yet it joins the toxic party just to motivate others that hate creates more productivity than peace or forgiveness. These individuals try to "arrive on time" only to realize that time is not the factor, it is through the engagement in competition, outdoing others just to gain praise, and making loyal friends into servants that paralyze the heart with envy.

If you have met any of these individuals or if you find yourself becoming one, step back and re-evaluate your purpose, habits, and growth towards forgiveness. In the previous pages, I taught on how forgiveness is learning to stay centered with your previous baggage and present baggage. When our emotional pain surfaces, we know that we have an unmet need or desire. Our unconscious mind gives us a preview of making life choices that will help us advance to the next level. When we improve our outlook on life, we will blame less and live more fully.

As I wrap up the chapter on forgiveness, I hope you have practiced the steps that I have laid out in the previous pages. Take your time and journal your progress. Having walked through forgiveness has taught me to be more optimistic, to connect with others, and to put my energy into interests that bring beauty and meaning into my life and to others. I want the same for you. Make a conscious choice that you will embrace your emotional conflicts. I promise you that you will feel renewed, and you will understand your personality on a broader continuum.

We cannot fail to recognize that our emotions help us to look deeply into life, not as a wish but as a purchasing power — maneuvering hate into a growing, maturing soul that yearns for love and forgiveness.

When the unconscious meets the conscious
thoughts, it must learn to rescript the
unmet needs into a courage of creativity.

ON WEALTH

Inherit Humility, not The Superficial Kingdom of Praise

How much money does it take to be satisfied with life? How many palaces and private jets must one own to live a happy life? The truth is it becomes a sweet poison to one's life. As time passes on, everything that was owned begins to feel like nothing. Without purpose, we lack direction. Wealth should be used to bring out a change in our society.

Wealth is quicksand for those that become the servant of gratification. Without an understanding, the fool becomes an expiration to his or her kingdom. Wealth for one is a palace of loneliness. Wealth for all is an investment that promises greater returns to those that you served.

Money has no personality.
The owner decides whether
it will be good or evil.

Inheriting a kingdom but being a slave to the impulses is the quickest way to lose all riches. Resist the temptation of putting a crown on a pig. You will slip and slide through an unworthy battle. Use your money to advance our human race. Bring positive changes with your money.

When success and wealth
enter your life, it becomes
another step in your journey.

When you are successful and wealthy, it is easy to get distracted with numerous estates, fancy cars, and private jets. Often, it creates a facade that one is better than the other. By focusing on the singular action of competition, we deplete our deeds and growth for the rest of humanity. When you have a lot of success and wealth, share it, and let others enjoy your company. We are the enlightened ones that grow out of a seed and blooms into a beautiful tree where everyone has their fruit of riches.

Voluntary concentration on one's title or accomplishments hampers the meaning of life. Whether we participate in sports, pageants, or become an entrepreneur, egoism can easily plunge into a dialogue of superiority. True humility begins when we adequately express our love for the welfare of others without pride in our titles.

The essence of a home is not only the shelter that we rest, but it is also sharing the piece of kingdom with others who are lost in their path. Through solicitude and unity, we can manifest a richer life that houses a driven purpose, one that is deeply rooted in humility.

Success and wealth are a guide with ideas, but at the same token, a confusion of chock-full of problems. Once we have reached the greatest level of success and wealth, we strike with our basement roots of, "I have nothing else to strive for."

When we pride in vain,
our humility becomes a skeptic.

In this development of thinking, we lose a valuable piece of our present and our future success. Therefore, let us reform our habits, exalting into a new altruistic Being that allows old forms of life to die away and for us to embrace the principles of an authentic life — one that opens new enlightenment in our hearts.

How many of you have attended a gathering and someone brags about their wealth? Humility is not warm to them, but rather, cold, and insecure. I have found to believe that when we engage in those affairs of bragging, we make up lost time for when we did not have riches. Thereof, we want to be recognized and worshipped for things that perish in due time. Humility is never the demise of personhood; it is the building of character that treats everyone with the same potential towards growth and success.

Show a dollar, a fool
will show you their investment of riches.

In the treasury of our pride, we have looked down upon the rest — claiming ourselves to be superior. To be glorified of riches and attention is to betray the welfare of our citizens. This generation has passed into a hallway of favoritism, engaging in drunkard pleasure, and feasting on fruits that have no juice to a meaningful life. Anyone who relies solely on wealth will begin to feel alone, with no one to share.

A true source of wealth has its beginning — it attains the possibility to obey the commanding heart to give back to the citizens who yearn for a common philosophy.

Opinions held by our society make little sense without understanding every citizen's biology, how they focus on humanity, and their relation to the world. If we are to select the steps from an existential approach, let us understand the empire that we are building. Together, we can enjoy the dance of life that brings us a peaceful eternity.

Remove the prideful taste in your mouth
before you drink the water of life.

The Lexicon of Wealth

Keeping sight of our divided tradition, we as citizens have a human drive to easily sprout that we are better than other countries or with our friends. Blinded by this realization, we reject humility, and instead, we invite the critical guest: The protractor of the ego. Through it, we sacrifice everything, even our international peace.

Today, let us move toward a path where we will no longer anchor through history, claiming the godless maximum of the last judgment of comparison. By looking upon everything with pride, we become weak and helpless. Raising the dependence on wealth becomes a chain that is locked around the neck; we become rattled by the whims of the idea of superiority while we bark for freedom.

Concentrate on what you would do with your infinite amount of wealth. There is plenty for all in our world. What you choose to do will greatly affect the pool. Satisfy on the wonderment on what wealth can do for a population of 8 billion people. Upon critical examination, we can categorize the weight of insecurity with the weight of a guaranteed, meaningful existence.

Technology makes it possible for us to connect with other citizens. We can share ideas, question the question, and we can lift each other to turn our efforts into numbers. Such security has been a pleasing revelation to snatch out the myth of passed traditions on how wealth was viewed as, "The rich are the rich and the poor are the poor." Men and women in their retirement are no longer hanging on the cliff to their social security checks. They are formulating new conversions to make their past family genes into a form of redemption.

Wealth is not the characterization of the same repeated vowels; it is action and ideas that help the world to gain a visible sign to climb higher. Without the hope of unity, we will continue to find limits in our environment. We must put an end to the stockpiling excess that one country is better while another country starves. I truly feel we can peacefully enable citizens to live with a full measure of assurance that our world can strengthen our bond through compassion and love.

The problems of existence are never fully understood. It is through our constant development of finding solutions that help us transform our nature. Through meaning and purpose, we can inherit a collective consciousness, motivating ourselves to understand the source of wisdom.

It is self-evident that we are trying to solve the riddles with a new dichotomy: To whom shall I serve? And how can I build a better legacy for this world and the generations ahead of me? Let us attempt a further step on how our global efforts of wealth can awaken and transform the meaning of life.

Wealth is a symbol of human history.
It either builds a new destiny or
it destroys the same history.

Perhaps, these times require us to globally unite with our talents to help each other manifest a new order of knowledge that springs to a primal source of meaningful action. We cannot deny this. Once accepted, we can gradually achieve social progress that is certain to grow organically through an extension of percipience.

Wealth and Personhood

We are conscious of wealth and the freedom that it gives us. On the other side of the spectrum, we address it as a form of podium — standing and looking down upon the rest who have lesser value than us. To the foolish, they give in to the consequences of wealth — easily manipulated and easily trained as a servant to obey the master. More painful than this is losing all riches without acquiring wisdom. The wise know that wealth is like taking care of a child. Once born, it requires constant attention and nurture. They also know that once wealth is grown up (in numerical figure), they know that it becomes a slow, steady trap to fall for an obsession with material beauty that has no meaning to the soul.

Whether in happiness or sadness, wealth cannot buy your soul. As beautiful and charming wealth may be, it will tempt you to come to the throne and to beg for comfort. Your wiser Self should be able to know that it is a temporary comfort — an escape to its whirlwind. You will feel burden with guilt, you will cry at night, and at times, you will profess to the Universe how wealth made you miserable.

When you have a lot of wealth, invest in greater things that will change the world. Do not be fearful when you donate thousands of dollars to a charity. Do it with great confidence because, in the end, the Universe will promise you greater wealth. It will be your responsibility to magnify our world with hope and love. The truly, humble citizens do not need recognition in the media or any other platform. Their confidence is spoken through their actions. There is never an expiration to their kingdom. Every action they take is understood through their wisdom. They know that wisdom is forever, and riches are not. Think about this for a minute. Of what use is it to have all the money, but stare at it through your hospital bed?

Of what use is it to have all the money, but selfishly spend it on yourself and left no abundance for generations ahead?

Every aspect of your life depends on the action you will take to advance our world to a new flourishing. Citizens complain about how money is suborned and evil while others are jealous because you have attained everything. Let's get this straight. The more you envy and complain about money, the more of the same gossip will come back to you tenfold. Do not bury yourself with hate or gossip about another person's wealth. Instead, go talk to them. Set up a meeting. Interview how they attained their wealth. It may seem silly, but its effects have a powerful energy that will be passed on to you.

I speak of experience. When I had little money in my bank account back in 2015, I knew I had to change my script and my energy towards it. Slowly, I began to be in love with money. I told myself all the great things that I will do with it. And lastly, I got involved with non-profits and through my time and effort, I was able to meet with several philanthropists. At that moment, I set up a date and a time to have lunch with them.

In my mind, I wanted to have their energy. In a nutshell, the more I hanged around with those people, the more I felt different. I viewed money as an agreement, not as a discussion.

If you find yourself lost in the road towards wealth, network with individuals who use the money to unite our society. There is something beautiful and magical when you listen to them explain wealth, leadership, and success. One of the greatest tools that I used and picked up from the social gatherings that I have attended is this: Use their success as gas to your vehicle of growth. If you wish to have their lifestyle, drive it toward your personality. Do not be exactly like them. Be creative on how you mold their headlines into your life. It will make a great impact on your well-being.

Our Myth of Wealth

Previous generations have whispered in the hallway, "Wealth is only for the elite. We as the people must continue to work if we want to live a comfortable life." These whispers have haunted our present Age, more so to those who are millionaires. Most fear with the trembling of war or pandemic, our food supplies, or shelter will phase out into the dirt. Being that we are aware of a New Era, it is important to study those myths from our previous generations.

As I said, many of them viewed wealth as a mystic cult or some poetic metaphor that they solved. Today, there is plenty of wealth to be shared. We have arisen successfully from the same rhetoric words that gave the same data.

The only limit to wealth is when you determine the outcome with the same terms and conditions of negativity, and a separation from your meaningful actions.

Humans are told that the elite are the only ones who accumulate wealth through world-class creativity. It remains a fact: real or imagined, wealth abstractedly seeks to bring forth the original truth to the present human experience. They who seek the truth will pass through the creative channel. From mind to mind, every soul who relates to the same enlightenment, they will obey the dictum that they promised themselves to sharpen social rational intelligence which most humans lack. With an obsessive concentration of helping others, we will devote to new stories on how the mind works — an alternating sequence of the architectural connectivity between our alpha state while at the same time, increasing the brain volume to direct its cognitive function with a higher level of mindfulness.

Wealth addresses the
obvious molecule in society.

To conclude this chapter, I want you to think about this scenario. Suppose in your neighborhood, you heard about a family who was trapped in a fire. They all got out safely, but their remains become non-existent. Tears are soft-landed on their faces, looking at you, hoping you have money to help them purchase a new home or at least provide food. But to your surprise, you do not have enough money to help them purchase a new home. You can only provide a week's worth of food.

Now suppose you have thousands or millions of dollars and an extensive network of philanthropists, you can look in their eyes, and promise them a new life.

On top of that, you can give them a check that is worth thousands of dollars, so they can buy new clothes and food. While you may debate that in the first scenario you are being a great friend who is there through moral support, of what good is it to give a hug and say, "I am sorry that this happened to you and your family." You want to be like the second scenario where you have thousands or millions of dollars — helping those acquire a greater benefit that leads to prosperity.

When you lack little wealth in your life, become familiar with an investment in multiple streams of income. As I said before, a lot of young individuals are making millions of dollars.

Is this a science?

No.

It is a new way of advancing our world to a New Age. An Age that ensues courage — heightening our community to the unfolding of human flourishment.

Passion supports your dreams.
But the action that is built on
wealth, you will leave a trace of
your humanitarian legacy.

ON AUTHENTICITY

A Solid Foundation of Awareness and Insight

The continuous existence amounts to the consideration of yesterday and today. Causes, choices, and the enactment of our free-will produces the observations which lead us to discoveries. Human reality is solely understood when we separate Being and nonbeing. Today, we see citizens organize a system that it "must" or "should" be this way. This fact is apparent in the descriptions that we see today. We often call them *motives and reasoning of action*. Generally, motives are the subjective ensemble of emotions that correlates to the environment. The reasoning is our inner historian which looks for everything, yielding to certain impulses which may abandon or add relations between causes and choices.

Our expedition should help us evaluate a practical bearing on what it means to be authentic. Each reaction that goes against the doctrine of authenticity is a provided aim to deplete our essential relations of Being. Strangely, most of us argue vaguely about what life is, yet we somehow modify ourselves to a charged emotion that destroys our society. It is like a careless smoker who says, smoking is what causes air pollution but continues to do it. This is what I mean about struggling with a bad conscience.

Authenticity should enliven the intention that provides a new joy and a new beauty that shapes the outcome into a moment of potentials.

We cannot, however, settle for superficial authenticity. When it comes to choices regarding how we want to live meaningfully, at times, we find ourselves siding with the majority. It is easy to get swayed by the pressures of calamity. Our fear causes us to take actions out of desperation, actions that we wouldn't normally take. This vacuum mindset chips away our good, moralistic authenticity.

I am Comfortable with Who I Am

The attempt to reach the hearts of many begins by knowing our darkness. Careful observations will help us course through our inner work and the works of others. Under these conditions, freedom inspires action, and contribution to our well-being inspires a new motivation to maintain a continuum of love and empathy. Our existence has wavered our personhood with old stories from our past, wishing for us to be "like them" or "to trademark their style." I remember a case of a young man in his early 20's who came to me for some mentoring and coaching. He came in confused. I opened the conversation by saying, "You seem to be puzzled." He said, "Yeah, I am confused. My girlfriend wants me to have a six-pack. She does not want me to be skinny. She thinks I would look hotter."

In these typical cases, especially with self-esteem and authenticity, I regard them as subject-object relations. The subject is Being. The object is how others want us to be. It is a mechanical drive to change our outer experience to fit their unconscious desires. It is selfish for the other person who wants their partner to leave their authenticity for something superficial. Many individuals, such as the one that I coached are often happy with their bodies. What poisons their soul is the entertaining ideas that their partner plays, hoping they piece them together, so it can create a dynamic fashionable couple.

What is damaging is when we compare ourselves to celebrities. Whether we idolize female models, male models, or athletes, we cannot structure ourselves to be like them. Each of them created their narratives based on what is fluid for them. Each tiny interaction they made with their goals lead them to their unique personality. Let's face it. No one is perfect. Each of us has flaws. Even those celebrities that you admire, they have flaws.

When you try to be perfect or try to be like them, you end up feeling like a ghost, non-existent to your personhood. Eventually, you doom your fate. Admiration for celebrities is a fantasy that is cupped with a flight from reality. Beautiful at times, but in others, it swallows your connection to who you are. If your sole motivation is to be exactly like a certain celebrity, then you are either restoring a loss of Self or suppressing it with shame. The only time you should admire celebrities is for their contributions to society. That is the only time you should use their inspiration as your fuel to inspire you to bring change to humanity. People like Bill Gates, Melinda Gates, Ariana Huffington, Warren Buffett, Jeff Bezos, Oprah, Mark Zuckerberg, and countless individuals who bring change should inspire you to do the same. That should help you restore your connection to where you are and to where you want to be in life.

Beauty appears polished from
the outside; but the true reality
is what is told from the inside.

In our childhood, we take in and play roles to whom we admire such as our parents or friends. At least in some part, we paint their morality and personalities into our belief structures. And when we incorporate them in our Being, it becomes a part of our written narrative. Thus, our self-image forms appraisals based on the creation that we developed.

Biologically, our limbic systems record our previous emotional reactions, which form our pleasure principle and habits. By pulling toward the biological center, our patterns tell us a story of who we are and what we unconsciously want based on our corpus callosum. It continues with other relationships, whether it is independent or dependent. Naturally, we have an unrealistic fantasy of becoming someone we are not. Do not get this confused about where you want to be in life. It is one thing to achieve your dreams and goals and another to be a statue of conformity.

If we divide our authenticity into two questions, it will be easier to realize whom we want to become in life. First, is it good for me to conform to what society tells me? Second, how is my authenticity serving others and of the world? The answer to the first question is a big NO.

Conforming to what society tells us binds us with nihilism. The answer to the second question depends on you. If I were to answer it, it would be something like this: *My authenticity is serving others and of the world by helping those who need growth and motivation to reach a new courageous life.*

This piece of authenticity is missing in today's world. Until we honestly confront this issue and work through our deeper meaning and firm truths, our Higher Self will hold us accountable. The undoing and rewiring back to our unique Self are long overdue. A lot of days are wasted on comparison, carrying an image of, "If only I was like that, I would have a huge following." No! You are perfectly amazing in this beautiful moment. Sharpen your wiser Self. Play out the part that you want to become; not what society tells you. Think differently. Question everything, even religion. Develop a curiosity and face the original set of wrongs that happened previously. Learn from them.

Self-discovery is the most exciting journey we can take. It leads us to a greater understanding of ourselves and to our life's mission. Our purpose in life is to be authentic. An increase of deeper meaning will allow us to live the opportunities that we longed for. Small or great, we can discipline our hopes and passions and open them to a new relationship with existence.

People who do not learn emotional geometry, they simply disappear to the meaninglessness and emptiness of existence. Constantly, they gravitate towards false passions, each encoding the same story to the same ending. Ten thousand times more, repetition instructs the individual to simply hold the secret of what is familiar around the world. They introduce themselves as someone who is not good enough. They feel that by tweaking their looks, they will be accepted by the Other. As time passes, they feel angst and nihilism in their personality. They end up betraying themselves. They pass away, not in spirit but into energy.

Their energy floats away, breaking up the process into mislead stages to their growth.

There should be no shame in being who you are. It is the most beautiful gift that you can walk with. For clarity's sake, refer to your wisdom and build it with action and growth. Part of this mastery comes from the notion of "waking up" to the fact that we are vulnerable and in touch with our Self. Beyond it is a remembrance of the powerful experience of authentic communication with the Self. Becoming oneself is a slippery road — often we slip into everything around us, feeling frozen to the useless forms that triggered us to change everything. But on the other side of the slippery road, we can stand firm, slide through it, and skate with our purpose of life. The long-term picture is more complicated than paralyzing to the conformity of society. Through the long-term picture, it helps us to stretch out of our comfort zone, helping us to provide more evidence that our strategies for staying safe are not required. What is required in our slippery road is to secretly put on our earplugs and ignore what society whispers in our ears.

When I Woke Up, I felt Alive

Do you ever have those moments in life where you wake up and you tell yourself, "Damn, I am back to being me." Or, you say, "Gosh, I love being free-spirited, lovable, and courageous." That is because you reorganized your priorities to live a life that is under your own will. It becomes empowering when we take back the life that was missed in the artificial world. In a place that is familiar to us, we become frozen, and at times, uncomfortable when we organize the Self to what others expect from us. They end up being the cocktail mixer and we end up being served by those who disable our thinking.

Feeling understood by the ones we love
can be healing to our human experience.

The first lesson in authenticity is to take ownership. It is your choice to repeat the unresolved hidden pain or to search for new beauty. When you take ownership, it liberates you from anger and resentment. The victim position can be seductive. It may provide a feeling of comfort, but on a moral compass, it will create a tragedy where you cannot resolve the issue at hand. It will fragment the internal experience with the outer-directed world. Maybe, to some degree, it will provoke you to continue to do wrong in all aspects of your life. That is why it is important to recognize when you are changing your personality based on the context of the Otherness-of-Self. A lot of people bind the human heart with a factory of defenses that allows them to live in a situation where life is on a pause. Denial, repression, and self-medication begin to work against those who do not understand the inner strength to tolerate oneself through the challenges of life.

Most of the childhood wounds stem from feeling insecure with ourselves. As we grow older, we repress the hurt with another personality, not the disassociation type unless, the individual was raped, then yes, it will mark different personalities. But the personality that I am talking about is one where we change ourselves to be exactly like a celebrity. Whether we want to look like Kim Kardashian, Charli D'Amelio, Addison Rae, or even Ariana Grande, it is impossible to be like them. Each of the individuals that we worship, they have their own way to connect themselves to the world. People get blocked around the idea that "I must talk like this celebrity." "I must walk like this actor." Individuals who conform have organized around their unresolved wounds, and they tamper with the evidence to create a new persona and a new name for themselves. In due time, they realize that all the quick fixes will bring them a haunting misery, one in which the pathos of the dark place rewrites the same manifesto history.

A quick way to get in touch with your authenticity is to ask yourself these three important questions:

1. Will I ever get what I want if I decide to mold myself to the expectations of the environment?

2. What does this say about my life and me for wanting to change my name and my personality?

3. How will this affect my present and future relationships with other people?

In my years of experience with individuals who want to change drastically, I have observed that when I put the mirror of logic in their face, they work better in approaching the eternal question: For whose sake am I seeking attention? Do I want to fit in the box, or do I want to live a driven, authentic life? Individuals seem to do better when they give up conformity and yield to a destiny that is open to new possibilities. I often teach them to embrace their beauty, and for them to foster knowledge and wisdom. A lot of us want to conform to be like the Other, but you must ask: To whose benefit? Most will answer, well because everyone else is doing it.

True beauty is when we have the confidence to continually evolve as a human soul. Reflection and spirituality seem to bring out enlightenment to those that integrate growth in their personhood.

You will find a great disappointment when you modify your personality to be like the Other, especially when you find out on TMZ or in E! Hollywood News that such and such was caught doing drugs or having sex with multiple people. Only then, you will realize and say to yourself, "Oh my gosh, what was I thinking? I am better off being myself. In no way am I like that person."

Nothing in life can come without an understanding of the connections that make us whole. We hang on to dear life, hoping that our previous sorrow will connect with a cure. Covering up hurt with superficial beauty is like someone stealing from a convenience store; the act of stealing is being caught, yet the person continues to do it. The same goes for your personality. Your emotional pain is a way for your Higher Self to watch you. The act of it is being caught. And once you are caught, you must motivate yourself to grow from the disappointments that caused pain in your life.

Stay emotionally current in your life. Do not undermine the pain or the troubles that you face. Each experience has beauty wrapped with more information to make you wiser and courageous. It is through those moments that your power responds to a meaningful life. Living meaningfully through an authentic grace, it will deepen your vulnerability to share your story with others. Rather than outsourcing to hate, you will enliven the hearts with love. Allow yourself to increase the capacity of wholeness. While many have difficulty to connect with humility, be that person who builds confidence as a sanctuary where beauty opens the heart of enlightenment.

Rather than spending your life
in being someone you are not, spend time
with your emotional wounds. Heal and
grow. With a compassionate heart, you
will realize that this life was made for you.

ON FAITH

Preserving the Quiet Voice of Optimism

What is faith? Philosophy studies it as a soul, sociology as social interaction, and psychology as nature versus nurture.

Faith is an understanding and a driven purpose pursued by the individual through their selective action. Our truth in faith is what binds our spirituality with nature. To live out our faith is to be confident with our end goal. At our highest level, we must not become the errors to our hearts that shouts revenge or hatred. Rather, we must secure ourselves toward the fountainhead of empathy.

Each level of faith is revealed, which calls for a new decision. We can be peaceful but end up causing havoc. We can live our faith but seek revenge. A combination of these brings out a perversion of impurity in our hearts.

In love, in war, and in unworthy tasks, citizens often act without regard to the end outcome of their decisions. When we obey the randomness of acts, we allow a drift to limit our stream of life. Most citizens call a preacher, but only to find out they are consumed with their sins. Shouting verses and commanding each soul to repent and to rebuke leaves them to put a bondage spell, leaving everyone captive in one large congregation. It is no wonder we are seeing more cases of neurosis, depression, and anxiety. Preachers feel obligated to tell stories of faith only to escape the emptiness of false passions. Communities circulate this idea that faith is a one-way street. And my gosh, if we take a yield, shame on us. We end up being labeled as sinners.

Our attitude towards faith should be based on the decision that makes our hearts command peace. No congregation should tell you how to express your genuine life. A reflection of God or whatever belief you have should remain distant from those that believe in the language of a phenomenon.

As believers, we live in the ambiguity of the obelisks and cloaks that mask the work of a greater willingness to search for wisdom. Patiently we listen, and yet our answers have not been resolved. Others say, "Follow this, and you will be healed."

When another flesh claims miracles on you, we know that it illuminates a philosophical discourse. It calls for questioning. Since every Being conceals on certain idols or beliefs, our reality cannot be based on their sensation of thinking. Ultimately, it will lead to arguments and perhaps, a defecation of nature — expelling the deepest beauty in our hearts.

Spirituality is a source of inner
strength that builds a connection with
an increased life of personhood.

Faith does not give; it awakens our lives to move us from our familiarity. It reminds us to anchor our understanding of existence. It teaches us the very essence of order, emotion, gratitude, and for us to be centered through the universal design. Too often, we place faith with religion, giving us an insecure revelation to our events.

Stillness in Our Faith

What clinches our fists are not so much the disagreements in our chaotic world; it is the defiance to compare faith with religion. A savage human drive that we take today is someone who proclaims that a certain God is better than another God. We fail to a degree to which our freedom drowns in nothingness. One's idea of God will differ in a multicultural lens. This is where we need to improve in today's age. We desperately want to shun the individual for praying to Nature or to Yahweh only because their beliefs do not coincide with ours. We cannot encompass this reality with the climax struggle to prove a point.

Authentic beauty should be certain for every individual who is in search of a new faith. The faith that they believe in should stand independently from society. If they decide to pray to Yahweh, let them. If they decide to pray to Jesus Christ, let them. If they decide to pray to the Universe, let them. And if they decide to share their beliefs with you, listen with a compassionate heart. Ask them open-ended questions. Get to know their culture, family dynamics, and subcultures. The most beautiful experience is to see the joy of another soul, glistening with a ray of sunshine, expanding its culture to the eyes of your soul.

Faith is communication that grasps historical manifestations through which we speak in Spirit. Excluding all doubt, we can have the attitude to conceive the life that we imagined for ourselves. Our true attitude of faith must press on even when we give voice to certain platitudes. When we connect our emotions to the experiences, we begin to feel a representation, one that begins to feel rooted in our consciousness. Mystery for some, but for you, it is an intimate silence between you and your haven.

The extinction of hateful desire is what stillness of faith is. It is being able to untangle years of emotional pain. The philosophical endeavor is to face the emotion through manageable steps that lead to spiritual healing.

Trust in the noble attitude that makes your faith possible. Clarify your knowledge, but do not assume that it will serve you a hundred years from now. Explore different doctrines. Question everything. Question science and religion. After all, even they had to modify their techniques in order to keep up with today's age.

The whole emphasis of your faith is to transcend symbols and signs into a completion phase that puts out a new understanding that you did not know before.

Today, we look to others to see if their faith is legit. And we also look to other beliefs when our foundation is broken. We find out who we become during the moments of chaos. Our faith puts everything in order so that we can take new responsibility that will extend onward to a new meaning of life.

When the comprehensive is circulated between the Self and the Divine, everything else stands in absolute manifestation toward the immediacy of empirical forms.

Gaining depth is a silence of speeches — contentment with the wanderings of the world, but at the same time, reflecting on the dubiety of secured knowledge. Rushing each answer puts us with the assumption that our human terms must meet the decisions that we made. Often, this comes with an imperative where we destroy everything, yet we saved one percent of obedience that puts us in the opportunity of flight.

When we remain faithful, optimistic, and unselfish, we will mentally retain the image of beauty — the door of second chances.

The desire to lead a great faith springs from the darkness in which we truly find ourselves to be vulnerable. With a formless ground, we can stare into the nebulous. When suddenly, we wake up in terror and ask ourselves: Who am I? What did I neglect to do in my life?

How will I know that I am getting closer to my faith? These questions should help us awaken to our primal source that deepens our inner action to demand more strength and precision.

A Whisper to Your Authentic Faith

The road to ambition begins anew, forging ahead with confidence that our lives must be present.

But what about the past?

The past is concealed with wisdom, rich in its context.

It has no control over your present behavior. What we gain alone is not as important as gaining unity as we trailblaze through life. Faithful communication must be realized. Without its adequate foundation, we stutter the vowels that make us reliable to our truth. Through the power of thought and intention, we can live a mindful, purposeful life.

In these moments, when you return home to your soul, you will flirt with the idea of memory and future. Tempting as it may seem to dwell on the future, reorganize your mind to stay focused on the present moment.

We anxiously wait for our death, and when it comes, we regret to not have lived mindfully and peacefully. Because of life's uncertainty, it is important to give your life meaning so it can extend its continuity. Neither shunning or suppressing your memories, it is okay to govern your vision or to question humanity. You will learn to not shy away from life's questions. Instead, you will be like a child building its first blocks, with excitement and eagerness to build a meaningful empire. Without any form of possession to old beliefs, you will throw away false arguments or illusory experiences that provided you an indentation to your darkness.

Out of the darkness comes transcendence. Exploring the signs of the universe will make your life beautiful. For it is not the message of another human flesh, rather, it is the message of the Divine, guiding you to the power of mathematics — connecting each dot and adding greater insight to the chain of experiences.

This, you must trust with your heart. More compelling than having your first kiss on a date is when faith presses to the astonishment of leading your path to what you envisioned.

Those who neglect the questioning of existence, they are no longer a seeker. They surrender to the cowardice of accepting life as is.

The false confusion to our faith is when the elements are produced at large: fanaticism, prejudice, and contrasts that one religion is superior to another. Similar tendencies critically hypothesize a domain of stubborn critical statements. Reflection on these principles should help us explore a genuine sense to listen, to test new beliefs, to reflect on new principles, and to invoke a direct counter with relativity than to suppose a permanent bedrock.

Presently, we are confronted with an ambivalent concept of faith. It has always been the case with every temple hall. It is public and accessible to everyone, but a secret lies within the windows.

Afar, everything seems wonderful, permanently preserved. Every discussion prevails, the body moves to its hymns, but more than ever, the individual encompasses a scope of an idea that yes, right here in this temple, I am the root of my happiness.

But as time passes on, the windows and the music that brought a glimmer to the soul are now robbed with public secrets, leaving every citizen burned into ashes. Truly, this is not faith. This is corruption. Made purely in vain is an activity that is wedged through a preacher's quest to limit the cognition that runs around, leaving others to feel inauthentic.

Consequently, every citizen follows the mistaken errors of faith. Our era sees a belief far into its distance, in its eyes, it sees achievement with greater opportunities. While at the same time, citizens blame faith for its evil corruption. Regarded as such, our human soul has relied upon the Word of faith from another flesh whose soul has a history. Whether corrupted in favoritism or corrupted with traces that left them open to a vista of controversial cases of child pornography, either way, without our innermost faith, every pursuit is lost.

Our pursuit of a meaningful life must continue, and every desirable outcome should bring humanity closer to universal love and peace. This does not take a prophet of a congregation to tell us a message on love.

Human thought must succeed in its function into a road of signs, indicating the direction of a transcendental faith. This profound discourse will speak to us directly, giving us a new source that was once taken away but has now come to life.

Faith, that is taught in school, it hypothesizes a signpost of entities that have transcended ossuaries into a religious system. We must not fall under the spell of the object term "religion." Religion is not faith. Faith is separate from an organized, systematic coercion. Once we understand this, we can grant a new entrance to a marvelous achievement of greater opportunities to flourish in our world.

How great would it be to stand in your own respected faith without religion imposing their desires on you? Pay no heed to the shepherd's crowd for they will substitute your wisdom with abandonment and protest.

ON GRIEF AND DESPAIR

Our Last Goodbye is Another Hello to Beauty

I was five years old when I attended school. I will never forget that day. I was nervous because it was my first time away from my mom.

I stood by the front door with butterflies in my stomach. I voiced my biggest concern to my mom, "How will I make friends?" "Can I stay home with you and watch the Walton's?" By the way, that was our favorite show in the morning. Nevertheless, she handed me advice that I carry with me to this day: Treat everyone equally and friendly. Smile and love openly. With her warmhearted advice, I felt a sense of peace in my heart. But knowing the way I was, I felt anxiety being away from my mom. I had mild tears in my eyes. I felt as if the polar ice caps were melting in my life. Looking at the clock, I rejoiced when I saw 2:50 pm and then 2:55 pm, and finally, at 3 pm, the bell rang. The class was dismissed, and I could finally return to my mom's loving arms.

Going back home, I could smell the luscious baked cookies, brownies, and cheesecake. As I walked into the kitchen, I would see all the pots and pans and all these amazing utensils that my mom owned.

I would always ask her, "Ma, what's for dinner?" She would respond, "It's a surprise." Boy, I played dumb. Mom could not fool me. I knew more less what she was cooking, but I wanted her to say it because she would always describe her food with such rapturous indulgence.

Another memory that I have of my mom was when I was in the fourth grade. It was a cold December afternoon. My teacher quietly asked me, "Luis, when is your mom coming over to the classroom to drop off the cookies, fruit punch, and McDonald's?" I responded, "I am not sure. Can I check through the windows?" With a soft smile, my teacher said, "Of course you can." Eagerly, I stood between the two pillars as I adjusted my eyes through the foggy windows and cold rain. Is that my mom, I asked? As I adjusted my eyes for one last time, I finally saw my mom parking in front of the classroom. I quickly went up to the desk of my teacher and said, "My mom is here!"

My teacher got up and went with me to help my mom bring down the cookies, fruit punch, and McDonald's. As my mom got down from the vehicle, she gave me the tightest hug and greeted my teacher with an infectious smile.

As we took everything down from the vehicle, we headed towards the classroom and all my classmates were waiting outside to see what goodies came in. All my friends would tell me, "Dude, your mom is awesome." "I wish I had a mom like that." "You are blessed to have a mom who loves you."

When I heard those remarks, I could not help but blush with gratitude. In my eyes, my mom was a superhero. She would substitute, volunteer at the school snack bar, engage in parent and teacher conferences, cook, help me with my homework, comfort me through my good and bad times, and lastly, she was my nurse. Whenever I was sick, she would comfort me with Caldo de Pollo (chicken soup). She would say, "Tien mijito, toma esto." Meaning, "Here son, drink this." My mom's ritual was for me to have two servings and everything would be great. At that moment, the thorns of my sickness became a crown of love that decorated my soul with riches and comfort.

A Touchstone of Loss and Meaning

On March 17, 2017, at 1:47 pm, my life was changed.

It was the day I witnessed my mom's death. Touching her hand, silently saying, "Mom, please open your eyes. I am your son. Please wake up." Hugging her beautiful body for one last time as they took her to the morgue made me realize, I will no longer have a mom. What now? How do I gain perspective in my life? I was thrown back upon myself to realize that I was in the courtroom of existence. I had no answer to the meaning of death until time soothed my soul.

A mother's love is fashioned and
packaged with humility. They
are the emblem of beauty that
gathers the family in unity.

Life is a brief candle; the splendid light goes on for a moment and it briefly passes down to future generations.

When I saw my mom in her final stages of life, it taught me that death is the greatest reset in life. It puts everything in perspective, and it gives life to those who rejoice in the awareness of personhood. Our seasons revolve and so does time. Each day is unique, and some may have its quirks. Seeing my mom on the confines of her bed, it allowed me to turtle wax my soul with a discovery of meaning. With tears in my eyes, I greeted her death with a handshake and said, "It is nice to meet you, professor." Death replied to me and said, "My young student, be not drunk in your sorrow for your mother's death will give you life."

Wishing for true wings and feathers, life told me, "Do not try so hard to get rid of the emotion. Your fountain of laughter, love, and forgiveness will come in due time." One could have easily settled down for the shades of the willow, but not me. Seeing my mom at the hospital taught me that we must unite as a family, to love openly, and to dust off the shelves of resentment and anger.

Seeing my mom's eyes, I felt as if she was telling me to melt hate and pain with love and forgiveness. Silently, I followed the experience of my internal Self.

Cast not the brimstone of hate. Cast the
grail of forgiveness that sharpens the
tongue with life instead of death.

Grief is not the end; it is another step in our journey to awaken the meaning of life. Do not permit yourself to wallow in self-pity nor do not use grief as an excuse that your life is over. Use grief to inspirit yourself with closure and wholeness.

The Dance We Take with Grief

Grief is an event that becomes strange to us. The affair with loss is different than any other feeling. When we are in love, we smile and kiss. When we are courageous, we take bold steps to live a meaningful life. But when we experience grief and despair, we feel a disrupted sense of Self. Grief is like a new kid in school; no one wants to converse and open the dialogue with, "Hi, let's get to know each other." Both grief and the Self are shy. It takes humility to meet the soul with a nakedness to nurture the experience of grief with a produced outcome of meaning.

Each morning will come, and the sun will set, and we will know that our loved ones are home with us in our hearts, carrying us through a new light.

One of the many lessons I learned through my mom's death is this, death is a paradox. It makes us feel we are immortal, yet we are gripped with fear. Filled with regrets, we tell the saddest truth in our tongue or through the pen, "What I could have been." Let this not be you. Your body is a guest. Honor your guest. Get to know your guest. Buried in our human eyes are not the tears of death, but the alienation of personhood.

Your body is a guest.
It visits, and it leaves.

Grieving for a person whom we have cherished is never lost in the continuity of life. It rises again but in the form of spirituality. Freed from guilt or past tensions, our subjective experience formulates a new outlook on life. Blaming, attaching, and grieving belong to the empirical time. Honoring and forgiving produce a new form of beauty in the subjective experience.

History does not stand in the way of the individual's meaning of life; it helps the individual to identify the distance between regretful tension and the degree of personal awareness.

An Acronym for GRIEF

What helped me get through my grieving was to wrestle between my superficial grief and learning to gain insight into a new world of possibilities. For those that wonder, what is superficial grief? It is a term that I coined during the process of my grieving. When I analyzed and studied those who grieved over a lost one, some of the remarks that I noticed were, "Well, my mom or dad are gone, I guess this means we can party and get drunk to honor them for one last time." Or "Losing my loved one means I will never push forward with my life. It is pointless." For me, I wrestled with the second statement for a while after my mom's passing. I felt as if I could not push forward with my life.

We must be wary of this type of grief because superficial grief cannot comprehend the conclusion of death. It cannot create or enjoy the process of grieving. The individual exaggerates the importance of banal pleasures that overestimates the growth of personhood.

Within three to five months, I realized I had to learn to switch my grief into purpose. This became the hallmark for me to gain insight into a new world of possibilities. It was then that I created an acronym for GRIEF: growth reacted to internal emotional feelings.

Rather than reacting with continuous despair, learn to switch it towards growth. This merge will give you a uniqueness where you validate the experience of the emotion. The liberation of despair will allow you to love and to smile again. When the time comes, you will understand the precious feeling of grieving. The feeling is unique to every individual.

In our discourse of human existence, an existential analysis strives to make every individual responsible for their reacted internal emotional feeling. By growing spiritually and emotionally, our limited time on earth will begin to feel like eternity. Grieving becomes a setting stage for love and forgiveness, a rebirth of hope that reorganizes our thoughts into a pathway of healing. Once forgiveness and peace take their stand, our wholeness can be rebuilt. When all is complete, we can extract from the worst of experiences such as losing a loved one and mold it into a new examination of life.

Beauty unwraps itself as we recognize the sense of fullness, giving us the soft expression to smile once again at life.

The Five Pillars of Reconstructing Your Wholeness

Before I present my new model for grieving, I want to shed illumination on my new model. The five pillars came about when I went through a painful breakup with my ex-girlfriend in December of 2015 and of course, the death of my mother. No psychological theory or philosophy or even a priest could water down my emotions. I had to honor my existential silence. As painful as it sounds, I did nothing but keep silent while at the same time honoring my emotional wounds. Mourners tend to rebel against the Self by taking sleeping pills or asking their doctor to increase their sedatives.

Most mourners commonly report feeling better after ten hours of sleep. But then they realize that grief is not wiped away from the soul. On the contrary, grieving breeds through consciousness, pushing the individual to feel the authenticity of emotions. Consistent suppression may protect you, but it will kill your inner biography. We cannot escape the absence of grieving nor can we pretend to "feel dead" to the public masses.

We must remain alive on the inside to make grieving meaningful. No event can be subtracted from life without adding meaning and growth to our experiences.

Our destiny suffers when we shape melancholy rather than shaping transcendence as a form of beauty that opens the window to growth.

As we all understand, relationship breakups and grieving over a loved one have the same effect on the psychological order. The difference lies in who is alive and who has died. Therefore, I was inspired to create *The Five Pillars of Reconstructing Your Wholeness*. For this model, I want you to use it daily. Practice the steps until you have mastered your clarity. This will take time, but the rewards will be recognized through your stalwart dedication to living meaningfully and joyfully.

For the following pages, I will guide you emotionally and spiritually to your centered Self.

Pillar 1: Honesty with the Self

It is the first pillar of insight, an awakening experience to the centered Self. At rock bottom, we learn to transform despair into purpose. By allowing ourselves to be in the moment, we can find a connection between the Self and the event of the emotion.

Often, we tend to ward off the first question of life: What can I learn from this experience? Such a question brings authenticity and awareness of the circumstances that are presented. It releases preconceived defenses that were holding us back from healing our emotional Self. The armor to this step is to be comfortable in this stage. As you heal, you begin to tie up your loose ends through soul-searching. By discovering your connection with the world, true nurturing begins to take root in your life.

In my motivational programs, I teach my students to *feel* the present moment. When *feeling* and *inner action* take place, the involvement with the event becomes a philosophical discourse between the confrontation with destiny and the relatedness of our environment. To put to practice, ask yourself these questions:

1. To what extent do I find my life meaningful?

2. Are my emotions "in" the world or is it trapped in my thinking consciousness?

3. When I make meaning out of this emotion, what can I gain from this experience?

4. By going through this emotion, what are some of the benefits? How can this help me mature and grow in life?

5. From what sources do I rely on? Was it from my irrational conscious, or was it from my Higher Self?

Taken together, this first step will allow you to withdraw from the bond between "what was" and the "after-effects of emotional attachment." Everything else will continue to flow once you begin to heighten new beauty toward the Self.

Pillar 2: Exploration of autonomy

For the second pillar, it is important to explore the autonomy of the Self. In this pillar, you will learn to rescript your dialogue, engage in your goals, and move towards congruence between creative expression and authenticity.

It is important to note that these pillars must be practiced when going through a breakup, divorce, or grief. The discovery that I made with these pillars is that most individuals found themselves influenced by the emotion rather than being influenced by the meaning of it. The meaning of events tells us how emotion and meaning equal to a dynamic, active phenomenon. When a couple breaks up or when someone goes through grief, the memories create a myth to protect the psychological order of the individual. This myth that I speak of can be in the form of fantasies, drama, or one's self-analysis. To put to light, I once counseled a couple who was going through a divorce. The husband was in denial whereas the wife was dawning on the fact that there was no union, no love, nor attention. The husband thought the relationship was fantastic which is why he was in denial.

In that level of denial, I asked him, "Could it be that you are creating a myth to protect your kingdom with your wife?" He kindly responded, "I can see where you are going with this. As a child, I used to love watching romantic movies. I would always create scenes in my mind as to how I wanted my marriage to be like." As you can see, we are opening a new revelation about the husband's past upbringing. As a child, he was enthralled with fantasies and myths.

As the session progressed, the wife looked at her husband and said, "I always wanted to feel sheltered in your arms, but you had this idea of how our love should be like. I got sick of it and eventually, I got sick of you."

After meeting with them for eight sessions, the couple felt it was best to get a divorce because they had different views on love. As the husband began to cry, I kindly asked his wife to step out of the room. As such, I started to work on rescripting his dialogue towards his meaning of life.

One of the activities you can use to rescript your dialogue is what I like to call, *changing the two poles*. This is an excellent technique to use when you are going through a relationship breakup or grief.

To explain, changing the two poles is a paradox between changing the language and the will to experience new beauty. In between the two poles, I have individuals write out their present emotions followed by the dialogue that they keep subscribing to.

Furthermore, I have the individual read the statement out loud until they hear how it sounds. Once they do, I have them shift their language from "This is awful" to "I am willing to learn about this experience. I have felt it before, and I am willing to learn my lessons as I make meaning out of it." Easily, 99.9% of the time, individuals begin to feel relief from their emotions. As it stands, the two poles imply love and death. Those two are inseparable because, in life, we need to experience the continuous struggle of conflict, creativity, and death. Without love and death, life would be insipid. There is no beauty without this struggle. As you move around your two poles, begin to engage in a congruent state between your creative expression and authenticity. In creativity and authenticity, we can find true beauty in our emotions. There is a certain zest when we accept this awareness as part of the maturing stage.

If we neglect this and concentrate on our troubles, we will sacrifice the vitality of mutual engagement between the Self and the relation to existence. The freedom to grow and to subscribe to new beauty in our lives will help us instrument the receiving end which helps us expand the totality of Being. This is called life's lessons. Rather than sleep-at-it-until-you-feel-better, wake up and feel your new arrival to a new insight through the gifts of embrace.

Pillar 3: Regroup your thoughts in the here-and-now

Emphasizing the past will put us at a deprivation towards the meaning of life. The tendency to be stuck in the past is comforting to most individuals. But to those who are willing to reveal the hidden structure of emotions are the ones who relate the present experience with a new manuscript of meaning. In my experience, I found to believe that when individuals "meet with the emotion," they begin to view it as if it were a friend. When our friends come over, what do we do? Do we ignore them, or do we welcome them? I hope you would say you welcome them. The same goes for emotion. The emergence of our self-consciousness yields to our capacity to think in terms of existence.

The here-and-now experience is a breakdown of the *what* rather than the *why*. The *what* reinterprets the growing aspects of your personality. The memories, the hurt, the denial, all form in the *what*. As the poet, Susan Musgrave wrote, "You are locked in a life you have chosen to remember." The formation of your emotions happens unconsciously, but nonetheless, you have a choice between myth or meaning.

Now, when I say myth in an emotional aspect, I do not mean that your emotion is not real. It is real, but your interpretation of the outcome is a myth. How many times have we heard the same phrases of, "Great, my life is over." "I fought for love and for what? It got me nowhere." These are exaggerated myths that present themselves in our consciousness. Mankind tends to revert to the past and somehow mold it to our situation. This is where we see trouble in the *why*. We begin to speculate our ideals, hopes, wishes, and characteristics of the Self. In a profound sense, it is much safer to collectively engage and reflect on your own identity. Even though we go through heartaches and grief, it gives us no excuse to use cocaine, heroin, or any form of drugs.

We must give assurance to ourselves and to the community that we share a common dream, carrying us through our existential dilemma.

The invisible chorale is the unity
of citizens, leaping each other to pierce
the night with sheltered love and growth.

Pillar 4: Reintegrate self-acceptance

Whether we dream and live or hurt and cry, we dwell among the occasional coming of life's events. A couple of years back during my internship, I had a client who was diagnosed with major depressive disorder with mild anxiety. The client presented as outgoing, sociable, expressive, and funny. In our first session, I opened the session with, "Gosh, you make depression and anxiety seem awesome. I wish I had depression and anxiety." He chuckled and said, "No, no. You don't want to have depression and anxiety like me." I asked, "Why not? You make it seem so effortless and awesome." By the way, I am using paradoxical therapy for the first 20 minutes.

He continued to say, "Well, my life sucks and it is meaningless. My wife died a few months ago. I am alone and I feel dead in my soul. All I do is drink and boy do I drink. I even had thoughts of suicide. I thought about slitting my wrist." At this point, he has cut ties with his relational output of life. He is "in-home" with his internal thoughts rather than "at home" pursuing his meaningful life.

To make my point, he never learned to be free as a child. He was grown up to be a man's man. He never engaged with other children nor did he parallel play in the playground. He lacked patience as a child. His occasional coming of a "child" was soon to be met later throughout our sessions.

A point must be made, when we have a need for attention as adults, not only does it curbside our personal youth, but it cries out in the form of attention and love. Most of our grieving gets complicated when we feel displaced with our feelings. When my mom died, I felt displaced. But somehow, I had to emblazon my search for a meaningful life. My mom's death has taught me to reintegrate self-acceptance whereas before, I kept finding my past for a secured guarantee in my life.

More than ever, I feel alive and happier not because I got over my grieving, but because I reintegrated parts of my lost Self into a new dialogue. Courageously, I learned to experience love and openness in the form of beauty.

We can experience a new destiny in our lives — a destiny that stretches out to meaning, putting us in the height of faith, helping us to respond to life's questions.

Pillar 5: A new reunion with the world

In my motivational programs, I always begin with my philosophical question: *If the mind is made better through presence, why do we live in the pulses of miserable aims?* Take a few minutes to think about that question. There are no right or wrong answers. Once you have answered it, ponder on your answer. You see, we are living in a time where beauty and courage have been submerged into chaos — wars against wars, an increase of divorce, a decline in education, and the most threatening part of existence, isolationism (us versus them). A choice confronts us. As citizens of the world, shall we withdraw in anxiety? Frightened by the phenomena of human life, shall we cover it up with nihilism?

If we do, we will have surrendered our participation with our meaning towards a greater future. We cannot forfeit our Higher Self for the pleasures of yesterday. As human beings, our influence is to bend evolution through awareness and creativity. We must have a firm belief in our faith. This will unsnarl the outlined emotions that we placed internally.

A chief characteristic of this pillar is when an individual knows how to participate in life. When an individual experiences grief, he or she is encouraged to leap into courage, forging ahead despite of grief. When we experience grief, not only do we follow the other four pillars, but we must create a new reunion with the world.

As newborns, we are born through attachment. Life begins in your mother's womb. Fluids exchange and your biological needs are taken care of. Through the mother's rhythmic beat of the heart, you do not need to worry about eating, breathing, or danger, that is taken care of by the mother. For you, existence is tranquil and effortless. There is a communion between you, the mother, and the universe. As you are taken out of the womb, you must create a "new reunion" towards life. Like all babies, they have no distinction in the early seconds of life. The baby cries and for the first few months, they coo and laugh.

As adults, when we go through grief and despair, we cry and mourn for our loved ones. Just as the child experienced unity with the mom, we experienced unity with the ones that departed from our sacred circle.

For whatever reason, our need for attachment never expires. When my mom died, a part of me felt empty. Again, it is the connection in the womb. Like a newborn child, I had to learn to create a "new reunion" with the world. Our reunions with the world will be different, but let us keep one thing in mind, our search for a meaningful life is universal. A sense of purpose gives us fulfillment in our everyday lives.

Again, I ask the same question: *If the mind is made better through presence, why do we live in the pulses of miserable aims?*

Through the connection of the womb, we were at peace and when it was time to arrive, we made our social presence known. As adults, when we go through a relationship breakup or grief, we somehow revert to emotional outbursts such as killing, fighting, or engaging in recreational drugs. This results in reductionism thus leading to nihilism. A point must be made, when we push ourselves beyond the forests and form new habits, let us leap into the unknown, without cowardice.

Let us be committed to our aims and goals in life. When despair meets courage, they will learn to form a club — exhibiting a foundation of rationality and intimacy with the world.

I can be what I can do and what I can
do is achieve the promised land
of a meaningful life.

Reservation of Tears

Society operates on many tearful levels. The first one is the cheerful tear where we cry out of celebration because we achieved a milestone. The second one is where we cry out of pain and despair. Whether we experienced a loss of a loved one or went through a divorce, we cry because we yearn for attachment and love. Lastly, we cry out for attention, which is what I like to call, *spontaneous confirmation*. Spontaneous confirmation is when we reloop our previous conditioned behaviors that yearn for attention. For instance, suppose your new purse tore. More than likely, you will text or call your girlfriends and tell them how awful your day is because of a minor tore. Or you will post the picture on Facebook or Instagram and hashtag it with "not my day." You see whether our purses tore or our threads in the shirt are coming off, we tend to emblazon minor shortcomings with beliefs that our life is over, and thus, we cry. Cultivating this type of behavior is what leads to a "me" society. Read my book on *The Five Virtues That Awaken Your Life.* I go into detail between the modes of me, we, and I.

In our reservation of tears, it is in a pure dialect that we form an abstract idea of what our tears mean to the personhood. The possibility of the relation can formulate when we ask ourselves, "Are my tears related to actual despair, or is it an emotional site that I learned as a child in which my tears became a disconnection to my personhood?"

Once the disconnection takes part in the tears, we begin to wonder, "Will this continue?" The answer is yes. It will attribute to the relation as a category rather than being an authentic form of despair. For example, a category of a reservation of tears would look something like this. Joseph has spoken about how awful it is that his friend broke up with his girlfriend. Joseph begins to feel his friend's despair, thus, causing unnecessary despair for Joseph. He feels depressed, begins to cry at night, and to great lengths, he joins his friend in drinking eight beers a night. In this relation of tears, Joseph destroys the possibility of being a thinker that composes wholeness rather than relating to the despair of emotion. Consequently, Joseph is not despairing properly. It is the beginning of an appetite, a regression of the past.

When a friend tells us a bad event or expresses a loss of a loved one, we need to be there for them, but we need to caution ourselves in not getting pulled in the vortex of their despair. Their despair is their unique event, not yours. When an individual despairs with another individual, we get rid of ourselves in the formula of authenticity. Therefore, the individual who joined the despairing vortex will make every effort stronger than the one before. This universality has set the ground for many centuries where we consume ourselves into other people's emotions.

We feel guilty if we do not participate in their despairing. This kind of participation leads to unrest and disharmony in our existence. When we carry this unrest, we secretly harbor a customary view of all appearances. This can either develop as a superficial view, a poor understanding, properly understood, or a category for each overstated reaction to the event.

To explain these concepts, let me share an emotional behavior habit when it was my mom's memorial visitation. Upon attendance, a great number of people showed up. It varied from family, friends, extended relatives, and former teachers.

To say the least, one of my mom's friends showed up. Lo and behold, she had not seen my mom for about twenty to twenty-five years. When she showed up, she began to cry and *feel* as though her despair was equal to mine. When in fact, hers was recognized as an overstated reaction; meaning, "If only I had hanged out with her more often, I would not be crying as much as I am now." On this occasion, my mom's friend reacted to my calm composure and said, "You seem to be taking this very well. You are not crying." In this stance, her friend wanted me to *feel* her overstated reaction. In every human relation, we want others to feel our pain and misfortune. They want us to be in despair like them. They begin by saying, "It seems like you do not care about me." "Why aren't you crying with me?" It is not that we do not care, but we care enough to reserve the tears that have a relation between personhood and Spirit. When I speak of Spirit, I speak of our relationship to our Higher Self, which connects us with a Higher Power. This relationship cannot be destroyed for it guides us in our earthly events.

Changing the Language of Grief

As we begin our journey through grief, the vestibule of alienation begins to quail toward the personhood, causing a moment of question, "What is the meaning of grief?" We concern ourselves with the meaning of grief, hoping to remove the wasps and hornets of the sting of grief.

On many levels, we must take the stage of grief. By exposing the traits of sorrow, we can understand the words that are being spoken, and we can turn the course from our imagined perils into a challenge that moves us *in spite of despair*. It is my perspective that a part of grief is to face the paradox — accepting the acceptance of grief or lose significance toward the Self. More people poignantly experience the second option: *He or she never knew their identity, let alone what their meaning of life was.* This is the basic dilemma of human evolution. In grief, we shift our void to sexual fantasies, multiple religious beliefs, or energy healing. None of this reaches a tableland of authenticity. It bifurcates the task to endure and to enlarge our scope of responsibility.

It is highly interesting to go back to classic literature and read how they dealt with anxiety or grief. Let's take for instance Dante in *The Divine Comedy*. Here we see an individual who vulnerably says, "Lost in my midlife, I lost my way in a dark wood. I started in a straight way but found myself in a dark wood." Dante cannot comprehend his virtuous life from his emotional standpoint. At a higher ground of understanding, he cannot find purpose in his life. To shed light on his totality, he has a companion, a guide so to speak to help him go from unconscious suppression to acceptance toward the Self. Throughout the long narrative poem, Virgil (the guide) tells Dante, "If you follow me, I will be your guide and lead you forth through a passage that is worthy to live for." Virgil as a guide leads Dante to understand his pale hesitation in making sense of life. Virgil tells Dante, "I understand your words and the look in your eyes, but this course is not a frightened horse or a shadow…it is a petal of a new warmth and light to your life."

This is reassurance for us in living through grief, anxiety, or despair. Like Dante, we have our emotional guide — it is the experience of the emotion that guides us to a meaningful life. Our modern Virgil is whatever emotion we are feeling. If we are going through grief, our Virgil is grief. Grief is telling us, "I am the content, but at the same token, I am a land of the underworld." Once we comprehend this, our human emotion can favor a new life.

Likewise, the event of grief or despair is usually paralleled with what I like to call *internal reminiscences.* It extends inwardly to the point where the individual feels compelled to narrate the same autobiographical description to the same story. Feeling sorry or feeling unnecessary guilt coexist in the human psyche. Traversing in this state will yield to a sensational embellishment made for the sake of nihilism. It is through beauty and connection that helps us combat the distortions that we inherited in our existential dilemma. Courage beckons when we attribute to the intentionality of meaning. Grief, in a sense, becomes a position in which we organize new beauty, leading us to carry out the understanding between conclusions and meaning-observer points of knowledge.

When we know the language and the anticipation of freedom, it gives us the power to build on our creativity, endurance, and spirituality. Unfortunately, most individuals split creativity with pseudo-pleasure, endurance with stagnation, and spirituality with meaningless brio.

As it can be seen, much can be learned from our language and to the relatedness of courage and sorrow. To bring out a change in your grief, try this shape-shift language. Instead of saying, "My life is useless if they are not here. There is no reason to live without their presence," say this instead. "He or she was a guest in my life. Like a guest, they visit, and they return to their eternal home."

Language and concepts give an individual
power to concretely interpret and to transform
their sorrow into inner freedom that
outwardly expresses enthusiasm.

By saying this, you change your separation from "loss" to "visiting." The relational dialogue between personhood and grief enlarges the foundation of the process which establishes a balance between guest and self-affirmation.

As I conclude this chapter, let me go back and briefly tie in Dante's journey and his guide Virgil to grief and despair in our present day. In our human experience, we have two guides: revelation and intuition. Both are cousins to our growth in life. Intuition can bear itself through life, but revelation must be guided by another entity — the presentation of emotion. For Dante, his guide was Virgil who helped him to see the illumination of life. Grief and every other emotion are like Virgil. They guide and pass through our hell of emotions. It speaks with reason, empathy, and love.

Our departure is the experience that
was lived in love, in time, and in situations.
Through it, we remain by chance to
recapture our lessons for different seasons.

Like Dante who uttered his conclusion with Virgil, "I placed my final goodbye to Virgil. He had gone but my wisdom is forever." We, like Dante, seek guidance to gather the fruit of liberty. When grief or any other emotion presents itself in your event, welcome it and say, "Hello, professor. It is nice to meet you. I am ready to journey with you."

By standing in this spectrum of life, you can reflect and pause to question your despair. The experience is more than tears; it is maturing and going through the private purgatory before you experience some sense of paradise.

As we already know, managing grief and despair appears to work better in approaching the eternal question, "Should I remain stuck in the past, or should I search for new beauty?" When we question it, it will help us to understand the meaning of life. By being vulnerable with our emotions, grief can become our guide and friend who interprets our empty halls of life.

Through each empty hall, we will feel a sense of anxiety, but the good kind of anxiety that pushes us to complete the quest — moving us to the experience of possibility, the consciousness of one's freedom as one emerges within oneself.

All through history, classic literature, art, music, psychology, and philosophy, they have taught us that by going through the brief smoke, we will reach a chance of heaven. The journey through grief and despair cannot be omitted. What one learns is a prerequisite to the arrival of a radiant life. Without this experience, there is no success in finding new directions toward the road of beauty.

Funeral sentencing is not only the burial of your loved one; it is a sentencing in which your sorrow must meet the process of vulnerability, courage, and beauty.

ON ANXIETY

The Existential Aspects of Personhood

There is no question that anxiety inhabits our well-being.

When we get bound and thrown into a flood of uncontrolled anxiety, our Being becomes clouded with confusion. Not only do we try to understand our anxiety, but we numb it with pills. Society has reshaped the same behavior for us to "be on time." "You have until 5 pm." "Hurry up!" "Be a little quicker!" All these statements made us highly anxious. For this chapter, we will observe anxiety from an existential, psychoanalytic view. Existential psychotherapy has been at the forefront since the Kierkegaard era. With my understanding and research, I will guide you carefully on the meaning of anxiety and how you can use it as your creative output.

Anxiety as Your Philosophical Professor

Anxiety has emerged heavily as a dilemma in our society. In general, religion, philosophy, and psychology have tried to explain it, but come back to the same answer: It is mind over matter. With such a weak statement, I will cast light on the meaning of anxiety. When we feel the heart rush, sweaty hands, stomach pain, or any somatic feeling, we tend to shy away, or in Freudian terms, we suppress it in our unconscious thoughts. While it may be beneficial in that moment, it somehow comes lurking back years ahead, taking the form of neurosis. In truth, anxiety arises when we become aware of it. Our possibility of confrontation becomes noticed when our nothingness contains an internal description of what we should do with it.

Even though clinicians diagnose anxiety, skilled psychologists, and psychiatrists leave out the coordination between freedom and choice. When our nothingness contains an internal description, most therapists blank it out and focus on wishy-washy solution miracles, having the individual remain passive to the symptom of anxiety.

An inquest of anxiety will be explained in this chapter. When we understand anxiety, we can understand its meaning. The forms of anxiety can be understood by the reflection of the feeling rather than a label of the symptom. When the Self is composed of relational aspects to personhood, the individual chooses the freedom of choice rather than the sickness of anxiety. However, being that anxiety is categorized as a mental disorder, I will challenge the notion. Anxiety is not a mental disorder, only to a certain degree. It is a dialectic aspect between the possibility of choice and the necessity of creativity.

Granted, anxiety is often masked as depression. When we position our emotions, we can view it as relational meaning. All speaking consciousness is decisive. The more consciousness we have, the more we enable responsibility toward the Self. The Self is always becoming something other than objective symptoms. When the task of anxiety becomes a relationship, the progress moves *through* rather than *away* from the scope of existence. Consequently, a lot of individuals despair over anxiety and remain chained to the emotion, not knowing that anxiety is freedom towards our creativity.

At every moment, we become a process of actuality. Simply put, the dialogue becomes a consciousness that wants to be validated. Every human is intended to become someone in life, and as such, we take that risk of becoming someone. Whether through business, sports, politics, or education, we strive to reach higher. And as soon as we reach higher, more responsibility kicks into the standards of achievement. If we alienate the path of courage, we increase the dependency of familiarity.

This is where we abandon ourselves and leave the scene of life open, hoping that someone will take over. Hence, anxiety withers, and depression kicks in. Since the external environment plays a pivotal role in our human behavior, we lose sight of our totality of wholeness. Engaging in our external environment is the most crucial aspect of the Being. Here's why. Because we risk our sanity in hopes of a better life. Heaping with consequences and authentically venturing into the unknown, we risk ourselves. If we ventured wrongly, we blame the environment that we are getting punished for not reaching the full potential.

Because of temporality and freedom, the individual will always have a reason to be in a state of anxiety. What separates the causality is when the individual honors the emotion with high esteem, absorbing each moment with a calculated possibility that the emotion can always yield to freedom rather than a disorder to the mind, body, and soul. Possibility, choice, and freedom are the necessary aspects to enliven the scope of existence.

When we stretch our boundaries, we grow and mature. But when we choose comfort over bold action, we stagnate.

The extensive capacities of anxiety are what I like to call *inter-social hostility toward the Self*. This develops when one blocks the pressure of anxiety. The hostility develops when it is channeled through the environment, friends, family, or the Self. Since the satisfaction is not present with the Self, it associates with a considerable significance of aggressive competition. This, in turn, creates a social prestige for the individual who wants to be remarked as a genuine winner.

These types of individuals will not change their character structure due to the control of what is left in their personality. Their anxiety is not just borrowed time, but it is their whole life. If one feels the pressure, they end up giving themselves vague emotionality to mask the present consciousness.

Anxiety and The Relation to Being

There is a considerable amount to take in as we relate anxiety to the Being. Awareness of the subjective experience is one key element, but the other element that is most often ignored is the personhood of valued construction.

The occasion of anxiety is a secure
threat that pressures us to turn to the
essence of creativity. By standing "in,"
we can master self-awareness.

I had several cases where clients presented to the session as feeling "dead," "anxious of the future," "stagnated," and "fearful." In these cases, I often ask them, *if you could divaricate the Self and the objectless emotion of anxiety, what differences would you notice in yourself?* This question often highlights their moment as they reflect on how their anxiety can be negotiable if they successfully follow the steps to a greater independence of life. What I have learned through my years of experience is that a lot of clinicians leave out the differences between separation-creativity and creation-of-anxiety.

These two are common in the present age. And we ignore it because we do not want to face the creativity-of-anxiety. Normal anxiety is valuable to our personhood. If we separate it from our human existence, we can cut the umbilical cord that ends the ties with fearful anxiety. As I said on the previous page, if the individual constructively rewrites their narrative from "I am nervous about the future," to "It may be difficult, but these experiences cannot break me," then, it will not only lead to greater autonomy but also a life lived with growth.

For the next pages, I will give several examples of how to use anxiety constructively, and how you can practice using certain techniques with your clients or with yourself. It will be noted that most of the anxiety that we face is not so much repression or conflict of environmental issues. It is a conflict between developmental creativity and producing a meaningful outcome. We throw away the potentiality of courage because we want to retire to the safety net of mechanical anxiety. When the pressure becomes too large, we yield in the direction of neurotic anxiety. This is where a lot of individuals give up on life. Strictly speaking, I do not believe that all anxiety is a form of neurosis. Yes, your biological makeup plays an important role, but when you compose anxiety as an overwhelming feeling, you no longer relate to the experience. Logically speaking, you become compulsive and irrational to cope with the situation that is presented to you. A point must be made. What confronts us is an open nature to actualize the capacity to discover, and to change the arrangement of anxiety into a central, personal awareness that enables us to live a purposeful life.

In our day-to-day experiences, we invent arousal anxiety in which there is no evidence of a threat. For instance, when you go out on a date for the first time, more than likely, you invent all sorts of anxieties such as, "My hands are sweating." "What if he or she does not like me?" "What if I upchuck my food?" "Imagine after tonight, I never receive a callback." This creates an emptiness in your subjective experience. The capacity is not justifiable because the invention of anxiety takes place as an *occasion* rather than pursuing courageous acts towards a meaningful life. The capacity to bear the occasional anxiety is to venture into those situations, to cultivate full presence and wholeness, and to be genuine towards the moment. The more original we are in the moment and with our service to the world, the more we will experience anxiety. Culture plays an important role in shaping our Being. It represents our progressive movement which adds a shibboleth to our viewpoints and aspects of action.

When the environment and the Being cross paths, it becomes an outlet for spontaneous consciousness toward the developmental growth of Self. Human beings vary in degree concerning their capacities of anxiety.

To one student, an entrance exam may seem just another exam to breeze through, whereas to the other individual, the entrance exam depends on his or her life towards career choices. Thus, this becomes a helix which produces two sides to the coin in which I call *content anxiety* and *suspended anxiety*. Content anxiety is when a person gives attention to the situation. They decide on how they are going to mold it and how to use it towards meaningful action. To them, it does not paralyze them mentally, it inspires them to distinguish the problem and the outcome. In a sense, they become the observer as if they are watching themselves from the view of a Higher Self. They take risks knowing that it may cause anxiety, but they know that they need this anxiety to succeed in life. Anxiety, for these individuals, it takes them from dread to growth; from stagnation to progress; from doubt to possibilities. They are the ones that say, "If I go forward with my goals, I know I will experience anxiety because I do not know what the outcome will be. If I remain stagnated with no progress nor meaning in my life, I will experience anxiety, mixed with guilt."

These people are what I like to call, *perception seekers*. Like a meat butcher who puts the meat on the table and carefully analyzes on where to cut and where to season, these perception seekers know exactly where to use their content anxiety and where not to.

As we can see, if we move forward, we will have anxiety. If we move backward, we will have anxiety. What is the difference? The difference is reshaping meaningful habits that will create new patterns in our lives. Moving backward will only stunt our growth. We will live with bad habits, we will have a negative attitude towards life, we will shut out the meaning of life, and lastly, we will blame everyone else.

On the flip side, we have suspended anxiety. This type of anxiety is when an individual "holds" internally to the emotion. The individual is aware of the creative capacities, but they integrate a symbiotic relationship between fear and remaining stuck in the past. They objectify an inner fear as a fear of life or on a deeper level, a form of insecurity that havocs a threat to personal growth and development toward the Self.

In many cases that I have dealt with, most individuals formulate the orientation towards nihilism. To explain, I had a woman whom I will call Savannah. She reported feeling skittish, had no meaning in her life, anxious about the future, and lastly, not knowing what to do now. To be frank, I asked her, "With everything that you presented to me, do you feel swallowed up from existence?" She looked at me for a few seconds and without hesitation, she said, "Yes, I do feel swallowed up from existence." After she went on talking about feeling "swallowed up," I tested my theory on suspended anxiety. I said, "Somehow, you feel swallowed up from existence but on the other hand, you told me how you enjoy crafts and baking. Am I right to assume that your correlation towards your anxiety matches with a newborn anxiety compared to your content anxiety which is enjoying crafts and baking?" With ease and less tension, she remarked, "My gosh, I haven't seen it that way. Oh my gosh, that is an eye-opener for me. Wow! I never thought of anxiety as newborn anxiety compared to what you said on content anxiety."

Throughout our sessions, we continued to ping pong between content anxiety and suspended anxiety. I am a big fan of leaving symptoms behind. When they present their issues to me, I ignore the symptoms and focus on personhood dialogue, metaphors, and constructing a new experience in life. The only time I take stock of symptoms is when an individual presents with bipolar, paranoia, schizophrenia, delusions, personality disorders, suicidal ideation, or eating disorders. With anxiety and depression, it is noticeable when an individual creates suspended anxiety (newborn anxiety). Like a newborn infant, they cry over attachment or when they need to be changed. This type of anxiety is normal for an infant who experiences a specific threat to their existence. But when an adult experiences this form of anxiety, they phrase it as, "I am anxious about the present and the future." They compensate for a weaker, less meaningful life. The chief interest becomes a dependency to rely on others for their freedom or at times, they surrender their life and they let others control their routines. There is no negotiation for them because they do not know how to divide content anxiety and suspended anxiety.

With suspension comes the responsibility to face the fear again. With content anxiety, it becomes enjoyable to the person who knows how to multiply social relationships and how to construct activity that has spontaneity towards their craft.

The crucial factor for a healthy personality begins with our subjective attitude towards anxiety, depression, or any other emotion that sets us back in our lives. Self-awareness is the hallmark that aides us to a discourse, prompting us to understand the passage, the ever-changing nature of growth. Our capacity as human beings is to gain new endeavors and emotional security in our dialogue. It is when we move away from the repeated narrative of, "I *am* anxious," to "I *have* anxiousness." Notice the differences between *am* and *have*. One is objective while the other is subjective. The objective mode is *am*. Such inferiority begins to take the form that the individual has a neurosis or is certain that they are weak. They accept the weakness or neurosis as a fulcrum of extensions toward the Self. This type of form leads to further neurosis, which leads to secondary mental illnesses. If we choose to focus on the subjective experience which is *have*, the product of emotion cautions the psyche to guide the principle of obtaining valuable constructions to sequence the inner contradictions of specific strengths, and specific weaknesses that need to be championed with new forms of habits.

It is then we ask, what specific purpose does anxiety serve? For the individual that blocks anxiety, they cue themselves to retreat with no responsibility towards a meaningful life. Whereas the individual who is creative with their feelings, they use anxiety as a motivation to further themselves to a world of possibilities. By and large, the individual develops a new attitude that essentially extends to the development of tools in which they utilize toward the subjective Self.

Empty anxiety never has meaning to our personhood. With my experiences in working with individuals with anxiety, one theme is common: power. Individuals who retreat from anxiety, they compensate it for power. Since their anxiety is too much to bear, most individuals strive for power to avoid anxiety. This will eventually lead to social hostility which makes the individual isolated from existence.

The meaning of anxiety is not to produce pseudo-panic feelings, it is to rewrite the narrative, to plunge in the experience with vulnerability rather than consequently passing through time wounded with angst and regret. Anxiety can be managed naturally once the bond is formed with intentionality and direction. Once the fellowship becomes congruent, it becomes of the world that affirms through insights and methods that lead to rational awareness. To reveal our rational and irrational functions is to understand it and to clarify it. The solution is not to ignore the specific form of anxiety, it is to open the door of creativity in which we have the potential to create a new meaning that molds the productivity of Self.

The discovery of anxiety begins with
an understanding of our individuation.
When meaningful content is built on
freedom, one can feel life again.

The anxieties of today are not in the form of freedom, they are in the form of competition, and through a lack of conditioned esteem. Today, individuals concern themselves with success, power, and wealth. They feel it is a form of self-actualization when they conquer success. Little do they know that love, empathy, forgiveness, and vulnerability are just as powerful than an individual's superficial fame.

It is necessary to note Sartre's concept of dialectical anxiety. Sartre purposed that our individuality has two openness toward the personality: freedom of development and world relations. To avoid confusion on what he meant, I will summarize it in layman's terms that we can understand. Freedom of development always involves the question of whether it will push us further to our goals or detract us from the isolation of guilt. The dialectic is the genesis of developing individuality, without being bound to the potential of fearful anxiety. It involves the freedom to choose and to formulate ideas that will join in harmony with the primary ties with our relationship to life. For instance, suppose you want to open your business. The sense of anxiety will be greater than the sum of individual action.

With that said, when you separate the anxiety into healthy purposeful anxiety, the action becomes meaningful. Even with the threats of anxiety, it pushes you to become aware as to why you started your endeavor.

On the flip side, we have world relations which is Sartre's second openness toward the personality. What this means is that when you have a strong purpose to your goals, you redouble the efforts to gain a relationship between the Self and the world. It adds motivation to maintain competitive individualism toward the Self. This is what separates competitive behavior against others. Competitive individualism is stretching the experience and learning to figure out the important factors of purposeful anxiety and creative anxiety. During this period, you will base your anxiety as a relation rather than a threat to your Being. When your secure base of Self is measured with the subjective experience, you begin to realize your selfhood as a moment of possibilities, not as a moment of nihilism.

You begin to heighten your spiritual relations with other like-minded individuals. You become courageous and constructive with your meaning of life, and most importantly, you strengthen each experience with clarity.

Anxiety and the New Freedom of Life

Far too long we have dreamt of a life of improving ourselves and the socioeconomic situations of our society. The dream became everything in our hearts. People sharing truths and ideas, struggling to create a new life for our earth. But then, the survival to create a new abundance became neurotic. The survival of "what" became a survival of conformity. We live life to the means of pleasure, not a means to a purposeful life. To fulfill our destiny, we must plunge inward to find the capabilities to turn our anxiety into a new freedom of life. Today, people cannot find meaning or purpose in their lives.

It becomes a motion blur when asked: What changes would you see if you added more meaning into your life? What I have learned through my clinical experiences is that anxiety will be at the center of our lives.

Whether one starts a task or tries to escape anxiety, the feeling will continue until you reach a new conclusion towards creativity. Self-transcendence is only possible if we turn our inner conditions into a new avenue of growth and insight. To paint you a picture, I will describe a case that I had with an individual who was addicted to alcohol and pornography. To preserve his identity, I will name him Ethan.

He presented to the session with a low affect and somewhat depressed. He was around in his mid-40's. I always start by saying, "This room is our energy room. There is no criticism, hate, or laughter toward the emotions." As soon as I said that, he felt welcomed and relaxed. To make my long story short, I will cut through and talk about his existential crisis. He was a smart man but avoided the tensions of life.

Primarily, the significant tensions that bring change to humanity. He served his tensions by allowing porn to numb his inner empty feelings. By no means, it served no purpose to mankind. So, I asked him, "Is it possible that you are in search of a new tension, one that brings harmony to you and the world?" He responded, "Maybe, but I have no idea what tensions I have at this moment." I went on to say, "Perhaps the tension to watch porn or drink heavily is creating the arousal of anxiety. The search that you want is never found in these pleasures, rather, it is found in creating something meaningful." With his head down, he slowly shed some tears. He quietly said, "I sometimes feel I have no purpose in my life. I see my friends doing great businesses in Texas, Chicago, or New York. And here I am, drinking my life away and watching porn."

By displaying empathy, I warmly said, "But isn't it true that if we compare ourselves to other individuals, we deplete our authenticity toward the motivation of creating something personable to ourselves rather than our friends?"

Quietly, he said, "Maybe you are right sir. Help me to find my meaning." In this case, you should NEVER say, I will point you to the exact meaning of life. Remember, existential therapists only direct and facilitate, they never give the person the meaning of life. So, I said, "I can help you relate your goals and guide you the way to a possible actualization through which you feel significant and happy."

It is important to note some of the main points that I have analyzed through my clinical experiences. These are some of the reoccurring points I have seen come up regarding anxiety and creativity.

1. Without the appropriate amount of creative tension, we reduce it with secondary pleasures such as substance abuse, recreational drugs, or pornography.

2. By allowing creative tensions, we allow a new emergence toward the personhood.

3. By not allowing our creative tensions toward the personhood, we retire ourselves to neurosis and guilt to substitute the specific tensions of life.

4. When we create tensions such as starting a business or writing a book, it gives us something to live for rather than living by objective pleasures.

5. When we have too much tension, it leads us to psychological trauma. Thus, causing us to have a mental breakdown such as a panic attack or severe depression. Thereof, we need the right amount of tension to face the specific challenges of life.

When we claim a need to measure up our totality of the chosen goals, we end up measuring our emotions with an interchange that prompts the anxiety to join the reservation of tasks that need to be accomplished. Insofar, not only do we end up facing our anxiety, we end up motivated to use anxiety as a gateway to construct the formed and the formless.

Formed and Formless Anxiety

In our open horizon, we have subjected our experiences to want more. Without appreciating life, we sometimes yield to boredom. This has become extreme in today's society. Wanting more and giving into boredom has become the leisure to spare out the creative tension from our personhood. Evermore, we find ourselves meaningless when we come to the obvious conclusion of submitting to artificial tension such as climbing Mount Everest or starting something, but then pausing and moving to the next task — repeating the same cycle. The high becomes great but then it becomes low within days.

By now, we know that anxiety is not only biological, but it is highly formed through values that mirror our relationship between the origin of involvement and the threat of not accomplishing our goals. For this matter, I present a hypothesis of today's anxiety: *formed* and *formless anxiety*. Let's talk about formed anxiety. There is a conflict in today's age. We cannot lie to ourselves that anxiety is only a mental disorder.

Anxiety is a side conflict of an inner working that is calling us out to produce a constructive stage between our meaningful contributions to the world and a change to the personality. The frustration, however, has been plotted as a threat to punishment toward the libido conflict as Freud suggested. Respectfully, the libido is not the threat to our anxiety nor sexual repression, the main threat is, the expression we give to our anxiety and how we relate the anxiety to the world. Formed anxiety is when we bind our inner personal relationship with measurements that benefit a closer examination of the structure and outcome. Ultimately, this will drive our instincts to serve the world with creative tensions rather than reacting with aggressive impulses. Fulfilling the encounter of meaning is always driven by the frequency of how we want to live through the output of our environment.

There are frequent occasions of "over-formed" anxiety, which may cause psychosomatic symptoms. In my experiences, I have seen individuals use their formed anxiety for their creative endeavors, but they end up oversimplifying the outcome. I once coached a driven female who started her business at the age of thirty-three.

To keep matters confidential, I will call her Aubrey. She had excessive amounts of persistence, positivity, and a goal to change the world with her business. Unbeknownst to me, she seemed tensed, had mild sweat on her hands and forehead, and occasionally had bouts of diarrhea when she was pressured to deliver for her team. Any clinical psychologist or psychiatrist would say, she meets the criteria for generalized anxiety disorder. But from my existential standpoint, I did not see a diagnosis in her. I saw a woman who was tangled between the formed and the formless anxiety. Through consistent counseling and coaching, it was evident that her formed anxiety started when she was fifteen years old. Her parents pushed her to achieve perfection. She told me, "Luis, as a teenager, I had to get at least a 97 or a 100 on my exams. If not, there would be some hell to pay." I responded to her by saying, "It seems you are tied to your teenage years. You have chosen to allow the past to cause a present disturbance to your goals. As an adult, it seems to me you gave the same conclusion as you did when you lived with your parents." The more I got to know her and her traditions of success, we slowly uncarved the hard shell of her personality. If my hypothesis were to be true, I had to put it to a test. Being that she had formed anxiety in place, it was my job to show her formless anxiety so that she learns to incorporate healthy anxiety that is suitable to her needs.

Truth must be illuminated before I go further on the differences between formed and formless anxiety. These two are good. At the same time, both can be harmful to your ways of living. To continue with my case of Aubrey, I will explain formless anxiety, and I will also explain how it can be harmful if we do not have the right amount of creative tensions.

Formless anxiety is freely chosen for whatever situation confronts us. On one hand, we may be confronted with a choice to break off the relationship with our partner, or we can continue to hurt ourselves emotionally by being in an unhealthy relationship. Formless becomes attainable with our rationalistic thinking which equates to the relations of our emotions. The more intimate we are with our experiences, the more revealing the answer becomes to our decisions. In this case for Aubrey, she formed her anxiety from her formative years. Thus, causing a dialogue between the ontology of categories from her past and the present affirmations that she is telling herself.

Nevertheless, if she had restricted her creative formed anxiety but had empty creative formless anxiety, the scenario would have looked like this. Aubrey would have formed the first assertion about the nature of her anxiety. I would have directed her path to a place where anxiety can be viewed as an awareness of one's Being. By forming the impression of the events, she would have formed the "creative anxiety" as a production of content. The effect of this measure would have educated her to view anxiety as an independent variable of fear. She would have emphasized the degree of reaction to her formed anxiety. As such, she would participate in existential courage and produce a new path that is meaningful to her personhood.

Now, if she had formless anxiety without the creative will, she would have experienced a spiritual and moral decay within her personality. The threat would have caused her to lose the ultimate concern of what makes life meaningful.

As you can see, formed and formless anxiety can be healthy to your Being, but it can threaten your personality if you do not measure up the contents of each scale of anxiety. If we cut off our creative participation with the world, we lose a sense of symbolic meaning with our culture. The drive weakens when we devote to the empty fate of a traditional content of, "Let me pop some pills to take away my anxiety." We are born to relate, not to separate our contents with pills. In a sense, anxiety is great for you. When we know how to manipulate the formed and the formless, we can plunge inward to form new conditions that bring out the best in ourselves. Courage and participation are the key elements to loosen the power of anxiety.

Between the connection of Self and
the specific meaningful tension, one
can establish the duty to fulfill the tasks of life.

Bracketing our Anxiety

In and out of the flux of emotions, we subscribe to empty lies or absolute threats that harm one's Being to a meaningful quest. At times, one feels frustrated about their culture while others feel passionately affirmed to a driven devotion that pulls upward to the human energy of creativity.

In the slightest sense, we realize that everything must have experimented action followed by persistence. The description of anxiety has been swallowed with traditions and emotional preferences. Seeking who we are is often challenged when we courageously take a risk upon life. Avoiding situations becomes a habit, based upon the separation from the totality of Self. In trying to identify ourselves, we surrender the richness of our present moment in turn for flat directions that disguise the details to examine the richness of beauty. The driving force of our anxiety produces anticipated depths in which we collectively achieve to advance our science towards enlightenment. The nature of anxiety has been brushed away into the nihilistic traits of despair.

Upon the givens of anxiety, I have come up with a solution that has helped countless individuals to realize that their anxiety is not a disturbance, rather, it is a connection of life that reveals messages that need to be completed in order to stretch beyond the creativity that is presented in our morally, puzzling world.

In the next few pages, I will explain my new exercise which I have called, *the ontological bracket of anxiety*. I will explain how to use it for your emotional freedom and how to recognize your anxiety from an intentional standpoint, which gives birth to meaning from an active state rather than a passive, reacted state.

The ontological bracket of anxiety begins in a mathematical equation; not the equation that we learned in our formative years, but the equation of philosophy and psychology. To explain further, suppose you had severe anxiety due to inner conflicts of a premature breakup. What I would advise is this, take out a sheet of paper or you can use your board, and begin with this equation:

Anxiety (A) + present emotions (PE) + my response to the situation (R) x the meaning that I will give to the situation (M) = adjusted rationality (AR). The equation would be this:

(A) + (PE) + (R) x (M) = AR. Now, how would this look in our everyday life? Let's delve deeper to learn this exercise. Suppose, Mitch and Sara had a conflict in their relationship. Sara tells Mitch, "I know we have been dating for three years, and I know we were supposed to get married next year. But I feel we are not right for each other nor do I feel this is our time to get married." Mitch may go on and say, "Where is this coming from, sweetheart? I know I have not been present or attentive to your feelings. I know I get caught up with work. But I love you so much." In this presented conflict, we can see the overwhelming anxiety from both parties. Both are defending their stance in the court of love. Everything becomes fragmentary to deal with relationship issues. In such a case, the couple would have to validate each other's emotional crossway. Second, they must listen without judging each other. Lastly, they must preserve the sacred circle of love rather than preserving the empty emotions of correctness. Because if they preserve the empty emotions of correctness, they will cling on to desperation, leaving each other with more potential reasons to leave the circle.

The canvas that was presented can be broken down like this:

(A)——+—— (I feel overwhelmed) (PE) ——+—— (I feel we should reconsider giving each other a chance) (R) ——x—— the meaning that we can give to our relationship is that we are loyal to each other (M) —— = —— I feel that our adjusted rationality could be a new self-affirmation where we defend the sacred circle of love rather than defending our empty threats of anxiety (AR).

In this example, you witnessed how to bracket your emotions. There is something powerful when we bracket anxiety, depression, panic, grief, or any other emotion that we may feel. By bracketing the emotion, you give it power and meaning. You decide the construction of your narrative by adding or multiplying a new outcome that will course through new healing with new customs to live a vibrant, courageous life.

If the experience favors the capacity to abandon the tragic aspects of our past, then favor the moment as you rebirth into something much more profound that vitalizes your life.

ON DEPRESSION

The Encounter with Creativity

Towards a New Discovery of Life

O n an afternoon of wonder at the pond, I caught myself in a curious fantasy. It goes something like this.

A person who is depressed enters a beautiful white room. As the individual enters the room, there is a big screen with a projector. The screen says, "paused." The individual looks addled as the screen says, "paused." As the individual gets closer to the projector, there is a squeaky noise behind. "Who's there, the individual asked?" It is me, your guardian HIGHER SELF. The one who sees and guides you to your customary life. The individual seems puzzled, "Wait, what? I am not sure what is going on." The Higher Self begins to take out his briefcase. "Let me show you the silent life you lived and the other life where you began your goals but stared into the nihilism of emptiness."

I am aware of the life I lived, says the individual. "I know I have been depressed and have not lived fully. I know that. I do not need someone to tell me how to live or what to do." The Higher Self looks closely at the individual and shakes his head. "Perhaps so. But the truly lived life is not a scientific form. Yes, you have fallen into silence which became darker. And yes, I am aware of your existential lectures of angst, confusion, and sorrow. If you stay with me in this white room, you will see all your revelations on the screen as I press play. You will see parts of your life where you could have acted differently regarding your goals. So, have a seat and relax. Together, we will solve the dilemma of human life."

The individual begins to feel calm and pulls up a chair.

The Higher Self takes out the controller and proceeds to continue the movie of the individual. In this scene, says the Higher Self, "You described your depression with a means to not live anymore. Remember this one? You broke it off with your wife. Both of you had your differences in the relationship. You paused one night and binged on whiskey. And at other times, you let the symptom speak to you rather than you speaking to the symptom."

I know. I know, says the individual. "I confess that I was not the best version of myself. And as a subject to my experience, I planted the wrong seeds in my life."

Now young man let's look further. "Everybody but you went and risked for higher ambitions to live a meaningful life. Around that time, you were contemplating on opening your business, but you let fear quail into your darkest fantasy of not working out."

The individual pounds at the desk. "What the hell is my dilemma? Answer me Higher Self. What is it?" Let me illustrate it to you in the next scene says the Higher Self. "Viewing and treating yourself as an object and being directed by your emotions rather than subscribing to meaning is merely a deadline to your Being. You treated yourself as someone who wanted to "fit in" with the sentences of life. In every relationship that you had, and for every setback that you had in your courageous endeavors, you suddenly got caught up with the alluring prospect of "thinking in depression," rather than "playing with depression."

You see, your human dilemma has suffered greatly with verbs such as *avoid, want,* and *wish.* When in fact, you should have focused on the two most powerful verbs: *acknowledge* and *have.* To possess the right form of possibilities, distinguish life from oneself to the environment around you. NEVER promise yourself on appearances. That has been the case for you, my dear young man. Late fruit always ripens with a sour pride that ends up being short-lived."

Your celestial Superior, "I have been placing myself as a deadline — mounting up with angst, fear, and nihilism. Liberated once more, not through medication or whiskey but through the power of your guidance. Quivering in every muscle, I am now free to possess a new measure of value that will prepare me to grow and to stand with the main clause that favors a meaningful life. If something were to stay in my memory, it would be this moment in the white room with you my celestial Superior. With a promise to myself and for the betterment of the world, I vow and take this oath herein this day forward to stand for a life that opens the window of enlightenment and prosperity.

To the beginning days ahead, my first duty of order is to CREATE. Being able to create and to manifest a new life will bring a new future that promises a long story to our greatness."

Changing the Trophy

As my fantasy ended, I began to reflect on my meaning of life. Like the individual, I began to give reverence to gratitude, love, and enlightenment. By shielding myself with courage, I can bend any emotion towards creativity. For this chapter, I will propose a new outlook on depression. Considerably, it has been clustered with an attitude of, "You will get through this." Pop Psychology views depression as a condition that can be handled in a 30-Day Daily Devotional Guide. A psychiatrist views depression as a mental disorder that can be handled with five to ten medications. An existentialist views depression not as a fraction but as a whole. We have reduced the totality of Being to a series of symptoms that manifest unconsciously.

When we shape our meaning and purpose,
our spirit gets nourished.

In its essence, depression is an intention to bring forth the appearance with a compelling story that you want to give. Society and commercials tell the story of depression as "sadness," "fatigue," "boredom," and "excess amount of sleep." The necessity to understand depression as a companion is to understand our *before conscious* and the *creative conscious*.

In both parties, they get tangled with the illusion of avoidance-limitation and creative-expression. Insofar, the before conscious derives from emptiness. It only conceives one idea and that is, to cause itself with more sorrow and guilt. Whereas creative conscious, it positions itself as a Being who is willing to discover that depression is not a symptom, rather, it is a relation to the world and to oneself. By questioning the subject, one can extract the sorrow and provide a foundation that consciously expresses a table of originality.

All the symptoms of depression are a consciousness of something. When we feel depressed, we animate the idea that we have nothing to live for. In front of this view comes the phenomenon of stagnation and over-medicating individuals, which results in a continuity of symptoms.

Between the engagements of our capacities, depression is aware of the gaps that lead to false expectations and intellectual creativity. As already pointed out, depression is nothing more than a narrative that has been imprinted with frames of orientation that lead to classical responses such as, "I came out like my parents." "My life is over." "There is no meaning to my life."

Conceiving these narratives imply judgment toward the Self. These bases of frames can be deconstructed when we move ahead despite the psychological symptom of depression. Our understanding of depression has crippled our world with an aimless drug that ruins the changes to our growth. Rather than letting ourselves be creative, we climb upward to the illusion that drugs will cure us. Even though drugs can control certain diagnoses such as schizophrenia, paranoia, delusions, bipolar, and the like, that is not to say that we should medicate everyone just because they have been sleeping more than usual. Yes, get checked with a doctor. Take a physical examination. But never impoverish your Being by comparing yourself to the Other.

Most practice a formulaic path — sprouting the same stories of how our generation is like the previous one, leaving us shackled with an unsuccessful life. Today, we live in a world where our mind is beginning to take notice of how powerful our thoughts are. Science has proven that when we enhance our productivity and clarify our meaning of life, we will emerge with a new mindset that will lead to greater excellence and vitality toward the Self.

Depression is an introduction to rank our
original content of feelings with a new
narrative that makes us live a meaningful life.

There are grave dangers when we admire and worship the trophies of depression. Experience has shown that when we create a mental picture, we begin to experiment with the landscape in our present world. In doing so, we paint depression as a negative scenery that has no meaning in our lives. Bearing this reality, we can rest assured that our creative endeavors will be distorted, leaving us lost and weakened in the battlefield of life.

Self-realization is our freedom to confront depression, anxiety, or any emotion to construct new possibilities that meet life with a new potential of growth. By removing the trophies of depression, we can begin to contribute to our growth. Within our reach, a positive solution beckons the light with new results to our dilemma.

The realization of depression cannot be brought together with a hopeless attitude followed by stagnation. Depression must be tested creatively with our values along with our abilities to move through the phase of depression-creative experiences. By and large, our Self will emerge, and we will be able to tolerate and to honor the emotions rather than fleeing from it.

If our meaning of life is to illuminate, then, we must confront depression with a qualitative leap that distinguishes from refusing freedom to an expansion of wholeness. Unfamiliarity is the acceptance and responsibility to involve depression as our seasonal companion. Increased selfhood, freedom, and mindfulness will enlarge our creativity, and it will reposition our frames of meaning so that we can establish a process that unfolds uniquely to the beauty of life.

Our expressions have
scars built on wisdom.

Popular Secret: What We Tell Ourselves

The mistaken notion that depression is for the weak is a foolish statement of ignorance. It shows a lack of empathy in the human soul. Behind every conscious thought lies a story. At times, it is told and in others, it is suppressed. To discuss the problems connected to the human mind, we must learn the stages of development and how it unfolds throughout the entire lifespan. Within the narrow frame, we carry out myths, messages, and secrets to describe our relationships with life. We restrict ourselves and deal with one percent of our problems rather than dealing with the whole sum.

From the cradle of the mother to the grave, we question and process our problems with reflections, doubts, and experimental action. Throughout our growing period in adolescence and adulthood, we begin to think of life as a dubious gift.

Everything in us begins to vacillate with the shrinkage of our possibilities to accomplish a meaningful life. In our natural happenings, we either widen our consciousness or turn away from the guidance of the Universe. The necessity to understand our emotions is an important task to comprehend the introduction to our narratives. We wish to make our lives simple. Though, the results will not be great as much as those who plunge inward, discovering their emotions, and rescripting depression to the clarity that it needs. If our problems and emotions give us a way to use it in a form of creativity, we will forget that we had depression or anxiety.

Several ways seem possible when the principle of questions belong to the domains of knowledge and wisdom.

To penetrate the darkness, we must summon the courage to indulge in the mystery of life's problems. Understanding life's problems require us to branch different knowledge for different seasons. Belonging to a private school of thought will only devour our growth with a special subject that will not capitalize on future gains. This extravagant thought is not to be charged as a natural happening; it is to be charged with our choices and with our psychological unique combination that makes up most of the special subjects of philosophy, psychology, and theology.

If consciousness were to arise fully, how would one act subjectively to the experience? Or to put in another way, if depression were to be conscious of the knowing, how would we establish contents to further ourselves towards healing? No one can be certain to give an easy answer to these questions. But we can find the answer with children. Every parent can concur that children are the explorers of their environment. When a child recognizes something, they either express it or get it. That is the foundation of "knowing" something.

As adults, we express our "knowing" in different ways. We recognize knowledge or emotions through the linkage of perception or through the experience of heartache. When something is established, we either ask for guidance through our friends or therapists or sadly, we numb the void with drugs and alcohol. Unlike children, we have more responsibility to know the "knowing."

Without consciousness, there are no dilemmas to solve the problems of human life.

To connect knowledge with wisdom, we must illuminate the observer stage.

On the next page, you will see a figure that depicts the "knowing" as an established event. By knowing the content series, you will get a better understanding of how emotions evoke.

Figure 1-4: The Cycle Bearer of "knowing"

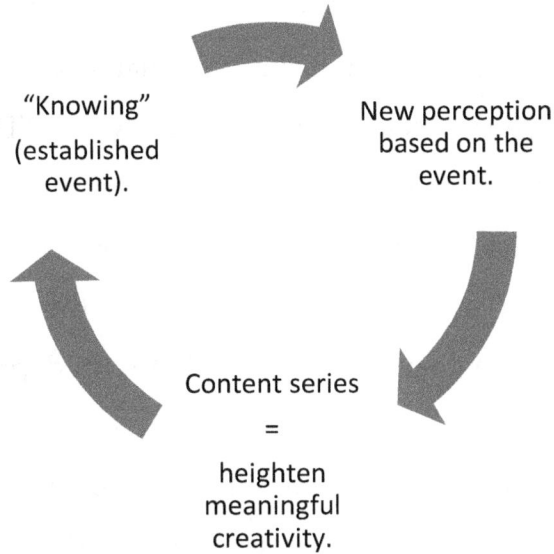

"Knowing"
(established
event).

New perception
based on the
event.

Content series

=

heighten
meaningful
creativity.

In the diagram, I explain the noticeable contents and the misplaced contents to our psychological life. The mere connection between "knowing" and new perception is learning how to observe and to connect new patterns towards healing. When consciousness is heightened, the content series elucidates a continuity of creativity to bridge the gap from depression to a magnitude of growth.

Often, our disturbances of depression come from the inner difficulties to adapt a new script that we can achieve through effort. In my clinical experiences, most of my clients had a difficult time to narrate what depression meant to them. When asked, "What does depression mean to you?" Most of the answers were, "Depression means there is no reason to live." "Depression is the final stage of suicide." "Depression is forever." "Depression is bigger than me." These are some of the responses I received from clients who struggled with depression for about five to ten years.

In my existential techniques, I provided various ways to cope and to eliminate depression for the time being. One of the techniques I teach people who have depression is one that I call, "If-what." This technique helps individuals to frame their emotions with rationality. To put in light, let me describe to you how this would look on paper.

→ *If,* it is true that I have depression, *what* would I do differently that will bring me closer to my wholeness?

→ *If,* it is true that I am diagnosed with depression, *what* short-term goals can I do presently to see changes in my life?

→ *If,* it is true that I am depressed, *what* can I learn from this moment? What meaningful actions can I do to see new roots of emotions take place?

→ *If,* it is true that depression makes me feel lonely, *what* responsibility can I take to guide me to a new set of principles that will make me grow and mature mentally and spiritually?

By framing depression with "If-what," it allows you to bracket and to phase out unwanted emotions that might impinge on your perception.

What people do not understand is that when we are depressed, it is not so much the circumstances, it is the popular secret that we tell ourselves. The popular secret that we tell ourselves often comes from the language of doubt and through a defeated mindset. What I have learned through my clients is that when you change depression from symptom-based to companionship, you open a new vista.

Therefore, in a way, depression, or any other emotion is a gift for us to unwrap in the respected season. To the extent that we adapt, we modify and process a choice between restriction of growth or a transformative phase of total fulfillment, which leads to the wisdom of meaning.

In conclusion, let us take another look at what it means to live in a false POPULAR SECRET. When we enclose and reserve our depression as something dark, we are living in the secret that depression will never change. But when we maintain a positive perspective, our growth towards depression becomes meaningful. We begin to design a new POPULAR SECRET that will interpret weakness as strength; sadness into purpose; and wounds into healing.

Depression may lead us
back, but our meaningful
actions conclude the concert.

The Modes of Doing and Allowing

Our chief concern in life is human freedom from determinism. The goal of existential therapy is to help individuals actualize his or her potentials that expand the process to become someone in life. Whether we want to be politicians or whether we want to be a teacher or a scientist, it is important to use our energy of depression as a context that stands alone. It will challenge us. But isn't the challenge of depression worthwhile? It teaches us to involve our human suffering with humility to surrender the ego for something much higher than ourselves. It is at this moment, we renew our strength with faith, leaving us open to a new change that will help us flourish. This is what it means to cut the loaf and spread the relationship between doing and allowing.

In my years of seeing individuals who have depression, anxiety, panic attacks, or simply feel confused about life, I have learned that it is not a repressed feeling as Freud thought. To me, it will always be an existential experience.

In any given relationship, our events are open with meaning, telling us to contribute a humble, loving gift that extends our faithful needs and to the needs of others. All aspects of existence are wrapped with beauty, tied to a sensitivity that says, "Unwrap carefully." The joy of this process becomes important because, with freedom and meaning, guilt is left behind.

Before going any further, we must admit that our existence is facing an existential crisis. Once we realize this truth, we can build a complete bridge between phenomenology and existential psychotherapy. Therefore, for the remaining pages, I will go into detail about *doing* and *allowing*. Once you grasp these concepts, you will increase your productivity and you will contribute to the ongoing preservation of human life.

There are two ways to think about doing and allowing. First, doing is doing something that proceeds to action. Simple, right? Second is allowing the experience in the now. Again, simple. It goes further than those buttered popcorn definitions of doing and allowing.

Of all the facts of life, depression is often recognized as a spiritual warfare between escaping the void and taunting it through daredevilry or reassuring oneself that life is not worth living. Participating in practices, occupying social roles, and establishing an authentic personality is difficult to maintain, especially when confronted with depression. Pursuing our meaningful practices dwell upon our courageous actions. As such, we inhabit a world of perceptive confrontation. Those who are aware of it learn the difference between staying with the experience and suspending the experience with excuses.

Unfamiliar aspects of the Self
often create the best examples of the
inner context of the world.

The tension between ontological depression and the division of Self (separation of Self with an emphasis on everyday recreational substances) is to translate and to construct the happenings of the emotions. Most deny depression through religious beliefs that it is governed by an evil entity. In some sense, depression is your friend, not your enemy.

Below, I will describe how depression can be understood through an output of meaning. On the next page, I will explain in detail what the figure means and how you can substitute depression with a new outlook on your life.

Figure 1-5: An Existential Output of Doing and Allowing

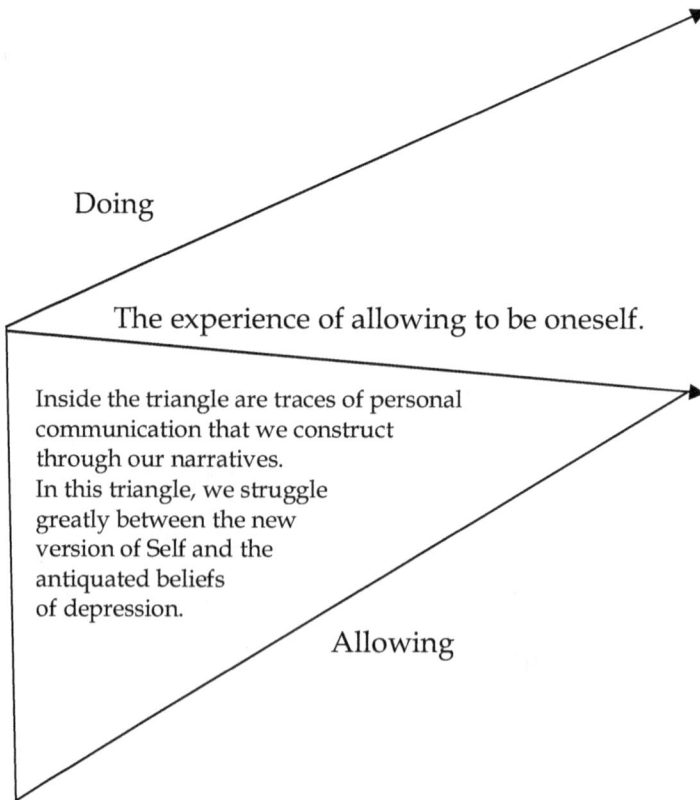

Doing

The experience of allowing to be oneself.

Inside the triangle are traces of personal communication that we construct through our narratives.
In this triangle, we struggle greatly between the new version of Self and the antiquated beliefs of depression.

Allowing

In the presented figure, I vividly show how the open triangle represents the freedom to choose a new translation towards doing and allowing. In the closed triangle, it represents our expensive compromise to derail our lives from output solutions to stagnation. Now, here are some statements to use daily to bring out your awareness of doing and allowing. Begin each day with these statements:

- ☼ I am *doing* something meaningful in my life and I am *allowing* my experiences to bring out the zest in my personality.

- ☼ I am *doing* management on my self-care while at the same time, I am *allowing* the connection of Self and the Universe to compose new growth and flourishment in my life.

- ☼ I am *doing* a major change in my depression that will cause me to make new bold changes in my life. Also, I am *allowing* my faith to help me rise above the clouds so that I can be determined to live a meaningful life.

Those are some statements that you can use as you rise in the morning. It is a quick reminder to tell yourself, "You know what, even though I have depression, I am going to turn it into something meaningful and creative. I will embrace it." When you can summon great energy and growth toward the Self, it becomes a hallmark to a new chapter in your life.

We often ride the passages of life thinking our revisions will extend small changes in punctuation. The truth is that just as simple changes have valuable footnotes so does the opposite outcome of doing and allowing. It is with great terror to cross-reference with meaning-making to the period of depression. An example of this cross-reference would be:

- I am *doing* enough work that helps me bring meaning to my life. But I am *allowing* my past and my doubts to ruin my human drive for greatness.

With this hesitation, earlier editions of the past begin to play prospect with your mind with pages of irresolute. Highlighting or italicizing the policies of depression gives us an unusual behavior toward the Self. One such as, "Be depressed and sleep for twelve hours." "Binge on ice cream." "Consider quitting."

All these policies are wrecked with havoc, leaving us with no introductory remarks to achieve the meaning of life.

If we are to achieve a greater destiny for ourselves and the world, we must continue to give a detailed description of the personhood. Arising from categorical descriptions of depression or to the formulated limited beliefs, we can begin to replace periods with question marks; leaving us to look at the question in the face and asking it: With further discussion, can I touch upon the fragmentary concepts of Being and the disturbances that charge my emotions with angst? The question will slowly understand your multiplicity of curiosity. And at that moment, what seemed dark is now a transparent map that guides you to become a distinctive, noble human being.

Screen Separation

Every inquiry to a purposeful life begins with a guided form of a question. Conceptualizing this inquiry reaches its crest through the Being-of-Self. This becomes transparent through knowledge and wisdom.

In the opening seconds to my therapeutic session with my client who suffered greatly from depression, she had a shapeless form to her circular world. Moreover, she was not suffering from the diagnostic depression, she was suffering from the contaminated pain that tipped her equilibrium. To continue my story, I will give her a fictitious name to protect her identity. I will call her Emily. She was a well-rounded individual with a lot of ambition. Intelligent and poised, but depressed because she could not move on from her past pain with her ex-husband. Without comment, I let her take the lead for the first ten minutes before I geared towards my existential technique.

"Last year, I was madly in love with my husband who is now my ex. He left his permanent residency in my heart. Damn it, Luis. I miss him. I almost considered killing myself through pills and alcohol. I thought, well, I cannot live without him, why live, right? So, here I am. Please save me."

Psychology can only establish human development and theories. It is up to you to actualize your life with depth.

The opening dialogue always intrigues me for any client that I meet. It gives me a private album to their world. By revealing their position in life, I can cross the land hoping to rediscover their lost treasures. At times, it won't happen. And that is okay. Even if they do not invite you to their private album, all you can do is empathize and reflect meaning.

She continued: "Oh by the way, before you save me, I am a porn addict."

I have difficulty when clients tell me, "Save me." "Fix me." "Work your magic." In the clinical profession of mental health, we have been utterly confused as gods who walk into your temple; shake your soul; pour healing water, and then tell you to go live your life. Far from it. We are individuals who understand the stain of a soul. We guide and explore the complications of human life. We inform but also, we question and answer the existential dilemma, hoping to extract new freedom that will push the union with a new form of purpose. I learned in my profession that the wishy-washy solution miracles or magic wand techniques do not work in the session. Nowadays, the profession has gotten lazy. Most of the therapists do it for the money and not for the dignity of human kindness.

Many therapists say, "Keep using solution miracles because it is easy and simple." When I listen to that, it haunts me like a house that has been abandoned in the field. One must remember this: psychologists, psychiatrists, mental health counselors, and social workers are a special fraternity and sorority. We are united with humility and servanthood. By being gifted with this LIGHT, we are deeply responsible to treat the mind with psychological methods that will precisely uncover secrets and truths about the unconscious mind. Since the mind is connected to the soul, we must lengthen our techniques that are suitable for treatment. Whether we use existential therapy, cognitive behavior therapy, or Gestalt therapy, we must gain access to the mind and honor the individual's suffering. It capitalizes on connection and empathy. To reside on growth, we must guide the individual to a path of stability that allows them to proclaim their purpose.

Going back to the case of Emily, she was not struck down with a clinical diagnosis as I said previously. To me, it was a faulty philosophical impediment where she repeatedly told herself: "I am only worthy if I am accepted by my husband. And through the acceptance, I will satisfy him with my sexuality."

This reminds me of the myth of Princess Aurora. She would cover up the castle from her authentic identity. She got lost in the castle with red flags of her own unconscious beliefs. Thus, it created a memory of a thorn, leaving her to repeat the vicious circle of "sleeping" and not "waking" to her beauty.

For about fifteen minutes, Emily muddled about her ex-husband. "Saying goodbye to him was difficult. I mean, we had everything going for us. I have no clue as to what happened. Was I too sexual? Was I too clingy? Was I too pushy? Was it his family that manipulated everything? I don't know. All I know is that he loved me, and I loved him. I cannot find my place right now."

"What do you mean?"

"Well, I cannot find my place in life. I watch porn. I go on many dates. I drink a lot but not as much as I used to though. I feel lost."

"It seems to me you are reaching out to meaning. You are trying to find your place in life. You are using porn and drinking as a coping mechanism to crosswind from what is truly hidden within you."

"Maybe. I think you are right. Explain more about me reaching out to meaning."

"Well, you are *responding* to your meaning through porn, and you are intoxicating yourself with alcohol. At some end of your pleasure, you are using yourself as an object and as a means to repeat the same directions to your road."

"That is interesting, Luis. You are onto something. Is there any way you can help me find direction or as you always point out, meaning?"

"Well, I cannot point out your meaning nor give you meaning. What *we* can do is explore why you reach the same conclusion towards your personhood. By maintaining a new depth on what you want out of your life, a new situation will appear."

"What exactly will appear?"

"The unfolding to your new destiny. A destiny in which you grow and prosper. This can be new shifts in your career, in your relationships, and everything else in between. By despairing over the man that left you, you will stunt your growth."

Before I go any further, I want to point out something. In every clinical case or consultation that I have done, repeatedly, clients will ask, "Can you help me find my meaning?"

Most clinicians try to play the role of a mountain God and command them to change this or change that. The truest art of existential therapy is when the word "we" is involved. Notice how I pointed out the word "we" during the session. From there, I touched upon her myths of acceptance. The elegance of existential therapy is when a clinician knows how to use storytelling, myths, parables, and connect it directly to the client's conscious thoughts. By and large, you can glide and dance forth with your client towards meaningful outcomes. Every meaning and every word that is spoken, you must pay attention to their syntax and how they express it. Meanings are unique; forever changing from seconds to minutes; hours to weeks; and months to years. When journeying through a session with existential therapy, it requires both the therapist and the client to recognize spontaneous creativity and challenges in which both transform tragedies into a human achievement.

For the next portion, I will nosedive into the myth of Princess Aurora and how she was "sleeping" and not "waking" to her authentic beauty.

By using this myth in the session, Emily can grasp the concepts between the thorns of her past and her present awakening to a new desire that will help her relate to the Being-of-courage.

"Yeah, I feel my life is useless right now. I know you said something about a new destiny unfolding, but holy moly, it is difficult to even see it or think it. My ex-husband was my life."

"Revolving oneself to another person can be challenging. But through these challenges, we can rise above and learn more about ourselves. Your suffering belongs to a different dimension and your meaning of suffering belongs to the work of life and love. It seems to me you are in a triangle where you are at the top and your bottom bases are pulling you together to dance with suffering and meaning."

"So, what do you mean about my suffering belonging to another dimension?"

"Well, your suffering is the *perception of suffering*. That means the philosophical issues that you face are based on the interpretation that you give to your suffering; not the suffering becoming the perception of suffering.

You see, when you give your suffering to the works of life and love, you take responsibility to choose the path of your life. On the contrary, perception of suffering is when someone encircles with determinism, which means that it ought to be this way and there is no meaning to my life if I don't get what I want."

"Oh my gosh, yes, Luis. Everything you are saying makes perfect sense. I see where you are getting at. So interesting to see it from that perspective. The whole time I was suffering from perception and not acknowledging the suffering through meaning."

"That's exactly what I wanted you to grasp. This reminds me of Princess Aurora. Have you heard about the myth of her story?"

"Umm...I don't think so. Is that from Snow White? Oh, wait, no. That is from Sleeping Beauty, right?"

"Yes, it is from Sleeping Beauty. Well, I am sure you are familiar with the myth, right?"

"Of course."

"The reason why I am bringing this up in our session is that you represent the traits that she had when she was daydreaming in her castle.

She was fulfilled and ready to face the day but at times, she was confined in a familiar place. In the myth, she was embraced for her beauty but felt lonely. With your case, like hers, you have been locking yourself into a "sleep" rather than "waking up" from your true authentic Self."

"To understand you much better, are you pointing out that when I went into the mode of suffering of perception as you said, is that me sleeping, per se?"

"Correct. Your perception of suffering is you "sleeping" per se, where you find a sweet sensation of the misery of the cycling pattern of past wounds. Presently, you arrived at a new development in your narrative. You are now "awake" and no longer sleeping from the same myth of wanting to be accepted based on validation from the Otherness-of-Self."

After our third session completed, Emily was not sure if what she felt was enlightenment or a sense of renewal in understanding the issues that troubled her. Either way, we had a lot of work to do for us to understand the discourses, systems, methods, standpoints, and every other main issue on how she mutually validated suffering over rational suffering on the stems of life and love.

Throughout the fourth up until the tenth session, we multiplied various tasks on what it means to be vulnerable and authentic to oneself.

Moreover, Emily was interpreting her formulations of questions through the continuity of composition. It was beautiful to see her transition from suicidal tendencies to a woman of meaning. Existential therapy creates this framework. When executed properly, your client's history or classical learning will be untangled as you guide them to human flourishment. As I said in the previous pages, solution miracles have no place in therapy. Washy techniques never leave the vehicle with gloss. There will be stains to wipe off and other parts to clean. Miracle questions are the gateway to lazy therapy. When the establishment of meaning, congruence, and empathy are introduced in the session, it will lean forward with the stages of creativity along with the understanding of independence to reach a new form of beauty.

To summarize her case, Emily was significantly less depressed upon the completion of her ten sessions. The onset of her suicidal behavior was extremely high when we first met but decreased dramatically after completing various forms of existential exercises.

Her self-esteem improved. Also, she successfully employed narrative exercises, plunged deeply into her existential world, and lastly, she was able to find beauty from her past wounds.

This is what I mean when I say, "screen separation." What this means is that there are two screens: *perception of suffering* and *the suffering of meaning through life and love*. Emily was in the first mode: perception of suffering. When you introduce screen separation to the session, it will help you and your client understand the dynamics of the personality. With every concealment, there is a secret to the human soul. Our duty as mental health professionals is to understand their narrative so that the session can take a flight to a new venue of awakening. It will be as if it were in a "baptism;" celebrating private events for the client that has surrendered their peculiar fantasy of despair.

Suffering with meaning includes everything with life and love. When we reduce meaning with suffering, we end up with an outward sign of retirement to our personhood.

RFID: Reacted, Feelings, Internal, Displacement

It is generally agreed that our imbalances are caused by disturbances that we project or tell ourselves. In acknowledging our emotions, we must grasp the concept of human nature. In various forms, our social outcry causes a special hearing for us to pay attention to. Exhausting at times, but our conflicts of opinions and false formulations color the painting with comparisons. We can never succeed in the long run if we surrender our minds to opinions or comparisons. If we were to exclude the opinions of a sheep, we would experience a spiritual balance of thinking and feeling in a rationalistic manner. Our obvious reasons to further ourselves into a well-rounded, rationalistic Being is to become the essence of vibrancy that leads to authentic feelings where they guide us to resolve life's dilemma. The wide approval for today's age has reduced our psychological equity with a narcissistic tendency to manifest a Being that we are not.

Stumbling upon this belief has caused our departure from our true meaningful selves. The main exponent is worshipping idols who bring out the worst in us. Whether we worship celebrities who drink and do drugs or whether we worship idols who mock modesty, we follow them because of the conformity that we want to be "them." This creates an internal displacement in which we position ourselves to their validity and their world. We mask a Self that is not truly authentic to our human experience.

Also, it is with this position that we wind up with a need of adjustments to win the majority with a strange, yet deplorable, reliance on the variation of congruity.

This creates a gross error for those who motivate themselves to the pleasure principle of contradictions. Undoubtedly, we will conform to the mistakes, hold the hand of grandiosity, and defy the human soul that makes us singled out to the meaning of life. I am inclined to believe that when we pin-point and ask questions on what makes our lives meaningful, we will taunt the basic attitudes that placed us on a precipice of superiority.

If we are at this level, let us acquire new habits from this misunderstanding. These attitudes show an ingrained passion for how our reacted feelings displace the attitudes with a degree of one side to the truth.

Stone by stone, we can carve the
preliminary stages towards human growth.
In time, we will welcome our stage
with a new history of prosperity.

The world of today reacts but never carries the form of consideration to nourish emotional pain with empathy. For this reason, we will delve into RFID. Like the radio-frequency identification, which uses electromagnetic fields to track objects, well, so does your internal thoughts and feelings to the world. Your thoughts and feelings help you track and identify the arena to your wholeness. For my version of RFID, it is simply reacted, feelings, internal, displacement.

Spontaneous psychological activity conjures up whenever the repressive depression state is congruent with rational contents. Often, when this happens, we are urged to connect the internal displacement with meaning. In society, we have learned that we react to feelings or emotions. I have seen this repeated pattern with many individuals whom I have counseled or coached. When introducing my model of RFID, I let them know that what they are feeling is not necessary the environmental displacement, but it is mainly their reactive state to the hesitations that they face. These pictures that they paint remain active unless meaningful motives are practiced with an ambition to widen the conscious mind.

A human being cannot grow into wisdom without an extension of lessons that are given by life. The necessity to grow begins with curiosity. When one begins to ask: How was I before when I felt depressed? Isn't it strange that I was happy two weeks ago and now, I am depressed? What changes can I make today to further myself into accomplished goals that make me feel alive? This becomes obvious when we begin to question our dilemma.

When counseling or coaching, my clients are entrenched with, "Oh well, this is how my life is. I might as well quit my goals and slouch around." With this belief, they realize the social failures that withdraw from a possible transformation. On the next page, I will guide you safely into a model that has worked perfectly for my clients. But before I do, I want you to ponder on this question.

Do we ever understand what we feel or think? We only understand our reactions to the event but never really understand the beauty behind it. On the next page, you will learn the RFID model so you can understand how our reacted feelings and internal displacement play a pivotal role in our social life.

Out of depression comes the new emergence of
Self. We learn to cultivate the necessary
prerequisites to pass on maturely
through the stages of life.

Figure 1-6: RFID: Attachment to Traceable Emotions

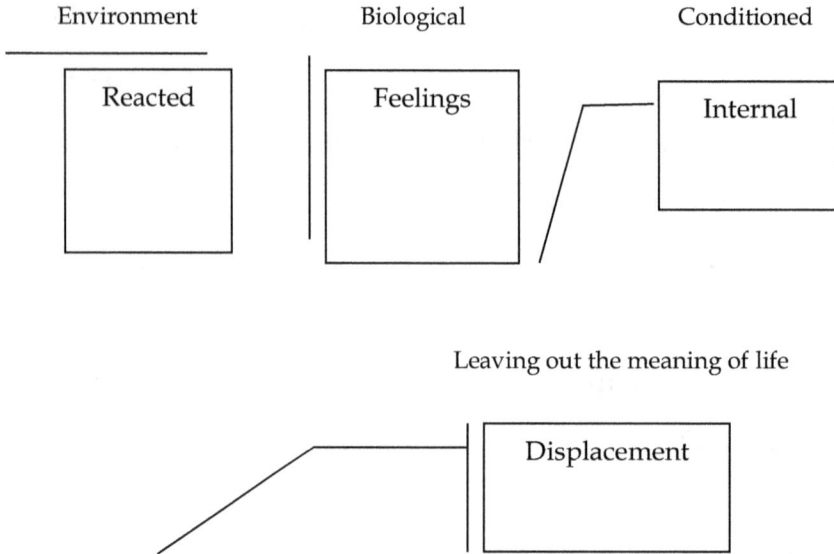

In this model, you will notice boxes with lines. These lines represent the internal displacement that shapes your personality. To begin, let us start with reacted. This is tied to the environment. Notice how the line is straight, facing forward and backward. This means that your reacted feelings are tied to your past which affects your present moment. The environment is a culmination of possible triggers toward the Being.

Next, we have feelings. This is tied to the biological system which makes up the synthesis and integration of placed patterns in your DNA. When your feelings are triggered with reacted expressions, your DNA gears toward the nervous system which accompanies neurons followed by the response of a feeling or a threat. These responses give a certain stimulus in your body and movement. Did you know that when you feel anxious or depressed, your body learns the rhythm with what you feel? If you feel depressed, you program it to the rhythm with slouch like behavior. But if you teach it a new rhythm, not only does your emotions change but your body posture as well.

That is why you will notice that for feelings, the line is positioned to the left because that is where your analytic thought, logic, and reasoning are made of. When you become aware of the iteration pattern, you can slowly change your biology, especially the epigenetics of your gene expressions. Truly, this is not impossible. It will take great courage to analyze oneself to understand one's inner conflicts.

Furthermore, we will delve into internal which yields to conditioned patterns of emotions. You will notice how the line starts from the bottom and slightly curves straight to the right. What this means is that your organized information, your context, and your emotions are positioned on your right side of the brain. Hence, you internalize both the left and the right sides of the brain. But for this matter, I will focus on the mode of internal. When I teach my clients or when I give presentations on the meaning of depression, I talk about how we must venture into the depressive conditions or anxiety conditions and learn to expose ourselves authentically. When we are genuine and constructive with our creativity, we can overcome depression, anxiety, or grief.

As I mentioned earlier, in most cases with individuals who have depression, it is never clinical, again, in most cases. What we know now about depression is that it is a connection based on beliefs on how we "ought" to feel. This inquiry is a slip and slide and you will end up trying to wrestle in the mud, only to find yourself tied to the same functioning of wanting to "get out" but refuse to upbuild yourself with a finer, rational, meaningful mind.

Lastly, we will learn about displacement. This correlates to leaving out the meaning of life. Far worse than cuts and minor sprains is when you do not give birth to the higher climb that helps you to reach new goals. When the morning sun sets in your eyes, you must speak of the day with truth, integrity, and boldness. It gives you hope when you nourish your mind with productive, meaningful habits. When you cut ties with the approval of the environment, you can measure up the atmosphere, taking stock of your impulses, emotions, feelings, and reactions. It is no wonder that this last stage starts with a line going up, then pulls straight, and ends with a big line that blocks both the line going up and going straight. The reason is because life, at times, will test our beliefs and our measures of courage and meaning.

Open-mindedness is the enactment to change
the faulty conceptions with new facts.
This will bring out new aspects of
living a good philosophical life.

People who experience tension and minor anxiety are the ones who cannot bear the inner conflicts. Their mind is divided between confusion and fear. These constraints result in suppression and prospects of punishment toward the Self and of others. This conflict will certainly produce power mixed with sexual impulses. Now, you may be wondering…umm…okay…I am somewhat confused. What does Luis mean by power and sexual impulses? To answer your question and to broaden your mind, when we take this route in the form of anxiety-suppression, in many cases that I have dealt with, individuals turn their anxiety into power which transitions into sexual urges.

To paint you a clearer picture, I will give a brief description of a man in which I will call Ian just to protect his identity. He was my client and was successful, smart, outgoing, had a beautiful girlfriend, and had many friends. Lo and behold, Ian felt depressed and had mixed episodes of anxiety. So, I presented to him the RFID model and I drew the model on the board to help him understand his relation to the subjective experience. Before I explained the model, he confessed this in the beginning: "I do not know how to handle my anxiety or my depression.

All I know is that when I control others, my anxiety goes from a ten to a two. I feel better when I am in control and when I have power."

When I heard this, I could not help but think about the displacement stage. Ian discounted himself with a half off Being rather than supplying new meaning and growth toward the personhood. Underneath his success and anxiety, he experienced depression. As he said in the first twenty-minute session, "Luis, at this point, I have everything. I mean, I am not a billionaire or anything. But I have money, power, and connections. Oh, and a wonderful girlfriend. But somehow, I feel depressed. I have no clue how this sprung up."

I asked him, "Ian, isn't it true that your success is perhaps lending itself towards temporary physical satisfaction like sex, but in this case, your total security and power?"

"Yeah, I suppose you are right. When you put it that way, it makes sense as to why I turned my depression and anxiety into power and sex. For some reason, it gives me gratification to know that my activities of power give me a higher esteem."

At this point, I challenged his belief and displacement with a new avenue of authenticity.

"Perhaps they do, perhaps they don't. What matters the most is how you deal with your conflicts in a way where you can have a dialectical relationship with yourself and with your community. Your social factors such as power, money, and connections are good for momentary purposes but at the same time, it develops into a measure of blockage in your developmental freedom. Without freedom, we cannot chart the independence to one's authentic relationship with other individuals."

Ian was able to recognize the differences between suppressing depression and anxiety and using it to gain power. Often, people will use their power to cover up their insecurities. This is when we need to surrender the belief that depression or anxiety is for ill people. This stigma has caused a lot of individuals to chart their path with secondary behavior that leads to more sexuality, more power, and more anger. Meaning and growth need to take place in the final stage of displacement. When the unfilled needs are carefully observed and carefully considered, we can begin to turn helplessness and conflicts into strength and resilience.

Toward the end of our sessions, Ian reported to me that his basic conflicts of power and control diminished when he developed meaning as a frame of reference. By providing him all my tools and worksheets, he concluded that his depression and anxiety were gone. He was able to focus more on his personhood rather than focusing on banal desires.

RFID, in my viewpoint, will greatly impact a lot of individuals who are struggling emotionally and spiritually. This model has a purpose. It is to carve out unwanted feelings of isolation, sadness, or any form of existential crisis. In any case, you will learn to clarify what makes your life meaningful, authentic, and vibrant. Nothing in life is easy. We will be tested. We will fall. At times, we will want to quit. But life is grabbing your hand and saying to you:

My dearest beautiful soul read me carefully. When the day ends, and you feel unsettled, begin to look out the window through your Higher Self. Without judgment, express your regrets, share the dream, and move towards forgiveness and healing. Only then, you will open a new window of freedom and wholeness to begin life for the second time.

Your Highest Honor, I am Guilty

The courts of existence are jammed with citizens who have validated hurt, anger, and jealousy as life's condition. Somehow, we feel emotionally and spiritually bankrupt. Like a timeclock, each hand resurfaces each minute and each hour. It puts everything on schedule. But with our vicious eight cycles, we cannot punctuate what is meaningful to our lives. We, instead, respond to our emotional triggers which deepen a flood of past rituals that recreates the darker side of human interaction. This has been our marriage as of late. It is no wonder the courtroom of life is packed with citizens who want to testify once more on the importance of living an authentic life. Somewhere in our minds, we remember the exhaustion and the complicated feelings that accompany them. But still, we want to testify in the courtroom to tell the story of the passages of misery that we accepted as our truth. As we outline the stages of meaning and growth, forgiveness shows up and brings along an expert named humility.

Together, they work in your favor to build a solid legal case against the lessons of life. It happens like this. You come in with your team: meaning, growth, forgiveness, and humility. You stand as you wait for the judge who is called Humanism to say, "Please be seated." As you do, forgiveness and humility whisper in your ear, "This case will be a slam dunk if you come forth on the emotional work that you invested in yourself."

You take a deep breath, and you say, "I understand but I would rather act out on my will through the awful feelings that I felt for these past years."

"No, no young soul. Listen to what I am saying. You already suffered. You realized that the human experience is to let go rather than hang onto an open void. Tell the judge the truth. Admit your vulnerabilities."

"All arise, shouts Humanism. How do you plead today young soul?"

"I…I… I plead guilty your honor."

"Fair enough. Tell the courtroom your case."

"Well, you see, I was hurt and furious to the stupidity of life. Everyone is puzzling themselves on the superficial aspects of human life.

What to wear. What bars or clubs to hit up. Am I handsome or beautiful? Why did you not give me a gift? All this your honor had me resenting life. I would get angry with people when they came to me for advice on superficial ideology. In my mind, I saw them as related conflicts toward the Self. Your honor, I went through a period of an existential crisis. I once asked myself, "What is the true meaning of my life?" To this day, I am searching for that strong emotion to tell me to proceed forth. The stupidity of mankind has me attached to the background consciousness."

"And what have you done about it, young soul?"

"Well, your honor I have made possible decisions to not open Pandora's box. Also, I have accepted myself and came to terms with my vulnerable side. Yes, I am a sensitive person. Does that make me a weak, less of a person? Absolutely not. I am human. I somewhat proclaimed to be a Roman God who had every problem solved. When it came to my fragility, I fell to my knees and realized, I am not a God nor a savior.

I am a human who is here on earth figuring out and wrestling with each dilemma to grow some sense out of it."

"And do you young soul believe that life is a dotted line that we follow, or do you believe that existence unwraps all the gifts, human frailty, and growth to us?"

"Your honor, I accept truthfully the second option, but I am guilty of the first option as well. I guess what I am trying to say is that we follow the first option, hoping to believe that we have a safety blanket in our hearts where there is no hurt or pain. All we do is follow orders. But what meaning is there if we follow dotted lines? Therefore, I have struggled and questioned my existence because I want to turn my unresolved wounds into beauty; sorrow into wholeness, and hate into forgiveness. As an act of my will, I have trudged through the darkness, anticipating to understand the great metaphors that I have been telling myself. Your honor, I have learned that human flourishing begins when we separate ourselves from opinions. Others will bark at you and say, "Life is gloomy. Deal with it." But to me, life is not gloomy. It used to be but now, life is precious. Like gemstones that we admire, my eyes esteem to the awe of life. Whether we accept ourselves or not, it is better to stay connected to meaning than to stay connected to anger."

Humanism looks straight to the individual's eyes and says, "Alright dear young soul. I am not quite convinced as of now, but I see that you brought a few members to your team. Would you care to introduce them to the courtroom?"

"Yes, your honor. To my left is forgiveness and to my right is humility."

"Forgiveness and humility, would you agree to your client's plead?"

"Yes, your honor."

"Fair enough. Carry on and explain why the court should believe that your client is guilty of living a life that was based on existential angst?"

"To begin, our client had parents who had their emotional wounds. Thus, it affected the genetic lines with more unresolved pain. The need to be vulnerable was not acceptable for the young soul. Living in a home where both mother and father played out their dysfunctional roles, the young soul felt crazy and at other times, the young soul felt suicidal. In between the flux, the fostering of meaning was not welcomed from the partnership of the unit."

"Go on."

"Your honor, as we stand before you as forgiveness and humility, our client never flirted with the idea of revenge nor did our client ever think about taking one's own life. Our client had unresolved issues that needed a second chance to work towards healing and peace. The young soul learned to surrender the dotted lines. Presently, our client faces the dilemma to hate those who mask themselves with pride and those families who ignore other related families due to economic status and intellectual superiority. As of now, the young soul has grown into empathy to understand that life can be intense, but with our partnership along with meaning and growth, our client gained awareness on the true power of forgiveness and humility."

"Very well stated points. Any last concluding remarks before we have your client present any final details?"

"Mm-hmm, we do have one more detail to add before we turn it over. Let this fact be known in our courtroom. When parents do not make it a goal to resolve their wounds from their past, it will tarnish the household with recycled patterns of hate and anger.

The secure attachment will lose the significance of a healthy bond. Like our client, we have seen those who have become dependent or too needy to their lovers due to unresolved wounds from their parents. Buried in silence is the closeness to the most available passages toward spiritual growth. When we partake in the enlightenment points of meaning, growth, forgiveness, and humility, our lives become richer and self-preserving. We must educate other citizens your honor on the power of forgiveness and humility. Ultimately, we will move into global peace where our past is no longer an assembly of division between our spirituality and the punishment that we induce to others. With all tendencies, we trademark our retribution with humor, leaving others with open scars. Acknowledging our history and present conditions, we know that emotional imbalances yearn to have the same roar that causes nihilism."

"Point well made, forgiveness and humility. Young soul, any last words that you want to say before we conclude this trial?"

"Yes, yes I do have my concluding message on the lessons of my life. In such a strange, yet unique existence, we know that the good, moralistic life is out there.

Like small pieces from different countries, we are shaped into our version of wholeness. Unconsciously, I have written a story of my life as a sin of my past — visiting the choices from my ancestry. I have learned that we live in a cycle of hurt, blinded by the passing pain from other citizens. Choosing our habits helps us to decide on what is meaningful and what is not. By turning the contents over to my Higher Self, I have understood my inner world. I was able to dig deep and plant new growth. As of now, I have confronted, explored, and experienced parts of my family's history. The exploration was difficult because I had many moments of countertransference with other citizens. The integration of meaning has taken me from the basement to a new visitation in which I call beauty. With this insight, I have allowed and used all my events as an opportunity to extract meaning. Without separating the past from the present, I have learned to move freely. It is a constant construction and deconstruction along with a reconstruction to build productive habits. And even though it got me weary your honor, I have gained an emotional center, and this has been this greatest gift of humanity.

From every perspective, my thoughts and feelings have grown into the changing youthful shape of empathy, love, forgiveness, and humility. This, your honor, is freeing to my psychological mind, body, and soul."

"Young soul, based on the evidence that has been given, you meet the criteria of being guilty. While it may seem as though you were hesitant to say otherwise, I am glad you came forth and admitted to me and the rest of the court on your honesty of plea. I can see how troublesome it was for you to testify as guilty. The extra burden became a false persona which amounted to your identity. You learned that your family's generation has nothing to do with you. Yes, they are your genetics but only you dear young one can change your genes. Without knowing where your journey would take you, part of the burden you carried was shed off with an understanding of your psychological and philosophical upheaval. You slowly wrapped yourself with an insight to give up the narrative of hate and envy. As to your other side of life, you went forth with meaning, trusting that forgiveness and humility will give you a sense of wholeness. Surely, it did. Before I conclude this day, I want to say something to you before we close the case.

As Beings, we make up personalities as we go along. We hope to weave in fabrics from other citizens who have their life together, only realizing the ongoing dialogue does not bring us meaning. Rather, it bifurcates the experience and your true narrative on who you should become rather than "be." Our experiences, environment, and connections are what make up the whole context of our lives. Reasons themselves do not govern the choices that we make. The link between worldly reasons and our independent choices lies in the tomorrow that we want to rejoice in. Part of knowing this comes from the different time zones of life. When I say time zones, I do not mean travel distances. I mean the engagement of our emotions. They all have different time zones. Once we fully acknowledge this, we can process growth at a greater height. Remember my words young soul: *I forgive but I will never forget* is an invalid recipe that is bound to give you a complicated soul. Never reduce forgiveness with a soul coloring that mixes layers with, "I will never forget." It may benefit you at the moment, but you will be hungry for more, always seeking out pleasurable revenge. Always…always…always forgive but most importantly, recognize yourself as a human of flesh, not as a God.

It is okay to want to believe that you are superhuman, but that is where your Supreme Divinity comes in. All you must do is surrender to history's stages and come forth to the measurement of a new security. Perhaps, then, you will truly live the abundant life that builds up a stable background of beauty and courage."

In this story, I portrayed a young citizen who went through turmoil towards life, towards the family circle, and having to face nihilism. Between the struggles, the individual had to differentiate historical setbacks versus current meaningful acts. By learning the subjective stages of life, we can learn and mature to view past generational mishaps as a reconstruction phase — engineering a solid foundation upon which the seeding of forgiveness takes place. By attaching the vines onto the foundations of meaning and forgiveness, we can soil new relationships with others while at the same time, creating better lives.

The ability to move forward with this spiritual awakening will help us to connect fully and authentically to the available passages that will serve us with an inner balance.

Despite our best efforts in suppressing our vulnerability, we will feel bankrupt toward the personhood. For our preservation, let us admit to the court of life that we are guilty. Guilty of hating one another. And guilty of feeling jealous of those who are succeeding. When we admit that we are guilty, life will work through your terms and conditions and will give you the necessary strength to understand the presented dilemma.

As it gets played out, old emotions will resurface, a certain song will play again, a certain scent will ravish you to be in that particular time, and above all else, words that were promised in your past will come back to remind you that you have an unfinished home to build. Time will evoke individual responsibility on your part. But also, it will find a way to make you feel disappointed with your growth. Unlike love, it does not fade to another human being. With time, it stays with you internally. In your mind. In your heart. And in your soul. Time has a way to reveal its position. Where it is given, it is due. When it is absent, we point out the relations of passivity and formula.

Every task in life becomes an orbit where we deepen our understanding of the unconscious mind. Often challenging, but in most cases, often thrilling. It prepares us to exert the influence of bravery.

When your life is tied with iron chains, your
soul will enter with strength and humility.

Now is the time to give this precious moment a significant search, a search for new beauty that strives your conscious mind with meaning. In motion, we live to practice our art, to become better citizens, and to learn through daily associations with our fellow contacts. Through this organized body of Beings, we come to terms with the same struggle and resistance towards human emotions. Isn't it time for us to make a profound movement from small thinking to meaningful thinking? Isn't it time to listen to the voice of faith so we can answer the questions of life? Learn to look beyond the world system. At a glance, it may look whole but look closely, you will notice the cleavage between the outer aspects of the world and the embodiment of your heart, mind, and soul. They are arranged this way to make the earlier aspects of your life more alert — an all-embracing horizon to your fulfilled destiny.

Adaptation to the
environmental surroundings
is the shield of survival.

We approach life from different perspectives. The philosophical life chooses to view reality from the standpoint of dogmatism, fanaticism, and determinism. Science takes the all-knowing hypothesis and turns it into a method that we can follow. Religion banks in many Gods to worship at the altar. Preachers go as far as playing God themselves, making each visible statement an etiology of torn conflicts.

Whether we go through depression, anxiety, panic attacks, grief, or any other emotional dilemma, preachers loudly say, "That they who fall to the traps of the dysfunctions of emotions shall not inherit the kingdom if their ways remain foolish. Banish the darkness of depression and you shall seek ye old faithful light to all the directions in your temple." Fundamentally, we can either agree or disagree, but most of my clients that suffered from depression or anxiety struggled with the preacher's demand. Preachers do not understand it from the subjective experience, only from the outer spirituality. To understand the darkness and every other emotion, we must relate to it just like the story I depicted in the courtroom of existence. When we endure the darkness, history will roam down to a few centuries and mock us that we are "alike" in our ancestry. Existentially speaking, individuals who suffer from depression become transparent when they say, "I am chained to the world." This is a profound statement to analyze.

If we were chained to the world, we would lack the speech and the true certainty of the practical life through which we see the world as a harmonious concert — each of us playing our part, sharing our strengths, and turning our fair share of emotions into one, eternal permanent residency of resilience.

As I wrap up this page, I want to remind you that depression is a blind devotion that we give it. True, we feel it. And true, we go through many events that will make us yield towards it. But what is not true is that you are not your depression. You are not the diagnosis that the psychiatrist gave you. You are not the medicine that you take. You are purely bathed in the LIGHT, concrete, and favored to pursue your meaningful life. As you grow in your personhood, you will see failure as a forward action; depression as a narrative; separation as a connection to old wounds; and lastly, you will view despair as a form of wisdom.

By the time you realize it, your frailties will not be a common objection toward the Self. It will, in fact, make you humbler, more accepting towards forgiveness and empathy. You will realize that all along, your experiences needed to be this way so that you can take a flight to a new form of beauty.

Vicious Eight

Our insight has revealed certain connections to our world. Namely, technological innovations, scientific research on mental health, new methods to cope with depression, and a new understanding of our social structures. Beyond its realm, we also find a connection from our previous generations to our present generation. It grows out of history and morphs into a natural process that unifies mankind.

In our way to wisdom, we cannot arrive with the strivings with violence or with a corrupted politics that dictates our lives. For this reason, we will focus on a concept that I coined as *vicious eight*.

We see, each of us with potential, rarely with a stale dialogue, but we see a sophistication of optimism in our Age. Enlightened education has become our theme. We modified ourselves to live a good life, one that does not blind in pride, rather, it quietly builds up the background into an empire. The view is not divided as one would imagine.

The view increases its distribution with philosophy and psychology. We become impelled to raise ourselves above the emotions of depression, anxiety, or the stricken panic attacks. Through each tossed chaos, we remain aware of the last judgment of humanity. There is no escape from our superior grace. By making history our own, let us move toward absolute independence which cannot be moved from our indifferences. Whether our emotions are conformed or isolated in passivity, we will clarify the antiquity which offers us a new narrative. With our personalities, let us remove the mask. The mask of, "Under all conditions, I must be this way for the public's pleasure." Freedom in our emotions, especially in depression has never been more challenging until today. We have learned our illusory terrors that we are "marked forever this way." Ambition, enlightenment, persistence, and meaning will guide us safely to the promenade of independent wisdom.

Our Being reveals itself through conditions that test our character. Mostly, when we feel depressed. In the next few pages, I will go into full detail and explain my diagram of vicious eight. It will help you understand the mythical perception of our retained speech toward the submission of depression. In every classical psychoanalysis, depression was viewed as neurosis, a dizziness that causes turmoil to our comprehensive whole. To use Carl Jung's term, depression is often an *archetype* symbol that articulates the unconscious needs. It embodies a transformation of growth — equidistant to choice and responsibility. Without this stage of adaptability, the individual will continue to rattle the doorknob until his or her church is open. And when I say church, I do not mean the sacraments from the preacher. I mean the church through which the individual is influenced and constrained by nihilism, orienting to a large extent of distress, resulting in a conceivable shade of uncertainty.

In this existential condition, the Being is in debt with guilt feelings along with the persistence of sadness. In whatever thousand ways the individual wishes to make, they realize that they are locked up in both the mind and the body. By the same token, they also experience another ontological guilt, and that is the fellowship of humanity.

Arising from this guilt comes along the questioning of moral strength: By escaping the challenges of humanity, what does that say about me? Let us go deeper, "What will humanity think of me once I cross to the afterlife? Will it view me as someone who viewed everything as unfair, or will it view me as someone who dared to plunge inward and found courage through despair?"

These moral questions must be considered if we wish to look at the world with fresh eyes. Many of my clients who came to me with the diagnosis of depression often came with various existential dilemmas. A lot of it was due to confusion in one's placement in life, another was understanding one's biology, and at times, it was trying to make sense of the world. By separating the three systems of placement, I was able to help them view depression as an interest in ontological meaning. Hence, the source of all information which carefully fulfills the potentials of the Being.

Each of us dialects with consumer products. Should I purchase this or that? Why not dialect with depression? The reason why we do not dialect with depression is that we fear that we will dramatically decrease our personhood. Depression knows how to strip us down naked through the fabric of Being. One must realize, this is a gift. If we are to become aware of this gift, we can easily segmentize the symptom formation with new constructive effects. Below, I will illustrate how we can fork the source of depression.

Figure 1-7: Vicious Eight — Symptom Repetition

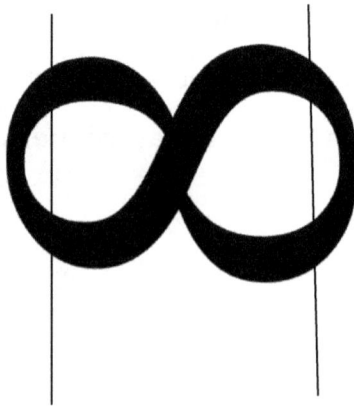

The problem that we encounter with depression is learning how to construct and view the potentials of existence. We pay too much homage to the deviations of the symptoms rather than focusing on the individual's position with existence. The problem of today's depression is that we objectify people with messages such as, "Get over it." "It will fade away." These messages, when viewed from the outer-directed world, it will quail into a collection of objectivity.

As we look closely at the lines, we can see two modes of reduction: the universal connection and the biological blame. In these two modes of reduction, there are significant consequences such as no participation in the Self and no participation in the actualized meaning. Now, you may be saying to yourself, "Wait a minute Luis, my family does have the gene pool for depression and anxiety. It traces back to my great grandmother and great grandfather. Even my mom suffers from it." While biology may play a part in your life, it certainly does not shape your endeavors toward self-actualization. Everyone who lives in the blame of, "Oh well, my family has had a long line of depression.

I should also expect to have it anytime soon," they yield to a deduction of meaning. This arouses the loss of a spiritual center. Every meaningful belief that breaks down the external events will be granted the sphere of a knowable culture.

A critical approach to understanding how depression affects our Being begins by the familiarity of the looped repetition which is seen in the diagram. The center is not touched because that represents your Being. Somehow, we believe in the world systems where we worship a voluminous text of restrictions that hold us back. I call them world-absorption-of-systems. We absorb the cruelty of over-medicating our patients. We absorb the flatness of how we cannot change for the better. We absorb superficial faith without questioning its ethics. We absorb the contents of humanity without seeing the syllabus. Bestowed upon us is our road, a road with casual relations, deeply seen as a brief outline of what's ahead. Conflicting possibilities on which road to take becomes a thrill. Discussion, partnership, and cooperation expand our era to a new enlightenment. Opinions about depression or its customs mean nothing to the conscious Being.

For the first time, we are slowly learning how magnificent existential therapy is. Without any superficial techniques, we can infuse deep meaning in this precious moment as we crush the myth of depression.

When we unify our emotions, we can understand our previous forms of depression, and we can turn them into a new narrative, one that speaks meaningful communication. Before we understand vicious eight, stop right now. Go back to page 386. Look at it. Observe it. Study it. Where are you in its loop? Notice how the loop makes its way to the universal connection and biological blame. I often remind my clients that depression, when understood in this diagram, we can gently remove its faulty power. Each of us has a self-will and a certain sophistication to grasp the instrument of meaning. The unfamiliarity has been visited before, we have seen ourselves stricken with war, battling nihilism while at the same time building a stable condition of beauty.

We must adjust ourselves with a new form of perception in understanding depression. Its true arrival will come at a point when we feel comfortable in knowing the emotion like a new student who was transferred to a new school. You will learn to introduce yourself to depression. You will get to know it. And you will understand where it is coming from. Maybe, just maybe, you will not be overwhelmed by the history of your biology or godless maxim that depression is the last judgment to test you.

The strangest affair we can have is with
our darkness. It forces us to examine the
current flows in our unconscious mind.
By discovering this truth, we can show
the LIGHT to other human beings.

Everything that I have explained about depression has led to a new truth: *suspension of depression.* We now know that we can suspend the emotion and bracket depression. When we fully understand the subject-object dichotomy, our knowledge can be transparent. In other words, our Being indicates that we are *here,* and it also implies that we were *there.* Therefore, depression is not only a vicious eight but also, a mode of here-there. The "here" is your present feeling through which you reference your existential dilemma. This becomes "mine" because by owning the present, it somehow builds capacity through the etymological process from the "there." The "there" connects to what is yours from the past to the present. The particular point in time is a space that distinguishes the Being from other Beings of the world. When we choose the full meaning of life, it becomes clearer that our "here" and "there" woven the existence of beauty. Rather than focusing on how depression originated, let us focus on how we can understand the potentialities of the emotion. Despite the difficulties, we can understand ourselves when we fully question human nature. Being aware is a challenge for most, but for those that are awakened, they understand the emotion as a connection to universal symbols with a throw-in of the dialectical relation to the nonbeing. Now, we often put depression as a Being, something that is part of us. What we need to understand is the emotion itself is a nonbeing. Meaning, it does not exist in our daily pursuits. The emotion is a visitation to let us know that something is off tuned in that specific moment. Whether we go through a relationship breakup, a divorce, or experience a seasonal sorrow, depression is there to let us know that we are off track with our emotional quest to a meaningful life. Most understand depression as an enemy to be warded off but in truth, it is our companion who gives us light and responsibility to understand what is meaningful and what is not meaningful. Haven't you noticed when individuals are depressed, they do drugs or get involved in reckless behavior, and somehow, they feel worse? That is because depression is saying, "Not so fast. You cannot escape me by numbing your soul with artificial substances." The nonbeing wants you to rationalize the original source to understand the dynamism and to become significant along the process of human growth.

Our human sense lacks. We have these tendencies to split the Being with some future moment that everything will get better with drugs or alcohol.

Those who engage in these affairs will realize the choices of the future are only an error of choice and speech. The primary feeling that we receive at this moment should be honored just as we honor the birth of a child, with awe and beauty. The experience of turning depression into a gift is like a mail carrier who delivers packages; we eagerly open it to see the product. The same goes for depression. It delivers to your conscious thoughts, so you can open the gift in hopes that your faith will carry on to a new chapter in your life.

To this extent, a moment's thought will show how significant the here-there and the modifications of "I am" is to the experience. This becomes fundamental as we develop a mature personality, where the sense of Being refers to one's totality. The "making sense of it" becomes apparent when one is rooted in the experience of depression, not alienating it with a reflection to the outside world. As the Being flourishes through depression, he or she will begin to feel life again, one where they believe they can do things again, to enjoy the simple pleasures, to terminate therapy and medicine, and to focus on holistic wholeness, filling the conclusions to a new ascension.

The signpost to live a meaningful life will vary from person to person. It is easy to drive the common road where the conclusive, identical answers remain the same. Give your attention to the goals that instrument the highest degree of authenticity. I promise you; you will inherit something that has not been underlined by others. That, my friend, is a gift you must share and embrace.

When we mature and understand

our inward freedom,

life becomes invigorating.

ON GRATITUDE

Take Me Back to Sunday Morning

In the beautiful sunshine, children are playing in the playground, adults are enjoying their picnic, laughing as if they saw Bob Hope's videos. On numerous occasions, there is no explanation as to why we love deeply, why we smile with a ray of light, why we go out of our way to help those in need, or why we say thank you to the smallest things that are given to us. What I know for sure is that gratitude is the Father of transcendence; epiphanies are how we experience the awe of life through beauty and connection. In each peddling moment, we can turn to gratitude as we aim for a meaningful life. Gratitude has power in words. Like a seed that is planted, it grows and blossoms with inspiration, motivating us to stubbornly open the heart of beauty. Multiple pathways to a meaningful life happen when we storm forth through the moments of prospect that unfolds a rooted discovery of transformation.

By using gratitude as your tool, you will erect the walls and gnarly parts of the unconscious mind. Your first word will be love, and your concluding sentence will end around the lines of, "My heart traveled to a distance. Sunshine complete, so is the moment of another day of giving thanks to the Universe." True and beautiful, the endearment of the sacred circle of gratitude brings out the victory to overcome anything. It is the most powerful spiritualization that constitutes the touring of the mind, body, and soul. When we connect the riddles of life, we can understand with a fresh perspective on how each lecture had a lesson. Once you comprehend the lecture and complete its assignment, your fractions will turn into wholes. And at that moment, a sense of renewal will build a new smile in your heart. Confusion, fear, anger, and jealousy will no longer serve your purpose. Love, empathy, and gratitude will speak its languages for your different seasons. It is impossible to observe each one in one day, but I promise you, lovable soul, you will extend your heart with a beautiful smile and say, "From my olden days, I discredited my vulnerability. Now, I am rewarding my soul with the thrill of acceptance along with a ceremony of new wisdom."

That, my friend, is the magic of gratitude. Backward and forward, we can pull ourselves upward to stewardship, servicing meaningful acts while banishing the dangers of a wild, freaky, imagination towards the tail of hate.

Something Carries Me with a Smile

Being propelled by some grace is what people believe. In my heart, I truly feel that gratitude comes in the form of a mature personality that shares the powerful, generous feeling that something beautiful happened. I hear people plead to gratitude that they want to experience the feeling of inner solitude. When gratitude ensues in us, it becomes a private visit, kind of like those shaman healers who come at night to heal the sick people. Gratitude operates the same way, but the main difference is that its duty is not to cure your psychological warfare, its main duty is to repeat the feeling of wholeness and to repeat the sensation in your heart. When the feeling of gratitude takes root, hold onto that feeling, and recapture its essence when you feel depressed or anxious about the present or future.

Learn to center yourself in the here-and-now. Give thanks to the Universe or any deity that you believe in and remind yourself how you want to experience this feeling again. I do not think there is a more enchanting feeling than to feel the superiority power of happiness and peace. Being in love with life and feeling grateful are the recipes to give our minds a permanent feeling of nirvana. Importantly, we must recognize the small encounters of beauty. Whether it is noticed or not, it allows us to trust the invisible force that paints thousands and thousands of stars upon our hearts. By showing up and saying, "Thank you for this magical day," we set ourselves up to visit the ballroom, where every guest is dancing to the song of gratitude, hugging in love, and engaging in small runs of praise. You might spend your entire life in question or in frustration as to why you cannot feel gratitude in situations that you may not understand. Listen to me beautiful soul, if you follow your path and give thanks to the Divine and show empathy and love to those who have wronged you, you will have an absolute completion to your life's journey.

You will have satisfaction like the kind where the Egyptians carved the pyramid; you will feel the majestic beauty of existence. In pure devotion, your courageous heart will divorce the possessions of negative emotions. It will give you a moment to your private eternity, helping you to glimpse into a new search of dawn.

Hope is the window through
which we glimpse the eternal beauty
that is yet to come in our lives.

Keep the Magic in Your Heart

Psychologists, philosophers, neuroscientists, and pastors have all acknowledged the immense power of gratitude. Most consider it as a healing agent to all diseases. There has not been any specific proof of study, but most researchers have taken into account to find data. While it is difficult to delve into a research of gratitude, let me share a story with you.

Aside from my motivational training programs and giving talks on how to live a meaningful life, I also donate my time to talk to patients who have been diagnosed with cancer. For this specific population, I focus heavily on children and adults. When I meet with children, they have the most beautiful smile on their faces as if they saw the geological history of the earth. Often, I ask the kids, "So, tell me, what makes life exciting?" To my surprise, they all responded with gratitude messages. Most of the time, children will yield to the sorrow of the diagnosis. To my impression, they focused on the wonderment of life. Two wonderful girls said, "After suffering from cancer, I was healed due to writing letters to myself in a gratitude form, and I created vision boards." It is amazing to hear stories about the power of gratitude. It extends onward to help us build evolutionary steps to a new social organization that we can call: A Portrait to a New Freedom.

When I met with several adult patients, some were agitated which is completely normal to feel. But others, they displayed positive traits toward the diagnosis. There is one special soul that I will always carry with me in my heart.

To keep his identity private, I will call him Steven. Steven is forty-nine years old and healed his cancer through gratitude and by reading a lot of self-help books. When I asked Steven about the meaning of life, he responded with this beautiful insight. He said, "The game of life is well worth playing. Whether we are ill or happily enjoying life, I feel that the meaning of life gives us a chance to connect with several events in our lifetime. It builds a sharper image of what is important to us. You know, we all havoc to look beautiful on social media, we all want to be accepted by others, but none of that will matter. Trust me. It does not take a major illness to figure this out. It takes a humble soul to unscramble the pieces of life. When we do this, our human potentials will become a beautiful opportunity to accomplish whatever it is in life that we want."

You should have seen my expression when he told me that. I had the biggest smile on my face. Individuals from all walks of life inspire me to listen to their personal stories.

It helps me to understand their suffering. It is reasonable to question the meaning of life or to question gratitude, but the dire possibility of a new life will admittedly give reason to evolve to a new chance of life. Let us grant this dream and let us permit ourselves to believe in a new wonder of a greater meaning. To make our argument much stronger, we must map out all the beauty of mankind. Rational and emotional, conscious and unconscious, we will learn our human patterns. We will learn to collaborate on projects and to bring peace to civilization. Each path will point the way to gratitude. Rarely do some depart from its gift. But those that depart, they will sink beyond the sea. Skepticism concerns the soul on whether gratitude can expand successfully or not. I say, take that risk and find out for yourself. Push ahead to its practical application. If you do, just remember this, before you were individuals who succeeded in solving the riddles of life which led them to an infinite amount of gratitude, causing them to have happiness, love, and wealth. Combine this puzzle with your faith, and you will have many reasons to be optimistic.

With every gradual emergence, you will increase your confidence like those before you. It is possible to track the steps of the good life — the good life that rears to a new entry of human consciousness. This will be found in your journey. It may not be today or tomorrow or months ahead, but surely, it will be found. The organized system never fails. It only fails when you change your neurons with specific orders that construct doubt and fear. Each thought, each feeling, and each wonder is the expression to change your thought program. Make it work for you, not against you. A strong additional advantage to this step will help you understand the intersections that follow the events from your past to your present.

What about the future?

Do not focus on that. Focus on occupying a new meaning to your life that will guide you safely to a new creation. This transcendence will help you illustrate the intricacies with a new direction that will propel your experiences with an upward form of human engagement. The biggest advantage is when you consciously decide to transform yourself into someone who wants new possibilities that become stepping stones to an illustrious life.

Those that have not practiced the immense power of gratitude, they have slipped to the conformity of social lies along with a multitude of fractions, which left them to feel limited to their truest selves.

Our minds consist of narratives. In each instance, we either tell a story of positivity or we tell a story of negativity. In either case, a flood of neurons will give us real information based on our thinking. It will mirror exactly as you engineer your contexts. A choice will be given by how you feel. Do you feel awful? Do you feel regretful? Has your life brought misery or meaning? Mentally and spiritually, do you feel confident? Are you satisfied with your finances? Are you happy with your love life? Are you happy with your health?

Our conscious mental life helps us get through an occasional crisis, giving us the initial choice to either produce meaning or to remain passive, being carried away by a near-obsessive burden of fear. As we already know, our conscious mental life is a powerful professor who gives us reviews, questions to answer, and provides real-life scenarios that teach us the effectiveness of the present conscious mind.

Free will, what a gift to unwrap. Without it, we would be confined like prisoners, ranting, and fighting against humanity.

One may ask, does gratitude exist in all areas in our world? Absolutely. It is not some operational sense where religion soaked in some scriptures specifically for this topic. It is by this virtue that gratitude is seen in the eyes of all cultures, beliefs, and practiced in many socioeconomic statuses. One could say, world religion, I call it supreme Divine intelligence. It is evident in all situations, in all places, and in all different time zones. We are completely free to entrain the results that make us feel alive.

The Invisible Medicine

Today, we speak of medicine to define our Western society when citizens experience the terror of phobia, the sudden outbursts of anger, or crying spells of depression. The source of this cause is an ontological relational Self and it is to some degree an existential aspect.

When we unite, and when everyone participates, we become an extension of each other's world. It shares the kindest, and loving pain where tears are put on the road. We drive them cautiously, using our wipers to identify the road ahead. Every human being will experience some guilt, perhaps even lengthy depression, or anxiety. If unaccepted in our dialogue, we will face a great deal of neurosis. Confidently, I say, embrace depression, anxiety, or any form of existential crisis. What I have learned through my mom's passing and every person that I talked to is this:

Emotional beauty is largely presented when we are aware of our purpose — yielding toward the stance of an altruistic, centered leadership that teaches others the meaning of life.

In every occurrence, it gives us the knowledge to interpret the meaning. It becomes our task to formulate questions in order to produce answers that are grounded with adequate, philosophical discourse. This makes our consciousness seek a fundamental aspect to possess an inquiry that stretches the structure of choice and responsibility.

When we give each moment more vibrancy and meaning, we will add a powerful mnemonic to our communication. If your life matters to you, eradicate the narratives that you ingrained as your "saviors" whether it was past relationships with your exes or with citizens who brought you no meaning to your life. Today, our beautiful world needs your compassionate heart. Let us become a one-world of love. Let us single out hate with a new, deeper aspect of expressions that lead to a new table of candles that we all can blow in harmony.

Cry not for the olden witnesses in your heart,
cry for the moment when our destiny wilts
into a path of sinuous waste that
leads to forgotten ambitions.

When we consider the medicine of gratitude, we will retain the image of a meaningful life. As its power increases, we can let ourselves go from war and envy and move towards peace. Our great decisions will speak of the just and the unjust to live to the principles of courage and humility to the hearts of our world.

Our conflicts have often been paid off with negative attention. It is no wonder we are seeing more citizens yield to the comfort of pills, alienating the Being that belongs to the world. The problem that we face today is a renewed appreciation of gratitude. Primarily, we focus upon the worldly news that causes our humanity to branch out into a division of fall. What I gladly propose for this chapter is to not only focus on gratitude but to focus on its meaning. When we give birth to gratitude, we must reflect on why we impregnated the idea of fullness. Once we have our deep reflection with our conscious thoughts, we can slowly move away from the "search of revenge "and gladly move toward the emotional LIGHT that is deeply rooted in our involvement with beauty.

As I said before, harmony cannot exist if we rise to the same compulsive behavior that forfeits the natural selection of our world of enlightenment. This world must be patient to grasp the knowledge of the angles that each of us takes. If one takes the angle of causes, we must recognize the havoc that will eventually teeter-totter to the external collection that arises with the division of our world.

Now, we cannot understand our world without understanding ourselves. The view of the outside is just as important as the view of our inside, conscious mind. What is required today is to eliminate the same foundation, the foundation of dissonance. The kind where we believe our bad behavior is a good one, but at times we believe the good one is also good but ends up being bad. The reason we endeavor to this route is that we strike directly at what "I" think is right instead of focusing on what "we" think is right for humanity. If there is any value to take from the medicine of gratitude, it is this. Faster than expressions are our languages that shape the imagination of our minds. Brilliant, yet clever to recognize the nature of existence.

Relating to everything will become a gift — playing in the sunshine, smiling at small and big moments, and writing our manifesto as someone who pocketed freedom when others doubted hope. Learning will also dawdle in your Being — slowly you will notice a-for-no-reason-to-smile, and others will be plagued by your LIGHT. This gripping picture that I am describing, I have witnessed its power in my life.

What are the secrets to your happiness and amazing vibes? I am often asked that question and my answer remains the same. It is gratitude. I demonstrate the increasing power of empathy, love, and courage for the sake of humanity. There is plenty of evidence out there. Some choose to beg for happiness; others strive for their path to be connected, meaningful, and purposeful.

The Search for Beauty

Life and I had a date the other day and we pondered on what makes life meaningful. Guess what life told me? Life gently whispered in my ear, "Luis, without experiences, how can one know life?" Wow! That was deep. It did not end there. Through calm breezes, brushing on my face, and the sun shining in my eyes, another message was benchmarked in my heart. Below and on the next page, this is what Mother Nature imprinted in my heart.

Rooted in our generations has been a story, a fictitious one if you will. Blinded with a raising arm that shouts "War! War!" We vaguely understand our purpose, but we only understand it when our world is shaken by an old system. Traditionally, when our world gets caught in the convulsions of war, religion, or gender equality, we suffer altogether in a spiritual nihilism. We no longer believe in the Sunday sermons or the accepted ways and means of society. Instead, we easily conform to dogmatism — giving up our authenticity in return for the orthodoxy of what is commonly accepted.

My young soul, pay attention to me as I am seen as Mother Nature. I know all and see all. So, before the sun sets in your eyes, I will leave you with this concluding message: However unpleasant it may seem in your world, just know that you can use your emotions as a product of creativity. Any crisis that you face or hear, know that your emotional shock is a dependence on your old Self. Wherever there is a shake in the world, allow yourself to use that to unwrap beauty and to fully emerge into a new Being that will transition from meaningless activities to an experience of self-consciousness. In great confidence, leap to my work. Make me happy. I will be watching you as you complete my work on earth. If you should find yourself lost or mildly sad, I will send an individual whom I trained to the highest degree of consciousness and that individual will be my representative. Go on my fellow LIGHT. Go on…

I do not know about you, but I cried when Mother Nature told me her message while we were on a date by a creek. I am not joking. I cried and pondered on the meaning of life. This is what I got out of the lesson. Like Socrates, we use dialect to search for truth, beauty, and good ethics. But even those get clouded when we admire fellow humans who have souls that are tarnished with previous encounters of bad dealings. Whether it is in politics, religion, business, or science, we somehow experience what Pascal called, "The swallowing up of a brief span." What this means is that we fill our lives with a small space and within it, we fill it with terror, angst, negativity, and hatred. This becomes a problem when we engage in gratitude. The estrangement between Being and nonbeing cleaves the purpose of life and the contemporary problems in the environment. Unlike psychoanalysis, existential gratitude focuses on the avenue that brings a meaningful understanding of our world. By understanding the problems, we can give history a new birth.

The full meaning of life becomes clearer when we keep in mind the simple things of life: a roof under our head. Water to drink. Food to eat. Being alive for another day.

Being able to move and to exercise. And being able to read and listen. Every time I listen to individuals who say, "This has been the worst week ever," I tell them, "But you are alive. You can eat. You have shelter. You have money in your bank account. Imagine all of that was taken away from you, your personhood would take you to the last sentence of, I wish I did not have to go through this."

Now that we know the significance of existential gratitude, we can shift to the healing contributions that it gives us. When faced with a sailboat of confusion, we can easily change our narrative to a broader painting that displays the message of, "You know what, I am not a failure. I just did not tweak my plans accordingly. Thereof, if I do this instead of doing that, I wonder what outcome I will get. And even then, whatever results I get, I know I am not a failure. By trusting in my abilities to continue to try again, I know I will be okay." This is the narrative we want to implement in our lives. This attributes to an understanding of how optimism, when backed up with faith, we can express the favored principles of an increased livelihood, one that circles each experience with beauty.

We need to reflect on each experience as a gift. The more we do; our Being will begin to flourish in harmony.

Do I have to be perfect all the time?

I get asked a lot of that question when I discuss existential gratitude. And the answer is no. You do not have to be perfect. All I am asking from you is to position your emotion away from the Being. Remember how in the previous pages I talked about nonbeing. Well, we confuse our Being and nonbeing. When we learn to separate our nonbeing from Being, we can carefully analyze what is profoundly important in this precious moment. It will enhance the agent of awareness that launches lovable messages to ourselves and to humanity. Our brain will begin to communicate in a new genetic code. Yes, this is possible. When we change our patterns of thinking, our regions, nuclei, and every firing neuron will stimulate the bodily sensations of gratitude. Thus, it will fire up to the brain, releasing dopamine.

Another implication of this analysis of existential gratitude is when our human experience describes itself as a world of "becoming" rather than "as is."

Chiefly, when our world is in the mode of "becoming," we are continually performing and operating on the groundwork of culture and connection. Theoretically, this is the most logical consistency that we can base off in terms of gratitude. It takes great courage to recognize social despondency, especially in the form of those who believe in the fate of determinism. As citizens, we know this truth, but we suppress the reality in turn for pleasure which gives no value to our individuality. With the quality of mercy along with an extended hand, we can press beyond the blueprints that were written for us.

Something, Somewhere Out There

Something within my heart takes hold. Without any explanation, it is somewhere in my soul, burning, and yearning for a new life.

What is this feeling?

It is the feeling of a splendid effort to interpret the findings of gratitude. At each moment, you argued against the examples of what is incredibly powerful and real.

And in other moments, you concluded that it was biology that gave you a history of emotions or some philosophy to make sense of life. This is true when we try to solve the riddles of humankind. We are wired to explain meaningful solutions. This is evident in gratitude. We say that it is some sort of energy, a Divine, a Light, a God, an Angel, or whatever it may be. We always try to explain how our test of faith moved into the mysterious streets of gratitude. We try to gain public prospects to prove our recognition that yes, gratitude is the healing power of life.

Let us center ourselves and humble ourselves to help others achieve wisdom with an unhurried soul. Our evolutionary stage requires us to attend private lessons with ourselves and with the world. Understanding our stories, and listening to each other's cries, we will no longer compare conceivable deductions. In all its probability, we will know to some extent the providence of chance.

This should motivate us to grasp and to understand the immense power of giving thanks to the world, to those that pushed us emotionally and spiritually, and to those that took the time to treat us out to a meal.

We cannot disquiet these precious moments. They give us a widespread need to show love and connection in ways that represent the closeness of humanity. Sociologically speaking, it connects us to the Motherland where we feel the affection from afar, exceeding each hour with the sweetest experience of reminiscences.

On the day that we should ever find ourselves in an old system of thinking, consumed with negative emotions, let us aim to the detachment of familiarity. Cozy notions will not emit the LIGHT that we need in our lives. It will visit us as a stranger, dusted in ashes, blown away somewhere in the blue skies.

Apply the teachings of gratitude. The ones that begin with, *let this day bring me love and grace. In all that I do, let my service address those who are thirsty and hungry, not just in spirituality, but in the world of survival.* By saying this, not only do you bring magic to your heart, but you also increase love and humility. Surprisingly, once we yield towards gratitude, we sustain moments of reverence — being open to a life that is sewn into the invisible lining of awareness.

Inwardly, we can lead with the ability to connect and to consider life as a blessing. In our exchanges, let us make a difference by prioritizing our relationships as a heightened sense of compassion for others.

On each occasion, when a prideful individual attacks you that there is no meaning to life nor anything to be grateful for, challenge the individual and pull out the words of faith and continue expressing them until the individual becomes a testimony to your credence. Lead it to behaviors that become an interrelationship with an excess amount of beauty. You might be scorned for smiling through the darkness or being optimistic. Let those sideline individuals witness your fresh life that unfolds uniquely.

Whether we insist on free association or giving credence to our free will, we must remember this: Gratitude illustrates the renewal of life. It is in the pause and through the moving periods that heightens the orientation of new ideas and new possibilities.

Given this emphasis, we can excite the moment and step forward to our surroundings that groups the communication of thanksgiving, putting us to a new reward system.

The greatest challenge comes, as always, when we bathe in materialism. Those individuals who are superficial only say thank you when their wishes manifest to their own will. Materialistic ideology has become a buffet; we choose and pick our entrée and dessert. We draw attention to the courses that excite us. This background is what I like to call *exterior orientation*. It is seen from afar but fades in its position due to poor leverage. Perhaps, materialism is not as powerful as we thought it was. Gratitude, on the other hand, is saying thank you no matter what. This will require work to train our minds to input the continuity of blessings.

ON GUILT

Relational Meaning and Its Path of Purpose

At its core, guilt is threatened by the encompassing ontological demands of responsibility.

Guilt condemns the Being to judge oneself for not producing the outcome that he or she should have done. In this outcome, we can easily witness anxiety and depression as cousins who relatively produce a circle of symptoms that separates meaning and values.

To a certain degree, if the Being cannot spring up new meaning or stand up against the guilt of emptiness, this will lead to neurosis and in rare cases, schizophrenia. You may be wondering, why schizophrenia? To make it simple and understandable from an existential point of view, I will share a case that I dealt with as I was called in for a consultation at a mental hospital. The individual appeared to have a disintegrated speech. At times, the client would say, "I am a billionaire. Look at my wallet and you will find an unlimited amount of cash. Go ahead and take some if you wish."

To me, this was an eye-opener.

At that moment, I knew he was struggling with a two-sided ontology: The Being who had a dream and secondly, the Being who surrendered the dream in return for a retirement of neurosis.

He could not affirm who he wanted to be. He could not distinguish human reasoning with an understanding of the values of reality. When the values are separated from the Being, guilt forms as a nonbeing which results in a spiritual warfare. The richness of nonbeing is powerful enough to put the Being into a disintegrated personality. I always urge my clients to recognize guilt as a gift of embrace. Because when we embrace the gift, we can open it without judging the size of emotions. It is in that moment when our freedom expands our decisions in the center of Being. Within ourselves, we can fulfill our destiny with a full scope of clarity.

Like the client that I was called in for a consultation, he could not come to terms when he was previously cognizant to know what essential Being was. And since he did not know how to produce the outcome of meaning, he gave up his moral reasoning to retire to the emotions of nonbeing.

Nonbeing, as I said before is anything related to the outer-directed experiences of the world. If both Being and nonbeing are not treated respectfully, you can expect to feel spiritual negativity that will threaten both sides of the picture: The philosophical aspect and the spiritual center to your wholeness. And that is exactly what happened to the client who had a voluminous of guilt for not promising the empire that he wanted to build when he was younger. The "voices" that he was hearing were not inspirational, they were regretful voices on how he could have been if he had succeeded previously.

Nevertheless, his voices were the only admission that gave him meaning. While the psychiatrists wanted to get rid of the voices, I had a different opinion. Instead, I asked the doctors if I could challenge his voices from another ontological standpoint. Granted with permission, I was able to see this client regularly for about six months. His voices were not out of this world. His voices consisted of accomplishments, building a better life, and at times, he had hallucinatory episodes that consisted of billionaires calling him out for lunch.

Again, seen from an existential point of view, we worked on unwrapping the meaning of his voices. Taking the approach of Jungian analysis, we were able to discover his shadow garden and the temple of punishment that he rejected as a Being. Moving forward with our therapeutic goals, I slowly worked on his duality of his tragic past and his present suffering to make sense of life. The first step I took was to avoid negative judgments and the expected moral demands of society. Once we agreed on that, we moved slowly to the extreme background of voices that he was hearing daily. By accepting the moral despair, we will not lose our self-awareness. Despite of extreme situations, we can creatively bend and shape our reality according to our narrative.

Going back to the client, once we worked on his duality, incrementally, he understood his situation with life. Without adding more guilt to his conscience, I asked him, "If guilt was not a factor in your life, how would you courageously own your present moment?" With a big smile on his face, he remarked, "Luis, I would not be here. I would be lavishing in the good life."

Is Guilt Good or Bad?

This is the question I often get asked from my clients that I coach or counsel or even doctors when I get called in for a consultation. To continue with my story of my client, I will answer it throughout the pages. As the client concluded his remarks on my question, I moved slowly to his ontological relatedness to personhood. Rather than perishing the classified symptoms, I used them as a creative expression to build his foundation of existence. With some anxiety in his subjective state, I had him focus on his present environment, which was the hospital. Nevertheless, I had him focus on short-term achievable gains. Besides his frustrated reactions towards life, I helped him to focus on how he can "play" with his emotions by deciding on how he would live his life if guilt were not a factor, paradoxically speaking.

However, we must remember to understand the client's world. This is where psychologists and psychiatrists fail. Because of their heavy training on the medical model, they neglect the existential approach toward the totality of Being.

Even when they consider the best treatment, they mix their professional practice with net gains. Like the client who I dealt with who said, "I would be lavishing in the good life," the psychologists and psychiatrists would view him as hallucinatory and delusional and would more than likely add a provisional diagnosis.

These contingencies sting the aspects of personhood. It also threatens the personhood with an excess amount of guilt and depression. The client will begin to think, "Why are the doctors giving me eight more medications?" "What did I do to end up here?" That will add an attack to the ontological foundation toward the Self. It is imperative to understand guilt from its meaning and emptiness. Guilt is an organized structure of forms and functions. One cannot leap forward to liberation without the demand of guilt. For every guilt feeling that we feel, we must process these important questions which can be found on the next page.

☼ To what am I guilty of? Is it relatedness to my personhood, or is it caused pain that I inflicted on another individual?

☼ Is the degree of my guilt due to the fact that I left my wife/girlfriend/husband/boyfriend because I wanted to grow as a person, or is the degree of my guilt due to the fact that I will be alone for a while?

☼ If I escape my growth towards guilt, will I achieve the meaning that I need at this moment, or will I despair over the unfinished business that I suppressed?

☼ By understanding guilt from an ontological point of view, what can I learn from it? Lastly, how can I move forward with a fresh perspective towards my life?

The first base to take when answering these questions is learning how to take responsibility for what guilt is demanding of you in the here-and-now. To paint you a picture, I will describe a situation that I encountered when I was dating a woman in August of 2017. She was poised, classy, and smart. You would probably think, alright Luis, this sounds like the perfect woman. What happened? Well, as in every story to love, it goes on to say that our seasons were matched for growth toward the personhood. As beautiful she was, she was a season in my life. But through the pain, I was able to come up with a theory on guilt. After expressing my feelings to her, and using "I feel" statements, and telling her how this is not going to work out, I began to feel guilty. Why on earth would I feel guilty if I am leaving something that is dark and toxic? Here's why I was feeling guilty.

The nonbeing, which is our emotions, they hate to feel alone. Guilt, being that it is a nonbeing, it made me feel worse than what I was feeling. I went through periods of sadness. I wanted to text her, call her, and express my love. But I had to realign my morals and values and stick to my word. That is when I asked myself, "Am I guilty for wanting to grow in life?" Another question I asked was, "Am I guilty because I will be alone, and I will not have a woman in my life to shelter me with her love and kisses?"

My guilt was not coming from the plane of growth, my guilt was coming from the fact that I might be alone for a couple of years. To say nothing of, my guilt was a good one because, at that moment, it was pushing me to create something new in my life. By doing so, I was able to interview people who went through similar breakups or divorces and they reported back the same thing as I did. They felt guilty for wanting to grow in life. It is then we feel the need to call back the person that we left and express our love to them. This is where people get confused between the boundary lines of healthy guilt and neurotic guilt. Healthy guilt is when you leave something toxic in your life and you process how you want to flourish in our world. You increase new habits, you seek fitness trainers, you eat healthier, you attend personal growth seminars, you start up your own business, and you read personal growth books. That is healthy guilt. Neurotic guilt is when you are attacked with messages such as, "Damn it. I messed up! I should have listened to him or her when they told me to text them back. I should have obeyed their commands and agree to their ways of life." Raise your hands if you all been there? I have. It feels horrible when you surrender your Being to another person who will mold you into what they want from you. You begin to feel guilt and a recycled pattern of anxiety and depression. The main reason why you would feel this way is that you know deep in your heart that your self-esteem is a sense of value and an important aspect of your life. When it gets objectified, your emotion overwhelms the cycle of guilt with an extension to the questioning of existence. Who am I? Why do I matter? Why am I living? To the outside existence, it seems like a compelling proof that your relationship is a solid bedrock but between you two, you know that one controls the sermon while the other obeys the commands. As dreadful as it may seem, this is where we witness neurotic guilt and bouts of depression. We are conflicted with a dissonance. Should I leave this relationship? And if I do, will I feel alone?

In this dilemma, you must figure out what you want in your experiences. Separate your processed emotions with an existential view. It will water down the effects of guilt. You will notice how your guilt feelings can be molded with a powerful carriage of concepts that you can toil with. Speaking from experience, I had to deal with my guilt when I left the woman that I was dating.

Being that she had a lot of dark secrets and knowing that she was acting shady, for my own sake, I had to remove myself from her world. It got to the point where I was feeling highly anxious because of the darkness that she brought into my life. She wanted to change my personality for someone she admired in Hollywood. At that moment, I called up my friend and explained to her my dilemma. We both agreed that it was best to leave the toxic energy to preserve my sanity. At that moment, I learned to LET GO. It was the most difficult part because if you are like me, I see the good in everyone. I see love, courage, and kindness in every soul. They may manipulate me or cheat on me, and somehow, I will forgive them and love them. But even with that comes sacrifices. The sacrifice of my Being. The sacrifice of my health. The sacrifice of my heart and soul.

Being guilty of wanting to leave that toxic relationship taught me two things. I am my choices. And the experience of my guilt was a manifestation of a history that created extensions of appearances. It had to do with the fact that I will be alone but not necessary. During that alone time, it gave me an output to do things that I would have put on the back burner if I chose to stay in that dark, toxic relationship.

I learned that guilt can be healthy and neurotic.

The paradox of guilt is duplicating the same emotion but twice the impact. Let me explain. If I chose to stay in that dark, toxic relationship, I would be happy because of the "idea" of touch and kiss. But in reality, I would be miserable because I would have surrendered my Being for the sake of lust and comfort. Now, this is where the guilt comes in. If I stayed in that toxic relationship but gave up my goals, then, I would experience a conflict in my personality where my dialectical interplay would have yielded between doing and wishing. You see, the pain of despair came in the form of a miracle. I saw the beauty behind the darkness that I was in. By expanding my logic and awareness, I knew I had to give up something. That is part of life. Look around you. We always give up something. When you break a glass or a plate, you give it up. When you lease a car and buy a new one, you give up the leased car to enjoy the new vehicle that you bought. Everything in life recycles and we must go with the motion. With that said, I gave up the darkness in return for a beautiful life. Now, here is the tricky part. By giving up the darkness, guilt quailed into my thoughts and I had repeated messages of, "Luis, you made the dumbest move by leaving her. She is gorgeous. She looks like a model. She is affectionate." I had all those messages repeatedly playing in my thoughts. Until I said enough is enough. I had a serious talk with my guilt. I said, "Okay. You are making me feel guilty because I will be alone. But didn't you promise me that if I gave her up, you would push me to create a better life? And, weren't you the one that taught me that when we feel guilty, we can outnumber the experience with a new participation in life?"

Guilt agreed to all of that. But it did not agree to make me escape guilt for good. The lesson I learned is that we need to feel some guilt in our conscious thoughts. When I chose to live a successful life over the darkness, guilt reminded me if I was sure that I did not want to go back to that darkness. If I decided to have gone back, guilt would have caused me to have chronic depression. Think of it as some form of punishment because we disrespected the promises that we made to ourselves to live a vibrant life. My guilt for leaving her had low minimal impact on my conscious thoughts. I felt better each day. I was focusing on numerous projects, starting new businesses with my partners, and planning a new master course.

As time passed, my guilt was gone. I was not yearning for her attention or her love. Spiritually, I wished her well. Presently, I continue to focus on building my empire and the empire of others. That is the gift I decided to give back to life. We are not always aware of our experiences with guilt, but during the situation of guilt, we can choose to live differently and more abundantly.

Push and Pull Technique

The understanding of guilt will help us illuminate the difference between healthy guilt and neurotic guilt. The distinction is not based on one degree higher or lesser than the other. It is the experience and the reaction that we are adding to the here-and-now. Given this light, we can understand guilt as a process of orientation, and as a situation that deals with the confrontational issues of separation guilt. In the next few pages, I will describe a technique that I came up with that will help you or your clients to achieve an increase of knowledge toward the personhood. For this matter, let us consider the six steps of the push and pull technique.

Step 1: Remain present without judgment

This is the first step toward the ontological awareness of the Self and the world. This is the most comprehensive step because there are areas that we must work on. Though some may be repressed, it is urgent to bring those issues to light. When you realize your confusion, particularly why you feel guilty, the more you will be able to make sense of it. The source of all guilt is empty. We as the Being arise them to a certain degree that builds participation and reasoning to fulfill that void. Dramatically, as I said before, it can lead to depression, anxiety, and in rare cases, schizophrenia. Every Being will experience some amount of guilt and that is okay. We need that ontological guilt to accept the new results that we want to live by; not live for. Vividly, feel the emotions at this moment. What is guilt telling you in the here-and-now? Are you guilty of leaving your dark relationship? Are you guilty because you spoke the truth? What is it about the guilt that makes you want to classify it as a threat rather than an experience? Ponder on those questions and when you are ready, move to step two.

Step 2: Analyze the perspective

Guilt is not the same as depression or anxiety. Guilt stands alone with its unique contributions. By accepting your guilt, you can learn new ways to construct your guilt through the courage of meaning. It is rooted deeply in the totality of Self and within the realm of growth. By changing the phrase of, "I am guilty and worthless," to "I may have guilt, but it does not end here. I am willing to learn as to why I am feeling guilty. I am curious to open up to the endless possibilities of shaping new meaning in my life," you are analyzing the perspective from an objective state that will help you to think independently. If you caused pain through your words, then yes, you would feel the wrath of guilt. If you are wise, you would forgive yourself and ask for peace to whom you inflicted the toxic venom. But if you feel guilty for leaving a dark relationship or for wanting to focus on your health and business, then I would suggest for you to invite that feeling, analyze it, and provide a new outlook, one that will create a dialogue between you and the world.

Step 3: Avoid assumptions

Do not assume that your guilt will pull together all the pieces from your childhood rearing. The point of this step is to avoid the assumption of guilt as being a justification for one's permanent address towards the psyche. Guilt is your companion. Whether you like that notion or not, it is your friend. Guilt has served me greatly and to the clients that I coached and counseled. The courage to accept guilt as a transformational process is to fully encounter the experience of the communion of healing. By asserting oneself to the healing power of healthy guilt, one can jump to a new relationship that stands in the individuality of growth.

Step 4: Focus on your present moment, your body, the world, and reinforce the meaning behind your dilemma

This, however, does not mean accept everything as is and move on with your daily rituals. In this step, I encourage you to take the time to feel your emotions. Do you feel a tight knot in your throat? Do you feel a weird vibe from someone? Do you have knots in your stomach because you know that your relationship does not feel right? Pay attention to all your cues. In whatever way you choose to illustrate it, make sure the experience of guilt takes form as a collection, not as a division.

It is equally important to learn the difference between focusing on the present meaning and hanging onto guilt. Anything more or less will greatly stunt your growth. From an existential perspective, this step will add a premium to the novelty of change; not a wishy-washy miracle expectation that we see in solution-based therapy. Open attentiveness to the meaning of life reinforces new alternatives that you are seeking healing towards your guilt. Through your insight and your deep absorption of your emotion, you will uniquely respond to the meaning of life. The job is to stay in touch with the present emotion. Attentively, you must undertake the composition of characteristics rather than resisting the sculpture.

Step 5: Investigate the past (push), but pull them back to the existential awareness (present)

Everyone manages their past differently. Some become a total stranger where one day, they forgive but inflict hate to the individual who did them wrong. While others are brave enough to investigate how the past affected the present. The decisions that we make can greatly cause a future shift in our world.

This is where most resist it or deny the change. They knew it was coming but chose to ignore it. Most individuals struggle with this step because they disown half of their aspects toward the personhood. It is highly suggested to investigate your suffering of guilt from the past in order to pull that wisdom to the present moment. The fundamental difficulty that I have seen with my clients has been accepting the moment and learning to dialect a new orientation of knowledge. Most of them duplicate the same sorrow which causes unnecessary guilt.

Step 6: Favor a new outcome for guilt

Unfortunately, in our last step, most choose to live in a that-is-how-it-is manner. Instead of favoring a new outcome for guilt, they choose to wallow in self-pity. I teach my clients to view guilt as a new painting to rescript one's potentialities namely, arising from the fact that guilt is not of depression nor anxiety, guilt is an extension of what we left behind in our goals or what we said to others.

The Three Modes of Guilt

Interestingly, with all the clients that I have coached and counseled, I noticed a repeated pattern with their guilt. One of the main importance was not so much the *feeling of guilt,* it was more of locking up one's true potentials which resulted in my **first mode: the guilt of correspondence.** What this means is that our guilt, when it is associated with something (correspondence), we tend to attribute to the passivity of Being. Therefore, we fail to bring ourselves to our authentic, individual concrete forms. When we lock up our mind, body, and spiritual center, we can expect to feel a periodic episode of depression. This mode applies to those who considered starting something new with their business or a new change of relationships but chose to ignore the extension to a new life. Kierkegaard described it perfectly as the "dizziness to our freedom." When our freedom is confused, it becomes a tug of war — both ends feel tight, but one end will eventually tear. It is imperative to know what your guilt is corresponding to. Is it the guilt of forgetting oneself during the process of growth? Do you feel guilty because you gave so much in your love relationship that now, you developed anxiety for not pointing out the importance of how you want to establish an empire?

Whatever it may be, let us learn about the **second mode: the guilt of Self.** For this mode, I have seen many individuals overlook the Self by self-scanning the alienation to their unconscious thoughts. This archetypal explanation can be seen symbolically when it is integrated with our personal experiences.

To explain, I had one client call me up to meet with me because she was feeling guilty about speaking the truth to her best friend. I asked her, "What was it about the guilt that made you feel guilty? Was it in the form of how you said it or was it the fact that you had to destroy your comfort qualities of anxiety in order to feel some peace?" She said it was both. In these typical cases, guilt can be removed once the individual realizes that guilt is not in the form of inflicting pain; it is through the degree of intensity to what one feels in the experience. Like my client, she felt guilty because she was being honest. Now, there is nothing wrong with being honest. It is better to open with someone who brings out your vulnerabilities and helps you to mature as a fully rational human being than to be clouded with the eyes of admiration. A great weakness we see with individuals who struggle with this second mode is pride. They reach for the tempting glow of pushing onward toward the qualities that help them agree to the experience, but they end up grazing themselves with the same mistakes, which they know is a lesson to act differently, to decide wisely, and to change the outcome into progress. For whatever apparent reason, they yield to a separation to the world, which brings us to our **third and final mode: the guilt of separation.** The individual detracts from the world because they have no appreciation for the meaning of life. This is what I call the *impulse of blindness*. The impulse of blindness detracts the individual from reaching the highest human potential. They belittle themselves and they get desperate to find an answer to their guilt. In extreme cases, the individual may consider suicide. They self-poison the mind with causes and consequences of what "could become" if they chose to systemically repress the here-and-now.

I have seen many times the blockage of reflection. Thus, it creates a consciousness of pretensions that remain concealed by great pride coupled with a faulty positionality of emotion. There is an existential proof that the relatedness, either selects and actualizes the moment or compares the guilt from a previous precondition.

Moreover, the values of nobility are always open to its entirety, not just in certain selected outcomes. By separating your guilt from the world, you separate the reflectiveness and fullness of one's directed essence. Reflection of guilt will help you to arrive at a concrete common ground with creative guilt by openly accepting the separation and moving it towards the completion phase.

The enjoyment of completion will move forward to a means of exchange — great or small, you will structure new motivation and indeed, the transitional goals will lead to solutions.

In whatever way we choose to illustrate it, this discussion on guilt should enlighten you to know the positive aspects of guilt, especially the movement to a new Being. While at the same time, it is important to recognize its dismay toward the personality. The conditions that confront us with guilt should fulfill us with new potentials. During the first days or months with guilt, it should be noticeable for you to rattle the doorknob, to shake the door, and to go in and discover the leftovers that were once recognizable to you.

Ontological guilt can no longer be grasped as something vague. This reduces the totality of Being into a decentering of individuality. To understand its complexities, we must first understand the language that we are speaking towards guilt, then, from there, we must understand how we relate to the world. Being together in the same world, we exist as an external collection through which we view from the outside but preserve the reality that is within. This marks the maturity in understanding guilt. It is required to have guilt. There is plenty of evidence in our world how guilt served us creatively, and at times pathologically conditioned us to become a study.

To improve our world, we must
question our guilt in order to find new
evidence that will help us solve the
preconditioned ideas of our history.

ON POLITICS

An Increase Toward International Peace

In our global efforts, we have come a long way in acceptance. The acceptance of science, technology, religion, LGBTQ, and education reform, so students can afford to pay for their classes. Truly, we have work to do to unite our nation to its prominent height. We are blessed to live in a nation of all remarkable degree, where we rise from our past and present tragedies. Our children will come to know our nation as one who does not perish nor be victimized of race, color, creed, ancestry, disability, or sexual orientation. Our destiny calls us to be culturally competent; to understand the history of oppression, and to be the voice of the human spirit.

As a nation, we have faced serious problems. Varying from war, mass shootings, air pollution, catastrophic storms, pandemics, poverty, rare diseases, and more. Beauty has taught us that we cannot crowd our problems "as is," but rather, as one that can be worked together, solving each dilemma with a rationalistic mind. We have secured hate far too long that our generation has passed on with an evening of cynicism. This is not the America that we know. As the setting light of our liberty, we are reminded that our morals and values must connect with the tender feelings of our neighboring partners across the world. Let us believe that we can grow and attain our expansion of life, so as long as we are true to humility, our story will be told for decades to come.

Continual progress requires us to forge ahead with faith. The thrill of this adventure is knowing that in every moment, it becomes a lesson for us to weave in our world. Inheriting the lessons helps us to reflect on our constant flow with life. Living out each moment with a smile and ensuing a childlike spirit, we can begin again; not by luck but through an interaction with the world that helps us to stimulate growth through the guidance of empathy and love.

Second Chances

The way we champion love is how an individual gets excited when cheerleading around Silicon Valley; hopeful and determined to bring a new ah to life. But this becomes contradictory because we proclaim peace and love, yet we address the sharpened tongue with a linkage of a powerful presentation of war, creating strangers among humanity, and hewing our home and culture to a contemporaneous theater.

Where doubt may seem present,
the hero is born again.

Closed eyes are how we imagine love, open eyes are how we enter battle, absorbing irrational acts that create a personalistic movement towards Mother Nature. All occurrences strike a connection with events that bring us sorrow. For instance, when we hear nuclear threats or a possible world war, citizens dig up the utmost pain and hurt towards humanity. They shout in protest how the government is unfair; they sacrifice another human soul to make a statement; and they participate in movements that follow meaningless acts such as, kill the government. Events that present themselves should help us rewrite our destiny. This is when we should break the irrational behavior with a coherence that enables connection and transparency.

Today, we find ourselves living in a law of duplication: speaking of voided aged experiences and repeating history with the same senseless attention towards war and hate. This duplication is a bad habit that sets fire in our hearts, following year after year with written speeches of anticipation and immorality.

Regularly, we observe events because we know something is *occurring* or is about to *occur*. Instinctively, we prepare for its coming.

The courses of events that cause havoc disrupt the balance of our world in a way that is difficult to fathom. In all circumstances, the human dilemma is never solved through a period of highly prized threats. Whatever was presented in the past somehow adopted to the present moment, and in most cases, to the future.

We as citizens display a laudable capacity for reason but in our conflict, we engirdle irrational behavior. We experience love and peace one day and the next day, we experience war and hate. Our freedom is not to take sides of liberalism, conservatism, or Marxism but rather, the freedom to believe that there is some faith to unite and to create a common cause of participation in our world. No doubt we have work to do. The task of a virtuous life is to clarify and to illuminate our human passage. This will require a lot of work, but I believe in us. I believe in second chances.

Between the question and the answer,
the result is you, not the external environment.

Second chances renew our courses of life with a period of beauty that transforms our nature with the observance of potentiality. Second chances enhance a new belief, a new way of thinking, and a new politics that serves a higher mankind — vouching for growth and guidance. It becomes an active force to search our past and to ask deep, existential questions: Why did we become this way? How can peace be maintained through international relations? By questioning the phenomenon, we can analyze each social interest that was deeply rooted in greed and power.

Our crisis in human existence is longing for an original revelation to place our world to a new flourishment. We immediately fall prey to the agreements of higher authorities, alarming us with a division that illustrates an ill-fate. Occasional threats appear on the horizon, heavy missiles being blown to other countries, dictators rejoicing at the privilege of being the middle to a personality that stands with corruption and destruction. It is evident that our present experiences are deeply rooted in blind power. Perhaps we need to restart again. Perhaps we need to set a balance on our earth to flourish in all aspects of life. Second chances allow us to reflect on the ego that we clung to.

When wars greet humanity, we immediately thrive to the decision to hurt each other rather than focusing on the welfare of other citizens. What I advocate for in politics is a new foundation — built on faith, recognizing our values of peace while at the same time, promoting a culture of resilience.

Biologically, we imprint on irrationality, imbalance, and envy. These are the culprits that divide our lives in a strange direction which creates a change in which we cannot move. It keeps us suspended in a lettering that we cannot capitalize on.

Some may advocate for peace while others advocate for a reaction. We know in our history that it results in a world war that reveals itself through the shattering of an inner life that weakens the leader's faith, making them insecure. Bounded by such recognition, they enlarge the backward current to instill a misplaced faith with a new age of reform. In periodic peace, we find a date with division across the world. Through war and separation, we cause an imbalance to mankind. Through international cooperation, we can observe the optimism to aspire to a peaceful democracy, where traces of prosperity etch to the human soul.

Peace Treaty: A Way to Increase Globalization

There will come a time when nations will gather to a momentous theater — everyone gathering for the final movie. Admiration, wanting to promote peace, increasing to a new frontier, this will be the experience of acceptance. The world will dispel from religious ideology. The world will come to know a new form of worshipping; the kind where enlightenment gives rise to the acceptance of all language, culture, and race into one universality. Every person will feel and think on a global ecosystem rather than selfishly engaging in the ego of Self. The Peace Treaty will be the seal that binds everyone into one timepiece, utilizing every talent to contribute to humanity. Building hope and faith will be a vital part; not the praises of wishing or manipulating others to believe a certain ideology. It will be a new faith in listening and empathizing with others whose attitudes may seem to fall short. Each citizen will assist one another to become whole again. The more open they are to each other, the more they find themselves in the journey.

Without spitting fire of "hurry up," everyone will extend the same attitude that processes life to a new orientation of beauty.

Evaluation of others will not be based on a hierarchy nor judgment. It will be based on a new system of competency and knowledge. This evaluation will be given to every citizen who is forwarding with their talents. Those who are stagnating, they will be asked: What is life for if you do not learn about your talents and contribute to humanity? What is life if you do not make every citizen think and feel differently? How can you hold such an inactive talent and expect others to express their respect towards you? While these questions may seem brazen, it pushes the individual to think about the complexities of life. It helps every citizen to trust the experience of enlightenment that is curtailed with wisdom. During the Peace Treaty, there will be a discovery, gradually engineering a new foundation of prosperity. Reactions and vague thoughts will carry on to extinction as they meet a new attitude that carries on the humble, creative aspects to the corollary learning that helps each of us to make scholarly decisions that give life meaning.

The touchstone of peace is to compromise. We must compromise at a higher form of consciousness. The approximation to peace is like saying the chef is in the process of cooking something new: both add new throw-ins that becomes more as a personal learning experience rather than increasing the authoritative lawfulness on how the activity should be.

Still, nations across the world lack direction. They come with a presence, strictly ordering subjective harm that somehow convinces us to engage in their unsavory recall. Potential enemies wait across the hill whose footsteps wrench our freedom. Distance away, hatred reveals the language to the pieces of concepts that suspend our world peace. It would be in vain if we assumed a certain religion would give us a necessity to objectify the power of corruption. Neither pretend nor projection, we can form globally if we remain congruent with the qualities of empathy and love. Other's presence may appear vicious or cynical, but one thing remains clear: Fleeing from original relations will only give us a strange freedom, one that seems probable while the other one seems artificial. Threats and war may glimpse, but in the end, our humility will touch the hearts of many.

And when it does, we will know that we have given up the enterprises that cracked the stairs to the ascension of a new life.

The Mockery of Russia and The Ego of USA

"General Secretary Gorbachev, if you seek peace, if you seek prosperity for the Soviet Union and Eastern Europe, if you seek liberalization: Come here to this gate! Mr. Gorbachev open this gate! Mr. Gorbachev, tear down this wall!" The words of our former United States President, Ronald Reagan evinced a strong, directional message that put the Soviet Union in a changing process that eventually would weaken their image. President Reagan trusted the philosophy of civility. The destruction of the Berlin Wall meant that we were motivated for change. In such a relationship of peace, Reagan wanted to limit the angst and confusion of Germany by regarding mankind as a form of togetherness — a close relationship that seemed reasonable, self-directing, mature, and composed of definable changes that would build responsibility toward the actions we take.

Whether troubled or maladjusted feelings toward other nations, Reagan showed a tough, genuine transparency on how world politics should be displayed. It is through the understanding aspects of personhood that integrates a unique Self that helps to cope with the problems of life.

But this was not the case for Vladimir Putin who witnessed the weakening image of the Soviet Union after Reagan uttered, "Tear down this wall!" In a short distance, Putin learned the new changes that were to come once the Berlin Wall was torn down. Not only did it make the Union of Soviet Socialist Republics (USSR) weak, but the leadership of Gorbachev had Putin questioning whether he was fit to carry on its legacy. Through the eyes of Putin, he felt the Soviet Union had lost its respect and position in Europe. Putin realized he had to sharpen a new leadership so that Russia would stand alone in its reign, separating from the other republics of the union.

In 1991, the Soviet Union collapsed, leaving Russia as one of the former republics to hold a considerable amount of power and influence. Today, we see Russia creating its own identity. Other nations fear their nuclear threats, leaving them hopeless to their power. One can say that Putin has a Gestalt void from the collapse of the Berlin Wall. Presently, he holds a denied feeling of anger toward the weakening position that Gorbachev took. By changing the image of Russia, Putin has positioned himself as one of the most feared leaders throughout the world except for the United States. Those two have had a history. And through their discourses, we have seen USA mock Russia through Hollywood movies such as Rocky IV.

In our Western culture, we pride ourselves on individualism, unaware that we are considered egoistical when it comes to sports, movies, and mocking other nations as if we are superior to the rest of the world. Out of this lonely road, we can classify this as narcissistic. We have taken the role as if we can accomplish anything with no limits to how much satisfaction we gain. This has been our story. Our attitude pierces with an establishment that misses out on the simple joys of life — the beauty to increase the support from all nations to bind towards empowerment and peace.

Toward the experience of universality, I genuinely believe the echoes of the past will be silenced with empathy. We watch too much news that creates an instability toward the personhood. We fear chaos. We fear a pandemic. We fear a global war. There is an emotion in each leader through which they carry blindly, open with pride but closed with wounds. The threats we hear from all nations come down to one point: a misplaced void. Each of them including our country has a complexity of issues that build a common desire for power. They desire power to mask the pleasing Self of others. I find that many individuals have inaugurated themselves by trying to please the loud noises from the Other. They move away from love and peace to a more rigid personality that leaves them to decide on the form of war and destruction.

The one who travels the path of emotional wellness will lead the culture of universality.

USA has played the heroic myth far too long. Every movie portrays aspirations, ideals, beliefs, the machismo role, and the courage to save the world from war and threats. This was created by us. Collectively, we wrote the narrative on the quiet courage to mount up with achievement that secretly sets us apart from other nations. The "me" philosophy overwhelmingly creates a materialistic society. It strikes us to be more ignorant toward the Self. It is like a finger pressing the water, the ripples grow larger and larger; leaving the person to press more.

This philosophy has passed by on many occasions — declining our humanitarian love. In searching for a new way of peace, and a new form of beauty, we must collectively experience the *what* of meaning rather than laser focusing on *isolationism*. When we focus on the *what* of meaning, we begin to look at the world through the eyes of gratitude, standing bravely to transcend our emotional lessons as growth. This is the principle towards beauty — the principality to do good for humanity without the ego in place. The ego in every leader has persisted in their unconscious mind to kill the music of the world with darkness.

USA, Russia, Syria, China, North Korea, and among others have lived in a myth that power is a secure foundation to voice destruction. The contemporary concern that I have for our world is the upshot to live in a final clause that carries through a suspension of a triangular situation, like the mother-father-child.

Leadership is not a paved path of totalitarianism. On the contrary, leadership is a form of connection and transparency that embodies a culture of possibilities.

An Open Window of Political Empathy

We have been living a vague life that increasingly betrays the human form of meaning. To be truly intimate with existence, we must acquire the habit of comportment — governing our behavior through the lens of altruism, helping every citizen to change their circumstances.

By one's willpower, one can make good resolutions, especially against the impulses of instinct and the deterministic party politics.

In America and the rest of the world, we have consequently built a pathway of division that severs our ties of connection. We pass on through appearances, coloring each moment with doom and gloom, leaving our citizens in a precipice of confusion. If we are to appear with greater credibility of social order, we must measure our conduct through the genuine road of empathy — enriching each other's stories and culture.

No doubt, our world has met the face of chaos and separation. Confusion has sprawled among us, leaving us a step back towards the meaning of life. The cry is rarely heard in our age but in every sorrow, love produces humility in our world.

Let us not forget, there cannot be any beginning without the togetherness of a torch that carries our existence with light and liberty. Our touchstone of humility is when we extend our hands to every citizen in our world. The greatest destiny is when we do not conform to gender superiority nor ideology superiority, but rather, a window that opens to the remembered films that we played long ago from our ancestors that fought in bravery, teaching us to rise to spiritual greatness.

Without threat or economic superiority, we must put behind us our political differences and increase the fabric of empowerment. I know, of course, this could be a challenge, but I am more than confident that when we universally come to an order of connection and empathy, we can yield to a new strength that will push America and the rest of the world toward a peaceful process.

Our democracy did not fail us. We failed to work together, to unify our policies with openness and compromise. Our voices can no longer clamor to our differences of political colors between red or blue.

ABOUT THE AUTHOR

Inspired by philosophers and psychologists, Luis Enrique Cavazos has devoted his time and effort to educate others on the meaning of life. Through his thought-provoking messages, he illuminates his viewers to think differently about anxiety, depression, leadership, success, wealth, and much more. In his first book, *The Five Virtues That Awaken Your Life,* Luis gave a snapshot of where our human dilemma is, and he provided a measurement of knowledge and wisdom. Luis is dedicated to helping others confront the human dilemma through a framework of meaning and formulation.

In July of 2018, Luis was awarded Best Author of San Antonio by the readers of San Antonio Current. Also, he was voted Best Speaker of 2018 by his local chapter in Toastmasters Club.

As a thought leader on human behavior, and as a clinical mental health therapist and empowerment coach, Luis continues to innovate new strategies and techniques for people to use throughout their lifespan.

Luis is also the founder of What's Your Exit? which is a personal development program for those who are searching for the meaning of life. In his program, he teaches individuals that we have exits, but the exits that we cannot escape are anxiety, depression, and grief.

Also, he is the founder of Sacred Purpose which is a collaboration of education where he invites guests to talk about health, fitness, psychology, holistic healing, yoga, communication, fashion, leadership, and entrepreneurship.

With his experiences in clinical mental health and through his devotion to existentialism, readers will establish a form of contact between personhood and existence.

His main goal is to have individuals blossom in their present moment by altering challenges into a revealing fruit, one that opens a garden of possibilities. His hope for the future is to have individuals comprehend human nature from the viewpoint of belonging, connection, and vulnerability. His messages and writings have helped individuals to modify their nihilism into the development of knowledge — guiding them to make small, incremental steps towards beauty and growth. By drawing attention to existentialism, Luis hopes that each of us will inscribe the spiritual enrichment of freedom that gives us the voice to our faith. By understanding our mental universe, Luis believes that we can construct an ideal life that favors an outcome that directs to the position of accomplishing great things. Also, Luis hopes that we can cite our experiences as meaningful rather than feeling angst. In his viewpoint, when we marry bravery and connection to our experiences, we will engage in full momentum, leading us to a purposeful life.

To learn more about Luis and his work, go to Amazon to purchase his books. Make sure to leave a positive review of Emotional Beauty on Amazon. Lastly, follow Luis for daily inspiration. Make sure to follow his social media pages:

Instagram: @luiscavazos.motivation

Facebook: LuisECavazos.Motivation

Twitter: @LuisECavazos

ONE FINAL MESSAGE

First and foremost, I want to thank you for reading every chapter, and for reaching this far. Writing this book was a labor of love. This book was written to give you insight, not for a brief fashion of pop psychology or pop spirituality of, "The Universe is guiding you." No! This book, as you already know, it made you think deeper than you have before. It is a fact that we face many challenges — whether it is through politics, religion, or in academia, we somehow lost the state of being the investigator towards life. You know, the existential questions that we ask ourselves: Am I a responsible person to evaluate myself objectively, or do I judge solely on the external environment? Can I keep a relationship vibrant with openness and love? Is the meaning of my life based on social conformity, or am I taking courageous steps to pursue the highest ambitions toward the Self?

Daily, we process an inquiry of weaknesses toward the Self — neglecting our complementary focus on our meaning of life. As such, we label ourselves as not "good enough." The encounter with existence is challenging because we are always in the process of growth and maturity.

In life, it is easy to side with the majority. It is easy to get swayed by adversity. Our fear causes us to take actions that we would not normally take. This vacuum mindset chips away our good intentions. In our search for beauty and wholeness, we must ensue our full selves into the question and answer.

Some of us may reap its fruits, and some of us will deny the voice of motivation to progress toward the changing production of emotions. Our experiences will contain a showering of an ever-changing, unowned, unrecognized, unvoiced, and at times, deeply rested in the unconscious mind. The dilemma is often solved periodically but at times, it demands another season to teach us a valuable piece that was partially solved.

Often, it seems dreadful to face the angst or an introductory paragraph of another lesson presented by life. These lessons will come in the form of irony — evoking the human experience.

THAT, MY FRIEND, IS WHAT EMOTIONAL BEAUTY MEANS.

It means to process a meaningful life that guides us to construct new ways to discover, to change, and to deepen the richness of existence.

Haven't we been living it?

Carry on...

www.ingramcontent.com/pod-product-compliance
Lightning Source LLC
Chambersburg PA
CBHW052027090426
42739CB00010B/1810